# LIVES

# LIVES

## Encounters with History Makers

### Giulio Andreotti

SIDGWICK & JACKSON
LONDON

This translation first published in Great Britain
in 1988 by Sidgwick & Jackson Limited

Translated from the Italian by Brian D. Phillips
Illustrations by Vincio Delleani

Originally published in Italy by Rizzoli Editore,
Via A. Rizzoli, 2, 20132 Milan, Italy, in 1982, 1983 and 1985,
in three volumes under the title of *Visti da vicino*

ISBN 0-283-99584-X

Typeset by Hewer Text Composition Services, Edinburgh
Printed in Great Britain by Butler & Tanner Limited, Frome
for Sidgwick & Jackson Limited
1 Tavistock Chambers, Bloomsbury Way
London WC1A 2SG

# Contents

Contents

# 1
# *Benedetto Croce*

One of the greatest thrills I felt on the first day I entered the Chamber of Deputies in September 1945 was the thought that I was a member of a body which included Benedetto Croce. It almost made me feel dizzy.

Because of my youth, I had the privilege of sitting at the same bench as the Chairman, for at the opening session the oldest of those present (a former member of parliament named Agnini) acted as Chairman and the youngest as secretary responsible for the minutes. From this vantage-point I could see very clearly the faces of some of the great survivors of a very different Italy – now reduced to an even more pitiful state as a result of the violent way it had been permanently crushed, or so it was thought.

Benedetto Croce was certainly the most illustrious of these figures. No so much for his political past (though that was eminent enough, since he had been a minister in Giolitti's cabinet in 1920–1, and again in Badoglio's government at Salerno) as for his international fame as a philosopher, which was so solid that fascism itself had been obliged to respect it. Indeed, fascism used it as a defence against anyone, anywhere, who denounced the brutality of the dictatorship and the iron hand of the censor in Italy. It was pointed out by way of riposte that Croce's journal *La Critica* came out regularly, in spite of the fact that in 1927 he had published the intellectuals' anti-fascist manifesto.

Even the Treccani encyclopaedia was unable to ignore the illustrious Benedetto Croce, but got by, as far as this aspect of his activities was concerned, by stating that 'Even after the advent of fascism, he remained firmly attached to a form of liberalism in which the basic tenets of his own culture held pride of place.'

1

Croce had been appointed to the Senate in 1910 – on the advice of Sidney Sonnino – at the age of forty-four. He rarely made a speech there. His greatest moment of notoriety came when he voted against the ratification of the Lateran Pacts; but even then he took care to make it clear that he was not at all motivated by anti-clerical feelings. He behaved consistently in expressing his disapproval of the inclusion of the Lateran Pacts in the Constitution of the Italian Republic, but stayed away from the session of 25 March 1947 when the matter was voted on.

As leader of the Liberal Party, Croce joined Badoglio's cabinet, as already mentioned, and was one of the political leaders who accompanied Badoglio to Rome immediately after the Liberation. He also agreed to take part in Bonomi's government, but only for a few days. When a government reflecting the wishes of the Committee of National Liberation received permission from the Allies to set itself up in Rome, Benedetto Croce took his leave, believing that his temporary role as active politician was now over.

I had caught no more than a glimpse of him the previous year at the famous meeting in the Grand Hotel. It was Croce himself, at any rate, who told De Gasperi and the other CLN leaders in Rome that, as soon as the King had arrived in the South of Italy, he, De Nicola, and Paratore had gone to invite him to abdicate. The unexpected reply had been:

'I cannot do it. There is no one to whom I could entrust such a burden.'

This seemed less than diplomatic, and very ungenerous towards his son and heir.

Croce could be quite severe towards the 'lay' parties, and even went so far as to accuse Parri of trying to arrange a second 'March on Rome', but it was in relation to the Christian Democrat Party that he caused a serious scandal, by writing that until his dying day he would never allow a Christian Democrat to be Minister of Education. A temporary solution to the problem was found by confirming the appointment of Arangio Ruiz, who was a Liberal, but when Gonella was proposed for the position, Croce raised no objection. This was the moment, in fact, when he took the opportunity of recalling that Sturzo 'all those years ago' had not wanted Giolitti back in power, and had offered Croce the support of the Popular Party if he would form a government. Croce had declined the invitation, partly because he had no wish to become Prime Minister, and partly out of friendship and respect for Giolitti.

Without wishing in any way to denigrate Croce, I have to point out that from the time of the Consultative Assembly he was 'guided' – in politics – by Renato Morelli, a Liberal who was at that time Under-Secretary for Emigration. Morelli was a man with a refined and charming manner who played a major part in building up a very cordial relationship between Croce and De Gasperi.

I have described elsewhere how Nitti had an extraordinary conversation with Croce and Orlando during the crisis of January 1947. During that vociferous three-way argument, Croce had said something which I found obscure. He had taken Nitti to task for the frequency with which he laughed at Croce's habit of quoting from liturgical Latin, for these concepts, said Croce, were too elevated to be within Nitti's comprehension. The significance of this reprimand came home to me when I noticed, at a meeting of the Constituent Assembly, that Nitti was the only one to smile openly (everyone else showed emotion and respect) when Croce ended a speech about the way the Assembly ought to conduct its business by appealing 'above all to your hearts', and quoting the great hymn 'Veni creator spiritus, Mentes tuorum visita, Accende lumen sensibus, Infunde amorem cordibus'.

It was in this same speech of 11 March 1947 that Croce returned to a subject he had spoken on at the Consultative Assembly. This was 'a vigorous rebuttal of Prime Minister Parri's astonishing rather than scandalous suggestion that Italy had never experienced real democracy, even before fascism'. On that earlier occasion (23 September 1945) he had recalled the efforts made before fascism towards improving the lot of the poor ('including the poor of my own city of Naples'), the way the nation's physical well-being had improved, progress achieved in setting up a health system, but above all the birth of political parties – including the Socialist Party. 'Like all true democracies,' he went on,

> it was a liberal democracy, for liberalism without democracy will wither for lack of substance and stimulus, while democracy without the liberal system and the liberal method becomes perverted and corrupt. It opens the door to dictatorship and despotism, just as the democracies of the medieval communes gave way to Renaissance tyrannies, and the first and second French republics gave way to the first and second Empire.

At the Constituent Assembly he developed this concept further:

> Nowadays one often hears political opponents being gratuitously insulted as fascists. But for me one of the real signs of fascism's evil

lies in this echoing of the scorn and vilification which the fascists poured on the Italy of the period 1848 to 1922. I see myself as a child of that Italy. It was within its beneficent and sacred freedom that I grew up and came to understanding. It is a child's duty, I believe, to defend the actions and honour of his father.

Meanwhile, a serious political crisis had developed, and De Gasperi had formed a government without Communists or Socialists. In such a tense and threatening political climate, Croce's views were of tremendous importance, especially since credit was being given on the Left to a rumour that he would not take part in the debate on a vote of confidence on 21 June 1947. But he did come, and he insisted on acting as spokesman for the Liberal Party in declaring its voting intentions. His speech was particularly incisive:

It is obvious that before a man can decide to be a Liberal or a Christian Democrat, he has to be *alive*; and Italy will have no opportunity to follow the one creed or the other if she dies, that is to say if she is subject to the economic, political, and moral collapse which now threatens her. The duty we have to save our country is greater than any other duty we have towards her. We therefore favour a Christian Democrat government, for that party has made such a duty its principal and present purpose; and we are united in the support we give to the pursuit of that principal and present purpose. The war of words between Right and Left throws little light on the real meaning of liberty and justice.

Croce's speech in the debate was not without its polemical and humorous moments. Turning to the leader of the Communist Party, he said:

Togliatti often recounts episodes from my life in his newspapers, thereby affording me the pleasure of reading a fictional account of myself. Yesterday, if I heard correctly, he said that when the government was formed at Salerno I opposed the inclusion of the Communist Party. But he forgets that he did me the honour of coming to my house in April 1944, and that he was the first to approve the efforts made, under my aegis, to remove obstacles in the way of forming a democratic government which should include the Communist Party amongst others.

And to those who had criticized his lack of republicanism in the past he replied:

I have only one credo, and I accept and respect the result of the referendum. It is certainly true that my past is not like that of those

5

republicans who had little republican emblems in their families as children, as well as childish republican games. They remind me of the dolls dressed up as nuns which were thrust into the hands of the little girl, in Manzoni's novel, who subsequently became the Nun of Monza. I was brought up in the tradition of the Risorgimento, whose last and greatest poetic voice was that of Giosuè Carducci, the author of *Piemonte* and *La Bicocca di San Giacomo*, and it was my duty to respect such noble feelings of affection.

Croce was made senator for life in the 1948 parliament, but he never spoke there again, and rarely attended.

When he died, on 20 November 1952, I was asked by De Gasperi to look up two essays on Goethe which Croce had written in 1919 and 1934. Though De Gasperi was very grateful for the political support which Croce had given him, he wanted to pay tribute to him principally as a many-sided man of letters and culture, who would be remembered by posterity even when the chronicles of Italian public life in the difficult years of reconstruction after the Second World War were faded and forgotten.

It was significant, too, that he was being commemorated by an avowed and very militant Catholic – but an uncomplicated Catholic, both in his respect for human nature and in his attitude to the Index of Prohibited Books, whose approaching demise he foresaw.

# 2

# Umberto di Savoia

In an interview with Giovanni Mosca on 19 March 1973, Umberto of Savoy made the following remarks about me: 'I remember meeting him when he was very young. De Gasperi introduced us. The best of my aides, he told me. He will be no ordinary politician. I am instilling a sense of the state into him. But Andreotti did not hear that last sentence.'

Umberto was referring to a reception held in the Royal Palace at a moment in 1946 when his reign was about to come to an end. It was in honour of the new cardinals, and was held in an atmosphere of antique splendour and great solemnity. In his capacity as Prime Minister, De Gasperi sat next to the King, and he called me over to ask me to postpone a subsequent engagement. That is how the introduction came about, but I didn't catch the complimentary remarks mentioned in the 1973 interview. Apart from anything else, I was anxious to return to my table in order to continue a very interesting conversation I was having with Francis Spellman, Archbishop of New York. It was on that occasion that we began what subsequently developed into a very firm friendship.

Some days later, I received a telephone call from Admiral Francesco Garofalo, one of the King's aides-de-camp, inviting me to a private audience in my capacity both as member of the Consultative Assembly and as delegate of the Christian Democrat youth groups. Perhaps whoever thought of arranging the audience wanted to use it for some minor electoral purpose. At any rate, the King made no reference to the question of the monarchy, but he did show considerable interest in the way the Christian Democrat Party was preparing to set out its constitutional proposals.

There was something pathetic about this forty-year-old man

who had recently been obliged to shoulder a heavy responsibility, which had all the bitter flavour associated with the fact that the rule of the House of Savoy was likely to come to an end very soon. Two years earlier, his father – now an exile in Egypt – had rejected the advice of Croce, De Nicola, Paratore, and other authoritative figures that he should abdicate, claiming ungenerously that 'the little prince' (as he was still popularly known) was not a suitable successor.

In June 1946, I accompanied De Gasperi to the Royal Palace immediately after that extraordinary meeting in the Salone della Lupa during which the Court of Cassation announced that the referendum result was in favour of a republic, but postponed its judgement on objections to another meeting. What happened in the next few days is well known. The King's immediate reaction was to have done with it and leave Italy, but at the same time he was aware that certain supporters of the monarchy wanted him to stay, on the grounds that the verdict issued by the Central Office was not final. He asked for time for reflection. Enzo Selvaggi had presented a petition to the Allies in which he argued that, since the people of Trieste and those prisoners of war who had not yet been repatriated had not voted, the referendum was null and void. Vittorio Emanuele Orlando did a juggling act with a variety of interpretations of the referendum and suggested waiting. Others suggested that Romita, the Minister of the Interior, had tampered with the records, and that the Court of Cassation should not confine itself to a consideration of objections, but start counting the votes all over again.

There was talk of a confrontation between the Ministry of the Interior and the Royal Palace, but from the time of his first meeting with the King, De Gasperi always looked calm to me. He was quite confident of the King's straightforwardness and good sense, but the same could not be said of all his advisers. De Gasperi was unusually harsh in a telephone call he made to Marchese Lucifero (but it has to be remembered that he too was under almost intimidatory pressure from the less reasonable supporters of the monarchy). Up to that moment, all had remained calm, partly because Togliatti, Nenni, and the trade unions all acknowledged De Gasperi's prestige. But who could be sure that everyone would calmly wait for the Court of Cassation to complete its work, surrounded as it was in the parliament building by tight security, and without anyone knowing how long it would take?

The cabinet brought the delay to an abrupt halt. It pointed out that, whatever happened about objections, the figures showed that the referendum favoured a republic. And, in accordance with the law, it declared De Gasperi to be Provisional Head of State.

So the King announced his departure, and left from Ciampino airport in a military aircraft supplied by Mario Cevolotto, Minister of the Air Force, and Admiral Raffaele De Courten, Minister of the Navy. As soon as I learned that the King had left behind a message to be broadcast on the radio that evening, I went to see Admiral Garofalo (who had behaved correctly by leaving the Royal Palace and taking up residence in a small hotel near Piazza Bologna), in order to have a look at this message. In this way, De Gasperi could if necessary broadcast a reply immediately afterwards.

Everything happened very calmly; and in spite of its history of internal strife and local squabbles, Italy showed the world that it could shed the monarchy in a painless way.

Umberto went to live alone in Portugal, while the Queen and their children settled in Switzerland because, so the official explanation went, neither the climate nor the school system of Lisbon allowed the family to live there together.

On 1 January 1948, the new Italian constitution came into force, and that meant the confiscation of the entire estate of the House of Savoy. Victor Emmanuel III, however, had died a very few days previously at Alexandria in Egypt, and was temporarily buried in the apse of the Franciscan church there. Since the confiscation related only to the male line, this meant that the heirs were deprived of only one-fifth of the family property (that is, what would have been inherited by Umberto). But the old King had voluntarily left to the state the valuable coin collection which he had personally built up over several decades. It was housed in the Palazzo Barberini, and Count Pellati was appointed curator.

Discreet inquiries showed that it was impossible – politically speaking – for the old King's body to be brought to Italy for burial in the Pantheon. It was publicly stated, however, that there would be no objection to burial among the family tombs in the church at Superga; but the family immediately vetoed that. Meanwhile Queen Elena went to live in France, and when she died in 1952 she was buried in the cemetery at Montpellier.

In the spring of 1948, I went to Spain – partly to see the Italian football team playing in a match there, and partly to make some ministerial contacts. The Allies, and especially the British, had in fact brought considerable pressure to bear to dissuade Italy from re-establishing normal relations with Madrid, but from every economic quarter we were getting reports that the Allies were in Spain in strength, for the very purpose of drawing up contracts and confirming commercial plans. The Spanish Foreign Minister, Martin Artajo, and the Under-Secretary to the Presidency, Carrero Blanco (who later became Prime Minister and was the victim of a spectacular assassination), gave me a long list of missions which were then active in Spain – some of them British and some belonging to other European countries. De Gasperi was much impressed by the list, and used it to damp down an anti-Spanish campaign being waged in Italy by political groups who were disinclined 'to look forwards rather than backwards', as De Gasperi wished.

Umberto of Savoy had come up from Cascais and also watched the match. I was told that he himself had asked not to be invited to the VIPs' stand, in order to avoid embarrassing the representative of the Italian government. And for the same reason (so he had me explicitly informed), he left Madrid at once and did not take part in the official receptions. I appreciated his tact.

In the years that followed, the situation in the Italian parliament grew considerably more difficult. The Monarchist Party was quite substantial, but it was not clear whether the leadership was effectively held by the rather authoritarian Commander Lauro or the politically more astute Alfredo Covelli. De Gasperi was afraid that the Monarchists might make a firm alliance with the extreme right-wing MSI instead of coming to an understanding with the Liberals, so he tried to persuade the Monarchists themselves to make a pact of non-belligerence with him, so that his new government of July 1953 should not be strangled at birth. His appeal was in vain, for both Lauro and Covelli knew that De Gasperi did not exclude the possibility of holding fresh elections in the autumn without modifying the 1953 electoral law which offered a potential bonus to alliances. In other words, they were not going to carry out an act of charity by allowing Saragat time to recover from his electoral disappointment ('fate is a cynical cheat') and re-establish contact with De Gasperi's majority party.

As for the fear that an effective alliance might be established between the Monarchists and the MSI, many thought such a thing impossible, in view of the firm stance adopted at Salerno by Umberto in his capacity as Lieutenant-General of the Realm, after the liberation of Rome: 'There is one prime duty which we have before us: to drive the Germans out of Italy, and to punish those wayward Italians who persist in remaining with the enemy, and

11

who can now only be regarded by fellow Italians as traitors to their country.' Now, it is true that the MSI and the Salò Republic are not the same thing, but the fact remains that the former did not repudiate the latter.

When Fanfani also failed in his attempt to obtain the support of the Monarchists in 1954 (as well as in a parallel attempt to woo the Socialists), the unintended fall of his government had the effect of smoothing the path towards a revival of the traditional four-party coalition.

The National Monarchist Party paid tribute to the illustrious exile in Cascais on frequent occasions; but, apart from odd messages of greeting and trips to as near Italy as he might reasonably go, it can scarcely be said that the ex-King entrusted these men who declared themselves to be the faithful with any specific representation of his interests. And in many respects the Monarchist Party was not homogeneous. That this was so could become a matter of public notoriety, when episodes occurred like that of the visit of Raffaele Guariglia, a senator and refined diplomat, to Commander Lauro. On his return from a visit to Portugal, Guariglia called at Lauro's house. He was kept waiting for some time, and was then shown up to a balcony where the Commander was sunbathing, unencumbered by any clothes. The picture one conjures up of the conversation between the ambassador in his double-breasted suit and gloves, and his host in the altogether, bears graphic testimony to the . . . striking lack of unity in the party's inspiration.

I once happened to find myself in conversation with Paolo Matarazzo about the risk that the parliamentary situation in Italy might take a turn for the worse, especially since it was becoming increasingly clear that no useful and constructive amalgamation of the Monarchist groups could possibly take place. Paolo Matarazzo was a Brazilian whose family originally came from Salerno. He used to spend many months of the year in Italy, either at Castellabate or cruising on his splendid yacht, the *Astra*, and would call in at Cascais on his way to or from São Paulo, for he was a firm friend of the ex-King.

A few days later, Paolo telephoned me from Paris to say that he urgently wanted me to join him for the coming weekend, in order to meet 'a common acquaintance'. I was taken by surprise, but curiosity prevailed, and two days in Paris are always a pleasant prospect. What had happened was that Matarazzo had told Umberto of Savoy about our conversation, and got the impression that he was willing and even eager to talk to me personally about these matters, especially since I did not have a government post at the time, and there were therefore no problems of protocol or politics. Hence the appointment to meet in a small villa at Neuilly. The ex-King told me that he had been deeply saddened by De Gasperi's defeat, not because he wanted to interfere in party activities or in parliamentary decisions, but because he was 'genuinely distressed at the prospect of serious disease in the Italian body politic'. He could certainly not disown those who still fought for the idea of monarchy in Italy, but no one had ever been authorized by him to 'confuse the monarchy with a political party'. He also mentioned in passing that it was true that the Queen had voted for the Socialists in the 1946 elections for the Constituent Assembly, but he gave no indication of how *he* had voted, and it would not have been polite for me to ask.

The political message was clear. The conversation turned to less weighty topics, such as the economic situation, the extent to which the Atlantic Alliance enjoyed general support, and the relationship between central and local government. He also asked me whether the situation regarding the final burial of his father was still unchanged at 'Superga, yes; Pantheon, no'. I said it was, and made a passing oblique reference to his strange habit of speaking frequently of his father and never of his mother, Elena of Savoy. He smiled and changed the subject.

He said not a word about the events of 1946, and expressed no reservations about the legality of the change-over from monarchy to republic. And his respect for De Gasperi was in itself sufficient to remove any justification for the excessively polemical attitude of some of his Italian supporters.

As he said goodbye, Umberto told me that he would be inviting me to the forthcoming wedding of his daughter Maria Pia to Alexander of Yugoslavia, though he was sure – he said with a smile – that I would not be in a position to attend. Yet family matters, he added with a touch of sadness, ought always to be kept separate from political attitudes and exigencies.

The wedding took place at Cascais on 12 February 1955. I didn't go, but I sent a telegram of sincere good wishes.

Every year, Cardinal Spellman used to organize a charity lunch for the benefit of the Al Smith Foundation, and he regularly sent me an invitation. Some time after Maria Pia's wedding, he expressed great keenness that I should go this time, as co-guest of honour with Umberto of Savoy. He thought he had hit upon a good publicity stunt in this way; but my views were different, and I didn't go. However, I recalled the ex-King's appreciative judgement of De Gasperi, so I sent him a copy of my biography of the Christian Democrat leader, and received a polite note of thanks, signed by Falcone Lucifero.

The following year I was surprised to receive, via Marchese Lucifero again, the congratulations of 'His Majesty the King' at my 'escape from danger'. To describe it as danger seemed a little exaggerated to me, for what had happened was that I had fallen through the stage into the basement of the Brancaccio cinema at the end of a political meeting. Too many enthusiastic well-wishers had crowded round me on the platform, thereby causing a small section of the floor to give way. It was very kind of him, but it was nothing serious.

In late 1978, I happened to be in Portugal to see my daughter, who lives there, when I bumped into the ex-King in a Lisbon street. He was very pleasant to me, but for obvious reasons we kept our conversation to an exchange of polite phrases.

I mentioned earlier that in 1946 Maria José had voted Socialist with a preference for Saragat. There were later occasions when she again chose to express her admiration for him. She sent him a telegram of congratulations when he was elected President of the Republic (an act of courtesy to the new tenant of what had formerly been her Royal Palace); and still more eloquent had been a hand-written letter of condolence on the death of his wife Giuseppina.

But when the ex-King was himself asked in April 1961 about the Italian Socialist Party congress which had just come to an end, he answered: 'All Italians are equal for the King. There are no political hues which can cause the King to make distinctions between one Italian and another. So I have no opinion to express regarding the political activities of Italian Socialists.'

I read this statement with interest, but it seemed to me too impartial (and not just in relation to the Socialists). I prefer the less impartial stance which I heard him adopt in our conversation arranged by Paolo Matarazzo.

At least in public, however, monarchs have their hands tied. I would like to suggest – if it is not too bold of me – that the practice of having the sovereign read the Crown's speech in parliament should be altered. In Queen Elizabeth's long reign, for example, she has found herself first having to say that nationalization of certain industries was the basic solution to the crisis and, shortly afterwards, that this time nationalization was the cause of a great deal of trouble.

In the closing period of Umberto's life, the debate was resumed as to whether it might be possible to relax the provision which prevented the ex-King or his descendants in the male line from setting foot in Italy. It seemed likely that such a relaxation might be achieved on humanitarian grounds, and perhaps it would have had the desired outcome if the proposal had been limited to the person of the old, sick ex-King, who wanted to come back to his country to die. But the passage of the necessary legislation through parliament was slowed down by its extension to other members of the family, and by some gratuitous and provocative suggestions that the prohibition was itself invalid. In any case, the discussion was broken off partly by the dissolution of parliament and partly by the fact that Umberto died in 1983. I thought it a mistake that on this occasion no member of the government was present at the funeral at the Abbey of Hautecombe in Savoy.

The suggestion that the entire article of the constitution should be repealed is inappropriate, because that would involve restoring the ex-King's property to his family, thereby annulling the tacit compromise of 1946, which saved the princesses' inheritance from confiscation. Nevertheless, if Victor Emmanuel III had died a week later, the state would have confiscated everything – a fact which led to the circulation of a rumour, utterly without foundation, that the King had nobly committed suicide in order to protect his daughters' future.

In his will, the ex-King left to the Italian state not only some important archive material, but also his coin collection, which formed a distinguished complement to what his father had already donated. And the Holy Shroud was left to the Holy See. To each his own. In this sad but responsible way, the ex-King took his leave of the world. When all is said and done, he was a gentleman, and a very unfortunate one.

# 3
# *Palmiro Togliatti*

The two names Ercoli and Togliatti were much bandied about in the Committee of Liberation during the German occupation of Rome, and for a while I thought they were two different people. On his return from Russia, nearly everyone was critical of Togliatti, because of the compromise he had proposed regarding Communist relations with the King and Badoglio's government, which was totally at odds with the intransigent attitude publicly adopted by the six parties in the Committee of Liberation. The severest critic of these 'two persons' was Don Porta (the code-name of Pietro Nenni who, like everybody else, had taken the name of the seminarist whose cell he was occupying in the Lateran). His criticisms were interspersed with appeals to certain saints in Romagnol dialect, expressed in a way not really suited to a seminary – much to the disapproval of De Gasperi, who was also staying at the Lateran.

My misunderstanding about the identity of Togliatti and Ercoli much amused Bonomi, who put me right on the matter. He pointed out that Togliatti's long career as an active Communist, and the positions of political responsibility he had held during his exile in Moscow, would certainly ensure that he became the leader of the Italian Communist Party. I was not to overestimate the importance of complaints made about him at times like these, even though they came from fellow Communists; and Bonomi's personal opinion was that such complaints were unrealistic and exaggerated.

The first time I saw Togliatti was when he came to Rome with Badoglio and some other members of the Salerno government, soon after the Liberation. I was struck by the deference which

Badoglio showed him, as they engaged in conversation in such thick Piedmontese dialect that it was even less comprehensible than a foreign language. But that was just a matter of form. It took only a few words for Togliatti to come to an agreement with the other parties over the changes in the government which the Committee of National Liberation was insisting on. There was nothing left for Badoglio to do but leave the Grand Hotel in haste (the meeting had been held in a hotel rather than a ministry in order to avoid giving the impression that the authority of the southern government could be prolonged), go to the Royal Palace, and offer his resignation to Umberto as Lieutenant-General of the Realm.

The new government was headed by Bonomi, with Togliatti and De Gasperi as ministers without portfolio in a sort of mini–cabinet in which each of the six parties had one representative. When permission was obtained from the Allies for a return to Rome (a hurried withdrawal to Salerno had been necessary as soon as the government had been formed), the ministers without portfolio set up office in the Palazzo dei Marescialli in Piazza Indipendenza, where the Supreme Council of the Judiciary now has its offices. Consequently, I often had occasion to bump into Togliatti, but it never went further than a brief greeting in a lift or in the corridors. In fact I never saw him chat even with his own colleagues, except at meetings and formal conversations. It was almost as though his life as an underground Communist was still going on, or that he was having difficulty in readapting to the Italian way of life, in which, as at the theatre, there are intervals between the acts. Indeed, his formative influence on his immediate aides was such that they became more reserved and circumspect with every day that passed. I noticed this happening in the case of Massimo Caprara, who remained as polite as ever, but was gradually shedding his Neapolitanness, and becoming a suave young diplomat of mid-European type.

Barely six months after the Liberation, there was a government crisis (the Italian practice of having short-lived governments was already becoming established), and Togliatti showed a lot more flexibility combined with decisiveness than many other party leaders.

He joined in the general protest at the British veto on Count Sforza, but since he did not like Sforza and was not planning to make use of him, he proposed a fresh start and a search for a different political solution. This meant that De Gasperi might become Prime Minister, and that the three mass parties would acquire greater influence than the others.

One evening during the crisis, Togliatti issued a press release to us journalists in which he declared quite firmly that while the outcome of the crisis was uncertain, one thing was quite clear: Communists and Socialists would have equal standing in the next government. Eighteen hours later, Bonomi was forming his second post-war government, which included the Communists but not the Socialists or the Action Party.

Only a man of great authority could allow himself to perform what might be described in motoring parlance as a U-turn. Nenni expressed his disapproval (he wrote in his diary that Togliatti was 'behaving like an elephant in a china shop. On he went with all the nonchalance of an elephant, and woe betide any china that got in the way'), but that did not prevent him from maintaining the left-wing alliance, which indeed – *crescit eundo* – was to come to fruition as the Popular Front in 1948, but without the figure of Garibaldi in its emblem.

Before the referendum on the monarchy and the elections for the Constituent Assembly, there was an inter-party meeting to which the Republicans were invited as well as the six parties of the Committee of National Liberation. De Gasperi took me there as a 'reserve Christian Democrat', and by chance I found myself sitting next to Togliatti. I noticed that he was intolerant of over-long speeches; he grew silently restive at the flowery prose of that colourful member of the Democratic Party of Labour, Francesco Cerabona (otherwise known as 'Ciccio'), and when Oliviero Zuccarini (a Republican) was setting out his views in somewhat excessive detail, Togliatti surprised me by whispering in my ear: 'Small parties have small ideas.' This was one of the very few occasions when I had what one might describe as confidential contact with Togliatti, and at the end of the meeting I took advantage of this to ask him how he could reconcile his acceptance of a parliamentary system with his close relationship with the Soviet Communists.

He replied that we had a rather limited understanding of democratic pluralism. In the Soviet Union, policy was the resultant of the meeting of the political wills of various 'social bodies', each of which had its own individual characteristics, its own internal hierarchy, and a certain amount of autonomy as well. And he cited as examples the armed forces and the *kolkhozniks*.

From June in that same year, 1946, until the time of his death, I very frequently listened to Togliatti's speeches in the Chamber of Deputies, and I read both his contributions to the work of parliamentary committees and articles which allowed me to forecast his party's attitudes; but, with one exception, I never had direct contact with him. Unlike other Communists, such as Di Vittorio, Amendola, Pesenti, and Giancarlo Pajetta, who would willingly chat to journalists and colleagues of all parties in the lobby outside the Chamber of Deputies, Togliatti was almost unapproachable. He was assiduous in his attendance at parliament, and at the end of proceedings would grasp his briefcase – which was always bursting at the seams – and make for the exit. If my recollection is correct, the only person he would exchange a few words with was Emilio Frattarelli, a journalist who had been a colleague of Amendola (senior) on *Il Mondo*, and had never lowered the banner of freedom. Apparently he was not all that communicative even with his colleagues, for Pajetta stated in a recent debate that on one occasion only, *in Paris during the 1930s*, did he have an opportunity to talk to Togliatti about seriously worrying events in Stalin's Russia before the war.

The fact is that two different Togliattis were beginning to emerge. I am not now referring to 'Ercoli', but to the contrast between the man of refined culture, well read in classical and contemporary literature, who would have discussions with Vittorini and Pavese, and attend theatrical first nights; and the cold politician who was not averse to using coarse insults if he thought they would serve to boost his reputation as a strong man and pep up his public. Amongst these gems of vulgarity, I remember his calling the Americans morons at a time when we Italians had extreme need of their help; and he invited some mountain farmers to use their hob-nailed boots for kicking De Gasperi.

He called me a nitwit once – in reply to an article I had written – but thereby succeeded only in giving me some publicity. I was displeased and surprised at his attack on De Gasperi, however, because I knew that he had a high regard for him, and I remembered times when the two had collaborated very effectively.

However, we learned many years later from Eugenio Reale's book that the Italian Communists were effectively put on trial by the Cominform for allowing themselves to be ousted from government in 1947; and they were taken to task even more severely when they lost the decisive election battle in 1948. With the benefit of hindsight, therefore, one can understand that they had it in for De Gasperi not only as their principal antagonist on both occasions, but also because they were subject to the influences and reprimands of the international Communist world.

As far as internal politics were concerned, Togliatti never took things to the edge of a complete breakdown of relations with the Christian Democrats. On more than one occasion, indeed, he adopted a policy of prudence and far-sightedness. This led him, for example, to safeguard the spirit of collaboration in the Constituent Assembly, even after the Communists were expelled from government. And it was in fact at the Constituent Assembly that Togliatti made the confidential remarks to me that I have already referred to.

The argument over the relationship between church and state had been going on for months, and had created a good deal of tension. The Catholics wanted the Lateran Pacts to be brought into the constitution, with a provision that modifications could be made only if they were agreed by both parties. It was also suggested that the odious concept of other faiths being 'permitted' should be abandoned, and that 'agreements' should be negotiated with other religious confessions, and then approved by law.

The 'lay' parties were determined to fight against any reference in the constitution to the Treaty and Concordat of 1929, which they considered fascist; and they naturally counted on the votes of the Communists. The latter, however, had given no indication of their intentions. At noon on the day when the Assembly was to vote on the matter, I received a highly confidential piece of news from Togliatti ('for De Gasperi only') to the effect that the Communists – though their *decision* would not be reached until the afternoon – supported the wording which the Holy See was keen on; and he was now giving us a few hours' advance notice of the public statement he was to make at the time of the vote, by explaining that it would be a serious mistake to create a religious question, when what was needed was national solidarity, in order to reconstruct Italy and repair the split over republic and monarchy which had become particularly marked in the South.

I immediately passed the message on to De Gasperi. It was unusual for him to play a personal part in the work of the Constituent Assembly, but on this occasion he made a speech on the matter of the Lateran Pacts, in which he took account of Togliatti's message without actual reference to it. This was one of the most dramatic meetings at which I have ever been present. Not because of physical violence, though I have known that occur, but because of the fury of the Socialists and 'lay' parties at the Communist decision. Nenni called on the Communists to think again, assuring the Assembly that he did not want a war of religion either; but Togliatti replied by icily inviting him to read *L'Osservatore romano*: it does not necessarily take two sides to start a war.

On 14 July 1948, I was speaking in the Chamber of Deputies about the perennial problem of the high cost of newsprint, when there was a shout of 'They've shot Togliatti.'

We rushed out of the Chamber and saw the attendants carrying Togliatti's apparently lifeless body into the infirmary. The many members of the Chamber who were doctors gathered round him and arranged for him to be rushed to hospital for an operation. A young man had fired several revolver shots at him at the Via della Missione exit from the Chamber building, and had at once been arrested. Togliatti had been in his seat only a few minutes earlier, but had slipped away, without even his bodyguard noticing, to buy an ice-cream at the Bar Giolitti round the corner in Via degli Uffici del Vicario.

I immediately telephoned De Gasperi, who went at once to Professor Valdoni's university department, to find out what was happening and express his sympathy. Then he went back to his office to arrange with Scelba the necessary measures to deal with any attempt to take revenge for the general election results, or to subvert the political situation. News was already coming in from prefects' offices in the provinces of scuffles and dangerous gatherings in a number of towns.

The would-be assassin was a man called Antonio Pallante from Catania. Initial inquiries suggested that he did not belong to a political party, and was not a professional killer, since he had failed to kill a defenceless target at a distance of about ten feet.

The trade unions called a general strike, and there were worrying rumours from local Communist organizations, but the news from the hospital was reassuring. The afternoon session in the Chamber of Deputies was very tense. The government renewed its expressions of sympathy, and solemnly undertook to carry out a thorough investigation. At one point it was revealed that Pallante had watched the first part of the morning session from the public gallery, thanks to a note of introduction from Francesco Turnaturi, member of the Chamber for Catania. He was in danger of being attacked. He rose to his feet in a highly emotional state and declared with obvious sincerity that he had only done what was common practice in acceding to the young man's request, without even knowing who he was. Even though the extent of its influence was subsequently exaggerated, it is nevertheless true that one factor which contributed a good deal towards calming the atmosphere in parliament was the announcement of Gino Bartali's signal victory in the Tour de France. The fact is that we Italians are not just a race of saints, heroes, and explorers (as Mussolini maintained – and his view is still there to be seen in the sculpture on the walls of the Palazzo della Civiltà at EUR), but we are incurable sports enthusiasts. What is more, the Italian champion had taken France by storm on the very anniversary of the storming of the Bastille, and the little nationalist imp in all of us was dancing up and down with joy.

There was a cabinet meeting for most of the night, but although there was news of local violence, and even deaths (at Civitacastellana, Monte Amiata, and elsewhere), there were three reassuring factors. Togliatti had regained consciousness, and the doctors, while remaining cautious, declared that he was out of danger. The trade union leaders had come to the Prime Minister's office to assure the government that the situation in the factories would remain under control, and would not be allowed to spill over. Di Vittorio was in America at an international conference, and had asked Bitossi to tell the government so, and to let the fact be generally known. Giovanni Porzio was strangely anxious about Di Vittorio's absence and, not knowing anything about the trade union world, anxiously asked who 'this Bitossi' was.

What calmed us all down more than anything else, however, was a telephone call (officially authorized, I think) which I received from Togliatti's doctor, Mario Spallone. I was to inform De Gasperi that the Communists had no revolutionary intentions, and that clear orders to remain calm had been issued from party headquarters.

Togliatti recovered quickly. The theory that there had not been any assassination plot turned out to be true. Antonio Pallante was simply a self-appointed executioner who had decided that it was his duty to get rid of the number one in the party which he considered harmful for the future of the country. The Italians, or at least those who could, went off on holiday; and life went on as before.

De Gasperi and Togliatti now went their separate ways, and for five years they communicated solely in the form of written or spoken argument. When Togliatti and Scoccimarro came to discuss matters with De Gasperi during the political crisis of the summer of 1953, you would have thought the two leaders were meeting for the first time, such was the complete coolness between them, with no margin for mutual understanding.

23

The next year De Gasperi died. Togliatti naturally expressed the usual condolences, but also wrote an essay about him, in which he was very critical of De Gasperi's political line, but was honest enough to recognize his personal stature, his devotion to his country, and his personal unselfishness.

Years later, after Togliatti's death away in the Crimea, a friend of his told me that there were two episodes in Togliatti's life which had wounded his sensibility and pride more than fascist persecution and Pallante's bullets in 1948.

The first occasion was when, unknown to him and in his absence, Stalin had asked the leaders of the Italian Communist Party – who had agreed – to release their Secretary, since he was wanted back in Moscow for an international post. Apart from the personal offence, Togliatti felt that his colleagues had made an unforgivable mistake; because if he was working in Moscow, no one would ever again believe that the Italian Communist Party was independent of Moscow. Furthermore, he knew exactly what working in Russia meant. He told the story one day of how for three years he had been sent to represent the International Committee at the Party Congress in Mongolia, and had always taken with him an elaborate letter of greetings and good wishes from a worthy old Mongolian Communist who had moved to Russia. He was shocked, however, to discover by chance that this charismatic gentleman had died several years earlier, and that the letters were fabricated simply because they were considered useful to the cause.

Christian Democrat Italy might have its defects, but its working practices did not descend to that level; and it had never crossed his mind that his own colleagues in the leadership of the Italian Communist Party would be willing to send him back into exile.

The other 'blow' was delivered by Kruschev, when he made his unexpected report to the Twentieth Congress of the Soviet Communist Party on the misdeeds of the Stalin period. What upset Togliatti was the ill-mannered way in which foreign delegations were kept out, and sent back home in total ignorance of this dramatic event. They found out about it only when Kruschev's speech was published – in America of all places. What particularly upset him, however, was the way he was personally implicated, because he had spent those now blackened years in the Soviet Union, and in a post which, at least by implication, involved him in power.

This was the time when Togliatti's sense of isolation became intensified. It led to what is in a way a slightly self-critical political testament: the Yalta memorandum.

# 4
# Assis Chateaubriand

In September 1946, I was in Paris, waiting for De Gasperi to reach an agreement with Grüber to remove the South Tyrol from the series of punishments meted out to Italy in the post-war Treaty. (De Nicola had sent me to tell De Gasperi, as Prime Minister, that Epicarmo Corbino had resigned as Minister of the Treasury, and he had told me not to return without De Gasperi.) While I was there, I noticed that, apart from the famous handshake given by Byrnes, the American Secretary of State, there was an atmosphere of diffidence or, at best, of indifference on the part of the twenty-one victorious countries towards the Italian delegation. There was, however, one exception, in the form of the Brazilians. They, and their Foreign Minister João Nevers de Fontoura in particular, displayed open sympathy and understanding towards the new Italy, their attitude being related to a cultural context in a way I much appreciated.

Five years later, I was grateful to de Fontoura for an invitation to represent Italy at the first congress of the Latin Union. This organization had come into being to defend at international assemblies the desires and aspirations of a group of peoples with common roots, to strengthen ties between the Latin nations of Europe and America, and 'to stimulate the interest of public opinion in Latin countries in ideas of co-responsibility and in a consciousness of the part which history has assigned to the Latin peoples in the evolution of ideas and events throughout the world'.

By a lucky chance, the congress was to take place a few days before the official opening in São Paulo of the first Biennial Exhibition of Modern Art, and the organizer, Francisco Matarazzo Sobrinho, had come to Rome to ask for an official Italian delegation, which could also re-establish contacts with the Italian community in the State of São Paulo.

The first part of the journey was disagreeable. The scheduled flight was in a slow aircraft which certainly could not be called comfortable, and the stops at the island of Sal and at Recife proved a great trial for my breathing, which was already upset by a violent attack of fever. I was grateful to Professor Tucci, who had just returned from an archaeological expedition at the back of beyond, and had got into the habit of carrying with him a small bottle of one of those concentrated herb extracts which the Cistercian monks of Casamari are supposed, somewhat irreverently, to use for raising the dead.

As soon as I arrived in Rio, I had to take to bed, and so I missed most of the congress. There was some consolation for me, however, in that my condition was shared by Edgar Faure, the French Minister of Justice and head of the French delegation, who was also staying at the Hotel Copacabana. We were able to exchange messages of greeting through our doctor, Elias Feigenbaum, a man of Austrian origin who had left his country as a result of the Nazi persecution of the Jews.

I was pleased to receive a visit not only from the Italian Ambassador, Mario Augusto Martini, but also from the Papal Nuncio, Monsignor Carlo Chiarlo, who spoke enthusiastically of Brazil, except as regards the great distances to be covered. For him they were prohibitive, because he was allergic to air travel (and I could scarcely disagree with him about that, in my present condition). But I also received a rather different visit. A coloured waiter came in, locked the door behind him – thereby causing me some apprehension – and, after asking me if I was an 'Italian senator', burst into a song which began by extolling Balbo and his transatlantic flight and finished up with a verse from 'The Red Flag'. All this was done to a samba rhythm, and with a crescendo of excitement which did nothing to calm my apprehension. It was perhaps the most extraordinary quarter of an hour I have ever spent. That was the end of it, however. With a sweeping bow, he opened the door again, and disappeared into anonymity.

Perhaps it was characters like this who caused the Italian Communist senator Francesco Leone to give up the idea of trying to organize a revolution in a country where would-be conspirators spoke openly of secret meetings to which they had been invited, but of which they got the date and time wrong, thereby causing confusion, misunderstanding, and danger. Years later, when I paid a visit to Egypt with the Defence Committee, I talked to Francesco Leone about it, and he implicitly confirmed – though without betraying the confidences of the International – that that was exactly what had happened.

The work of the congress, to which I had sent a paper in Latin with a facing Portuguese translation, was closely followed by Professor Tucci, whose academic prestige was very considerable in Brazil, as well as by Nicola De Pirro, who took advantage of being in Rio together with Cassuto, the Chairman of Unitalia, to improve the penetration of Italian films on the immense Brazilian cinema circuit.

A special train had been arranged to take all the delegations to São Paulo for the opening of the art exhibition, but I was advised not to take advantage of it, since the total failure to stick to timetables made every journey hazardous. This proved indeed to be the case, for the train left in the evening and reached São Paulo early the following afternoon – two hours after we did; and we had slept as normal at Copacabana. Moreover, because we travelled by car, we even had time to visit the interesting little town of Guarantingueta, and stop for refreshment at the 500 Club, more or less halfway along the road named after President Dutra.

I enjoyed hospitality at the home of Dora and Paolo Matarazzo, the latter being the brother of the keen patron of the arts who was the king of the castle for these few days.

Italy was well represented at the exhibition. There were works by Domenico Cantatore, Renato Birolli, Corrado Cagli, Renato Guttuso, Giuseppe Santomaso, Antonio Corpora, Ennio Morlotti, and Afrio; and the sculptures included eleven works by Giacomo Manzù, two by Lucio Fontana, five by Pericle Fazzini, and three by Luciano Minguzzi. There were also some fine engravings by Giorgio Morandi, Luigi Bartolini, Mino Maccari, and Renzo Vespignani. I probably failed to note everybody's name in my diary, and I apologize for any omissions.

In the Japanese section, I was more intrigued than impressed by some panels with a suggestion of flowers on a pale gilded background, which were rendered very odd by some real Coca-Cola bottle tops in two languages, mercilessly embedded in the panels. Was it pop art, or just a sign of post-war dreariness?

The social side of our activities was beautifully organized. There was a splendid race meeting offered by the Jockey Club of São Paulo, and a lunch in the rooms of the stadium. I shall never forget the display of multi-coloured orchids used as a table centre. It may be that the Brazilians look upon orchids the way we look upon daisies, but the effect was amazing. I bet a few *cruzeiros* on horses with Italian names (Biancaluna, Fuga, Lia, and Enrico di Savoia) and ended up even. It was an unforgettable race meeting.

In the evening there was a reception given by the Italian Consul-General, Alfredo Nuccio, followed by a gala dinner at the home of Count Raul Crespi. Here I received two surprises. The first was to meet Dino Grandi, the architect of Mussolini's downfall on 25 July 1943. For this reason he was disliked by the more recent immigrants from the Salò Republic, with the result that he made a point of openly fraternizing with Italians who had left their country in bad odour with fascism. So it was Grandi himself who introduced me to some 'ex- Socialists', 'ex-members of the Popular Party', and 'ex-Liberals'. You would have thought he was the president of a Committee of National Liberation during the Resistance. In Brazil he was working as a colleague of Agostino Rocca in the Techint Group, apparently with some success.

In another room our hosts wanted me to meet Senator Assis Chateaubriand, who was the owner of an important television network and the biggest newspaper and magazine group in Brazil. I noticed that he was treated with particular deference by the Governor and those Brazilian politicians who were present.

Chateaubriand's comments on Italy were not confined to the normal compliments one expects to hear on such occasions. He declared that he was self-educated, but amongst the learning that he had acquired, he gave pride of place to the culture of Latinity, and consequently to his love of all things Italian. Chateaubriand's conversation ranged from the tribes in the Amazon basin which had not been affected by progress, to the beauty of the sunset seen from Trinità dei Monti in Rome, but he ended – as though struck by a sudden idea – by saying that I was the one person who could enable him to fulfil the greatest desire of his life.

I couldn't imagine what on earth I could offer this Brazilian millionaire that he had not already obtained from life. For a moment it crossed my mind that perhaps he was a bit deranged – a suspicion which was not totally allayed when I learned what it was he wanted. He wanted to give a talk in Rome on Roman Law in the presence of Vittorio Emanuele Orlando. At least it wasn't a difficult thing he was asking, and when I returned to Italy, I spoke to Orlando about it. He willingly agreed to the idea, but in view of the amateur nature of the talk, avoided using a university lecture theatre. What we did was organize a dinner at the Hotel

Ambasciatori, at the end of which Assis Chateaubriand, now in his seventh heaven, was able to read thirty sheets or so of a survey – and a quite interesting one at that – of various Roman jurists, such as Modestinus, Papinianus, Cicero, and so on. Orlando brought the evening to a close with one of his little eulogies, which almost made our Brazilian guest's heart burst with pride and joy.

After that day, I had no further direct contact with Assis Chateaubriand, though I heard news of considerable ups and downs in his fortunes.

As a man of humble origins, I was at any rate left with the real satisfaction of having given free moments of joy to an interesting personality from Latin America. He was also given a reception in Rome (where he made another speech, of course) by Ambassador Ugo Sola as President of the Italo-American Institute.

Dr Feigenbaum's orders were that I should return home from Brazil by sea, in order to avoid a recurrence of my lung trouble. The English steamer *Andes* on which I travelled was a bit long in the tooth, having been used as a military hospital-ship during the war. On the sea journey to Cherbourg, at any rate, I enjoyed eleven days of peace, not to mention the pleasure of meeting Pierre de Gaulle, Mayor of Paris and brother of the great General, and Raul Yrarrazeval, former Finance Minister of Chile, who was on his way to the Vatican as Chilean Ambassador, accompanied by his wife and seven noisy children. I also very much appreciated the attentions of the chef, Gino Fiorentini – a native of Tivoli and the only Italian in the whole crew. He used to send special sweets to our table, with written messages which were anything but complimentary to the navigation company. Before we disembarked, he came to say goodbye to us in the company of the purser, who was in an advanced state of inebriation and offered us boxes of ginger, saying that we wouldn't find ginger like that anywhere else. Partly, perhaps, because it had never crossed our minds to look.

# 5
# *King Farouk*

'We are the same age, you and I, but when you were going to secondary school I was ascending the throne; and, believe me, it's easier being a schoolboy than a king.'

I told Farouk, perhaps rather daringly (but his reference to our being the same age had put me at my ease), that I knew nothing about that, since I had never been a king, and had no desire to be one either.

It was February 1951, and I had been sent to Cairo to represent De Gasperi at both the opening of a magnificent Italian book exhibition organized by Francesco Sapori, and the eightieth anniversary of *Aida*. Both occasions were very appropriate ways of supporting and raising the morale of Italian nationals who had stayed on in Egypt after the war, and still had to live with the memories of long years of internment and other wartime troubles.

During the audience, the King told me he was adored by his people, and that the intensity of their Islamic religious feeling was an infallible antidote to any adverse propaganda. If I had heard any rumour to the contrary, I was not to take it seriously; there are always a few defeatists in any country.

I was indeed much struck by the contrast between the vast numbers of the evidently poverty-stricken (at every street corner there were swarms of beggar children with flies buzzing undisturbed about their eyes) and the gross ostentation of wealth displayed by certain families. The wife of the Prime Minister Nahas Pasha, for example, appeared at the theatre so laden with jewellery that she looked more like a luxury jeweller's shop than one of its smart customers.

King Farouk lavished attention upon the two Italian events. He was full of praise for Italy's work of reconstruction and also for its cultural renaissance, which was symbolized in the exhibition by Professor Tucci's splendid work on Tibetan painting, recently published by the Italian state publishing house. He even went so far as to say that in offering refuge to the Italian royal family he had not intended to act 'in a partisan manner or in support of fellow royalty', but rather as a mark of friendship towards Italy, which his father had taught him to love ever since he was a boy. Indeed, one of the best friends of his youth was an Italian by the name of Antonio Pulli, to whom he had later granted Egyptian nationality, in order to save him from the concentration camps ('the British were tough'). He had even gone so far as to give him the title of *bey*.

There were almost legendary stories about the influence of this son of a court electrician. To quote Dante, 'he held both the keys to his sovereign's heart'; and this is no mere literary reference, for it conveys very well his twin roles. On the one hand he showed a connoisseur's skill in selecting girls for his lord and master, and on the other he acted as special courier on the Cairo–Zurich run, to deposit the savings of his friend the King in Swiss bank accounts.

Antonio Pulli Bey must have been away somewhere when I was in Cairo, since I didn't see him either during my visit to court or at any of the various ceremonies. Nor did he turn up at the gathering of Italians. Had he been there, he could have joined his fellow Calabrians in applauding Mario Cingolani, who gave a sparkling address in which he referred to all the Italian regions one by one, stirring up enormous enthusiasm as he proceeded. Fortunately no one noticed Nicola de Pirro's barely suppressed laughter when Cingolani began in stentorian tones by calling on the 'Italians of Cairo'.

The performance of Verdi's *Aida* was intended to commemorate its first performance in the same theatre half a century earlier, on the occasion of the opening of the Suez Canal. It was an outstanding success. Gino Bechi in particular was received with endless applause, and at the end of the performance there was general acclamation for all the singers and the conductor, Vincenzo Bellezza. As I sat beside King Farouk that evening, I had occasion both to appreciate one of his positive qualities and to be scandalized by a piece of vulgarity.

I was perfectly well aware that he was a keen imbiber of the best brands of champagne, but in public he always displayed a rigid observance of Islamic abstemiousness, going so far as to sing the praises of the concoction of banana and other fruit juices which we were offered. A splendid example of 'If you can't be good, be careful'!

On the other hand, when the wife of the Italian Ambassador presented the singers to him and was praising Virginia Zeani's costume, we were dumbfounded to hear him make the following anything-but-regal remark:

'Where women are concerned, it's not their costumes I'm interested in, but what's underneath.'

Both the Ambassador's wife and the attractive singer blushed, without His Majesty feeling any need to apologize or even to modify his unfortunate remark in any way. Perhaps if he had gone to secondary school in the 1930s instead of ascending the throne, he would have behaved better.

However that may be, his optimistic assessment of the extent to which his people adored him was pure illusion. For when, a year later, General Neguib accompanied him to the quayside at the port of Alexandria and dispatched him into exile, thereby creating a new Egyptian Republic, there was no popular reaction.

Since Victor Emmanuel of Italy had gone into exile in Egypt, Farouk's choice of Italy as his place of exile constituted a sort of exchange; but he seems to have waited in vain to be joined by Antonio Pulli Bey. Neguib had had him arrested, not so much for any crime he had himself committed, as because the deposed King's Swiss bank accounts were on two signatures. There was no way the ex-King could draw on those accounts by himself. I don't know what happened subsequently, but I do know that Farouk was not particularly well off during his stay in Italy. Indeed, he tried to persuade Professor Valletta to get him a consultancy with Fiat – a purely honorary one, maybe, but with a handsome fee attached.

I myself never had occasion to meet him again, in spite of the fact that my family holidays were spent at Grottaferrata that year, not far from his chosen place of residence. On just one occasion he sent me greetings via his private secretary, who came to see me about some small family matter.

The people who saw him frequently were the clientele of night-clubs, for he would spend whole evenings and nights there in an effort to forget. He had certainly forgotten those banana-juice drinks. *Le Roi s'amusait.*

He was soon to die, however, and the manner of his death was both pathetic and sad. He was struck down by a brain haemorrhage as he sat at a restaurant table.

# 6
# Umberto Nobile

General Umberto Nobile's name is one of those which, if associated with some strong youthful impression (and in my case it was infancy rather than youth), are never forgotten for the rest of one's life. I remember that my brother wrote to him after his first expedition and received a signed photograph in reply, which he used to show very proudly to all and sundry. And I hope it won't seem shocking if I add that for me the word *Norge* conjures up not so much the airship of Nobile's valiant enterprise, as the delicious ice-cream we used to get on holidays, and a rough woollen pullover which an aunt gave me as a present. Everything was called 'Norge' in those days.

However, I learned a bit more about him at secondary school. This much publicized gentleman's second airship (to make matters worse it was called *Italia*) had broken down north of the Svalbard Islands, and he was accused of having left some men to die on the ice, while he and his little dog returned safe and sound to Italy. Those same authorities which had heaped him with honours two years earlier now gave him the cold shoulder by expelling him from the engineering branch of the Air Force, where he had enjoyed rapid promotion (but he had gone there from a university chair of engineering). Not even the city of Milan, which had financed the expedition, came to his defence.

So off he went to Russia to make airships; but I have no knowledge of their capabilities or technical merits.

When I made his acquaintance at the Constituent Assembly, I supposed it was his 'exile' in Russia (though in the early 1930s the Russians were not on unfriendly terms with Mussolini) which was responsible for his Communist ticket in the 1946 elections. But he

33

himself put the matter straight. Apparently Sullo had refused to have him on the Christian Democrat list at Avellino (he was born at Lauro in the Province of Avellino in 1885); and therefore – to use racing terminology – the jockey had switched horses, his second mount being the Communist Party. Earlier on, he had been readmitted to the Air Force, in spite of fascist objections.

He played an active part in the Constituent Assembly, and indeed often showed a willingness to depart from the party line by putting forward amendments of his own, which he was nearly always the only person to vote for. And the regulations at the Palazzo di Montecitorio didn't even allow him to have a little dog for company.

It was the isolation surrounding Nobile which caused me to approach him, in spite of the difference in our ages (he was sixty-one to my twenty-seven), plus the fact that my education had been a world away from aeronautical engineering.

He was grateful to me for this, and at Easter 1951 sent me an article, which I read only in part, in which a foreign writer by the name of Tryggve Gran recounted the dramatic events of 1928 in a version quite different from the official fascist one. In it, Nobile was described as 'a first-class commander', and, reading between the lines, the author had it in for the Navy, which apparently hadn't given all the assistance it should.

This caused the whole argument to flare up again. It lasted for many years, and since it involved organizations rather than individuals, it was one of those debates that can go on indefinitely. When I became Minister of Defence, I was personally dragged in by Admiral Adalberto Mariano, one of the survivors of the expedition, who made a vigorous protest that in a reprint of the findings of the Committee of Inquiry of 1929, headed by Admiral Cagni and with De Pinedo as one of its members, pages 115, 117, and 118 were missing.

These pages contained a eulogy of Commander Romagna Manoia, who was in charge of the polar expedition's base ship at Spitzbergen, and Lieutenant-Commander Zappi, who had 'organized the charts and maps service to *perfection*'. But the highest praise was reserved for Mariano himself, who was a commander at the time, and second in seniority to Nobile:

> By bringing to bear outstanding tact and personal qualities, he succeeded in maintaining suitable discipline and unity amongst all the members of the expedition, even at the most difficult and

dangerous moments. . . . He was a splendid example. . . . In spite of acute physical pain, temporary blindness, and the inability to move as a result of frostbite in one foot, his outstanding spirit and presence of mind, and his amazing courage, remained intact throughout, thanks to that limpid and manly faith which is the precious privilege of the strong. . . . Thus Adalberto Mariano brought honour to the Navy; and Italy can feel a sense of serene pride at this achievement of one of her sons.

Admiral Mariano was not asking that some procedure to obtain redress should be set in motion; he simply wanted me, as Minister of Defence, to be aware of the situation, particularly as regards Zappi and Manoia, both of whom were now dead. Admiral Cantù, who was Deputy Chief of Staff, told me that as far as Mariano was concerned he considered that, having taken this action, the matter could now be considered closed.

Protests were also being made by Nobile, however, for he did not think his readmission to the Air Force in 1945 was enough. He was asking that a new committee be set up to review the Cagni–De Pinedo report. Now, apart from the difficulty of reopening the matter after so much time had elapsed and with many of those involved, as well as potential witnesses, now dead, the Navy would have been up in arms about it, and we certainly could not allow ourselves that sort of luxury. I kept explaining this personally to General Nobile, and on each occasion he seemed convinced, but then a month later he was back again asking for the matter to be raised again.

A mutual friend acted as intermediary. This was Federico Comandini, a lawyer who had at one time been a member of the Consultative Assembly, and later of the Supreme Council of the Judiciary. On 24 July 1965, I received the following letter from him:

> I apologize for reminding you about the General Nobile business. I think that if it were possible to give him some sort of honour, on the basis of his achievements on the two expeditions with the *Norge* and the *Italia*, then the matter could be resolved without ill feeling; and an old man, who says that all he wants is to leave to his grandchildren an untarnished personal reputation, would be immediately satisfied.

Comandini assured me that 'General Valle is among those who would be very happy if this could be done, for the old quarrel is now forgotten, and he and his adversary of former days are now on friendly terms.'

I was able partially to do what was requested of me; and, after various preliminary discussions, it was found possible to make Nobile a Grande Ufficiale on 27 December 1966.

The old fellow lived on for another twelve years, and continued to frequent the Chamber of Deputies from time to time – especially the library. He set an example by doing so. No political party had offered him the chance to stand in an election, and as far as I know, he had not asked for this.

He died in midsummer 1978, and shortly before his death we were able to give him a different kind of reward, as an alternative to revising the Cagni report. The Italian Republic issued a stamp to commemorate the 1928 expedition. This was perhaps an indirect but certainly an eloquent way of bringing to an end a controversy which had lasted for fifty years. With the death of Umberto Nobile it was now permanently buried.

# 7

# *Charles de Gaulle*

I must be one of the few Italians who never liked General de Gaulle (though I have enjoyed friendly relations with some of his best aides, especially Pierre Mesmer). I set out my unpopular opinion in writing at a time when his star was in the ascendant, and even the secretary of an Italian political party said, on his return from Paris, that 'except for a couple of thousand political leaders' (*sic*) the whole world admired de Gaulle's personal charisma and authority. When he imposed the constitutional reforms which still operate in France, they were greeted by a chorus of praise. 'Outmoded supporters of parliamentary government' was the label given to those who forecast that under the new system a slight electoral swing would allow a minority to grasp literally complete power (unlike in the United Kingdom, where there are continuing checks and balances between executive and legislative, which the Queen has a certain role in maintaining). Today, Mitterrand and the Socialists have total command of the situation, though Mitterrand received only a few per cent more votes than Giscard d'Estaing in the presidential election, and only 30 per cent of the popular vote. It may be claimed that this makes France easier to govern, but to me such claims are rhetorical oversimplifications.

It may also be claimed that no other statesman was capable of solving France's worst overseas problem: that of Algeria (worst, that is, after Indo-China, which Mendès-France had dealt with at terrible subsequent cost to the United States, to the West as a whole, and to the freedom of the people of that country). De Gaulle's policy towards Algeria, however, involved a total change of direction, from insistence on 'Algérie française' to the declaration that Algeria was for the Algerians. The story goes that a young

Algerian with a stammer was prevented by his speech defect from expressing his solidarity with the 'early style' Legionnaires. He tried and tried to get it out, and finally succeeded, only to discover that he was now behind the times; so he still got kicked by the French soldiers, whose orders were now the opposite of what they had been before.

When de Gaulle was in London during the war, he skilfully succeeded in finding a role for France, in spite of the military defeat which followed the collapse of the Maginot Line. He had not been given full membership of the little club of the Big Three, however, and he was never going to forget it. The haste with which he re-established relations with the Soviet Union and, later on, his partial military withdrawal from NATO, and the costly setting up of an independent nuclear strike force, cannot be explained without reference to what happened in London during the war.

In 1952, France introduced stern new regulations on election posters. Up to that time, as in Italy, they could be put up anywhere, thereby wasting a lot of money and periodically spoiling the appearance of towns. Now the Communes had to provide a certain number of hoardings and reserve an equal amount of space for each party. It was strictly forbidden to put up posters, bills, or banners anywhere else.

De Gasperi wanted to know whether this reduction in visual publicity would cause a reduction in electoral interest. So, to my great joy, he sent me off for ten days to observe the French election campaign. In this way I was able to be present at several of de Gaulle's election rallies at a time when he was boosting the Rassemblement du Peuple Français.

The organization was perfect. The rallies were all held in the open air, but with seats for everyone. Proceedings began exactly on time. A leading local Gaullist – the mayor or a local councillor – would take the platform first, to be followed by a member of parliament, and when at last the atmosphere had been enlivened by swingeing attacks on their opponents and a promise to right every wrong in France, de Gaulle would make his appearance and speak for no more than twenty minutes, almost as though his speech were designed to fit neatly on to a record. After recalling the war, and France's humiliation and subsequent redemption, he would make a bitter attack on the party system as making it impossible for French men and women to bring their political will to bear, and he ended with an eloquent declaration that the Americans were allies and *not masters*. Then the General joined almost ecstatically in singing the

'Marseillaise'. Whereas he had appeared at the beginning from directly behind the platform, he now left through the audience, shaking hands as he went, and distributing smiles and polite expressions in generous quantities.

One day in Calvados, I noted that de Gaulle 'stirred up' and then satisfied the expectations of four towns in little more than two hours.

But the content of his speeches disconcerted me. In the first place, there was a contradiction between his criticism of the political parties and his promotion of a movement which, except in name, was as much a party as any of the others. There were generalizations about economic affairs, and ambiguities about foreign policy. I don't mean to suggest that he descended to the level of Poujade, but it was all too clear that he was taking advantage of fame and reputation which sprang not from political ideas and policies but from the inheritance of the Resistance.

As Minister of Defence, I accompanied de Gaulle a few years later at the celebrations for the centenary of the battles of San Martino and Solferino. I tried to bring the conversation round to the subject of the Rassemblement du Peuple Français and the elections I had observed. General de Gaulle frowned and cut me off with a curt 'That's all in the past, all in the past.'

As a matter of fact, the Rassemblement du Peuple Français was quite successful at the elections, but its lack of coherence in both ideology and political programme soon brought about an internal crisis, with the result that de Gaulle abandoned the battlefield and made one of his frequent tactical withdrawals to Colombey-les-Deux-Eglises. From here France would regularly call him forth, reserving the right, however, to send him back again, perhaps by voting against him in a referendum, as happened over the question of devolution.

It was understandable that he should seek special powers at moments of crisis; but in my opinion he should have limited himself to that, and insisted on constitutional reform only in relation to the role of the President.

There was no doubt that he was a well-balanced, upright, and dedicated man, but there was no reason to believe that the de Gaulle model would automatically suit his successors. They might be smaller men than he (they could scarcely be taller!), and look silly in military uniform. I once had an opportunity of pointing this out to him – in the politest way – by jokingly referring to the Vatican custom of preparing at least three different sizes of robe when a papal election was taking place. He smiled, but replied that the Italian 'mania for proportional representation' would cause us to meet the same fate as the Fourth Republic in France.

As regards the Holy See, I recall that on the death of Pius XII, de Gaulle wrote a splendid letter of good wishes to the Patriarch of Venice, in spite of the fact that when, much earlier, this same man had been Papal Nuncio in Paris, he had proved a skilful swordsman in defending the bishops against government accusations that they were behaving with unpatriotic weakness. It was Cardinal Roncalli himself who told me he had received this message, but he hastened to add that General de Gaulle's good wishes did not mean that the French bishops would vote for him.

The funeral service for de Gaulle in Paris was an international political triumph; but the General had arranged for it to take place in his absence. Those who wanted to pay homage to his person had to make the journey to his home town in the provinces. Never again would anyone go there to invite him to save France.

Jacques Chirac is an important political figure, without the pomposity of the founder of the Gaullist movement. It is in terms of his success or failure that the future will tell us whether Gaullism was a valid political formula, or whether this was just a case of another outstanding personality making his presence felt in French history.

# 8
# Dwight Eisenhower

When Dwight Eisenhower came on a state visit to Italy as President of the United States, I managed to exchange only a few brief sentences with him when I accompanied him to pay homage to the Unknown Soldier. What is more, it was pouring with rain as we went up and down the monument steps, and as soon as he got back to the President's Palace, his one apparent desire was to change his clothes, which had already got soaked on his arrival at Ciampino airport. I did, however, manage to get a reply to the question that most interested me – and it is perhaps one which every Italian would have put to him, given the opportunity.

'Why on earth', I asked him, 'did the Allies abandon Italy to its fate after the announcement of the armistice on 8 September 1943, and why did it take so incredibly long to cover the few miles from the Anzio landing to Rome in 1944?'

Eisenhower replied that if an airborne invasion near Rome by an American armoured division did not immediately follow the announcement of the armistice, the Italian High Command must be held responsible.

A few inquiries revealed to me that a message sent from Via XX settembre that evening had been drafted by a colonel (who was later to become a three-star general and Commandant of the Carabinieri); but it must have originated and been approved at a much higher level. The message informed the Allies that the airfield agreed upon (I seem to recall it was the one at Furbara) was not 'safe' because it was occupied by the Germans. I suppose it was only right for them to say so, but since this was a war operation and not a holiday trip, it seemed ridiculous to me that a prearranged military

43

support action should be abandoned without an alternative solution being sought and suggested.

At lunch, Eisenhower expressed great admiration for De Gasperi, saying that he had been one of the foreign political leaders who had impressed him most favourably during his time as Commander-in-Chief of NATO forces, both at ministerial meetings and on a previous visit to Rome. And I recalled that De Gasperi had said he judged Eisenhower to be 'a humanist above all else'.

# 9
# *Totò*

It must have been in the summer of 1957 (or perhaps a year earlier or later). The Nice–Rome sleeper had not long crossed the frontier, and I was peacefully enjoying my evening read of a detective story, when there was a knock on my compartment door. The days of terrorism had not yet come upon us, with escorts and all other necessary precautions, so I took no particular care in opening the door. There stood Prince Totò and Franca Faldini.

'They told me you were here, and I felt I had to come and wish you goodnight.'

Having got over my momentary surprise, I apologized to Franca Faldini for being dressed for bed (Totò, on the contrary, being just back from a cruise on the Côte d'Azur, was wearing a smart and imposing yachtsman's uniform), and thanked Totò. We then embarked upon a very enjoyable conversation. He really didn't want to take advantage of the Minister of Finance since he was on holiday, but he had certain pressing problems and would be delighted if he could come to my office to explain them to me.

'We all like to be overvalued in this life, but it's only the taxman who overvalues me.'

After a whole fireworks display of such jokes, Totò gave a slight bow and took his leave, it having been agreed that he would come and see me at the ministry at midday on the following Monday.

I had first met Totò in 1950 in Milan, when Remigio Paone had introduced him to me at the Teatro Nuovo. I ought really to say introduced me to him, because Prince Totò had let it be known that he would be glad to receive me in his dressing-room. At that first meeting, I found him to be a man of great dignity, with an evident air of superiority over a mere Under-Secretary of State like me. He

was a completely different person from the one who, a few minutes earlier, had had us in stitches during the grand finale of his show, when he had several times rushed up and down the catwalk at ever increasing speed, wearing a *bersagliere* helmet and feathers and rhythmically reciting a slightly modified line from Dante's *Inferno*: 'Oh Pi – Oh Pi – Pi – Oh Pisa, vituperio delle genti...'

Totò's success was all the more impressive in that it depended on three or four simple ingredients: mechanical, almost puppet-like movements; the insistent repetition both of jokes from a deliberately limited repertoire and of certain amusing catch-phrases ('Do you mind', for example); the use of a heavy Neapolitan accent; and a way of rolling his eyes that only he could manage.

Was it easier to make our generation laugh? Perhaps; but the fact that young people still enjoy his films, which are still frequently shown on independent and state television, is confirmation of Totò's great artistic value. His comic verve is destined to last, precisely because it is based on simple and natural qualities.

Apparently Antonio De Curtis (to give him his real name) took the defence of his princely prerogatives very seriously. The applause and affection of the crowds seemed to act as a substitute for the honour that was due to him as a prince of the Holy Roman Empire.

We once had a conversation about the moral aspects of comedy in the cinema, and he made an interesting distinction. Obscene *images* were to be avoided because they arouse passions and can be disturbing (especially for children), but one could make free play with *language* because each of us interprets it in proportion to the state of cleanliness of his own mind. As an example, he mentioned the famous scene where he has trouble sharing a sleeping compartment with a member of parliament (nothing to do with our meeting on the Nice–Rome train!). There were lots of fairly explicit allusions in it, and it was enjoyed equally by those who understood all the *doubles entendres* and by those who simply laughed at the cases being thrown out of the window one by one or the spray of saliva which landed in the member of parliament's eye when Totò tried to get his way by shouting.

'With all due respect,' Totò said to me, 'if you didn't miss anything, you must have had a dirty mind in the first place.'

Totò was not really vulgar. Even the phrase 'I've seen this face somewhere before', used with reference to the area at the base of the human spine, was said in such a way as to appeal to the ear rather than the eye. At least, that is what I think, and when I said so, I received the amusing reply, 'I would never go as far as the sculptor Canova.'

He had an immense capacity for work. For many years he made films at the rate of one every two months; and he was also very precise in his work, giving a real professional example to actors whose modest accomplishments were inversely proportional to the airs they gave themselves.

Totò's best – and genuinely princely – quality, however, was his generosity, which was all the more praiseworthy in that it was applied in silence and without ostentation. No one who applied to him for help was turned away. He was particularly sensitive to the needs of unlucky artistes, who spend their lives waiting vainly for an engagement, and animal lovers, would would write to him about the difficulty of looking after a dog or even (it really happened!) fifty dogs.

If anyone pointed out to him that, given the avalanche of appeals to which he responded, some people might be taking advantage of him by inventing needs and states of poverty, he would reply that he was aware of that, but 'not to trust people is saddening'.

When he came to see me at the Ministry of Finance, he mentioned the 'meanness' of the taxman precisely because he failed to take account of this rapid and unrewarded recirculation of the large sums of money which he earned. He had been told that in America you can deduct gifts to charity when you declare your income. But if it meant publicizing the act of charity, he considered it unfair, both because of his respect for the beneficiaries and because it was in poor taste to be ostentatious about one's acts of charity.

He also complained about the long time gap between earning money and receiving a tax assessment. He had recently received a file from the tax office containing astronomical figures going back as far as 1949–50. Nor did he think it just that the rate of tax for actors was so much higher than for bankers; and for a second time he referred to America, where film companies save even their most famous stars a good deal of tax by putting them on the payroll.

Since I knew that what he had told me about his personal circumstances was correct, I spent some time trying to convince him that it would be fair enough to take his word in his case, but that the tax authorities could not ignore the all-too-common tendency to keep quiet about one's income and evade tax. As for America, what he had been told (about deductions, salaried work, and so on) was true, but they had a steeply increasing scale of taxes;

and there was no doubt that the overall tax burden for everyone was heavier there than in Italy.

Was he really sure, anyway, that actors would prefer to move to annual or longer contracts, thereby tying themselves to a single producer? I doubted it.

The only useful outcome of our conversation was my advice – which he followed – that he should ask to pay his back-taxes in instalments, a widespread and quite normal practice.

He went on acting in films until the last day of his life, in spite of becoming almost blind. Once he had been taken on to the set, he brightened up and managed to move about and keep to the script almost as well as in earlier days. He *had* to keep earning, not so much for his own personal needs as to keep his munificence towards his fellow men up to its usual level.

Off the set he needed to be guided, and concealed his loss of sight behind large dark glasses. I passed him one day in the foyer of the Grand Hotel, but although we were only inches apart, he didn't see me. I didn't have the courage to greet him and say who I was. I know he would have felt humiliated.

I don't think the estate he left when he died was very substantial; and I received indirect confirmation of this some time later, when Franca Faldini came to interview me for Radio Monteceneri, where she had taken a job.

# 10
# Jacques Maritain

Nice airport on an early summer's morning thirty years ago. The Rome flight is several hours late; and almost all the passengers go up to the restaurant, grumbling about the airline, but cheering up at the thought that the delay will at least get them a good lunch. It is still the days of the old franc, and the exchange rate is tolerable even for the Italian lira.

The sudden crowd in the restaurant created a few difficulties for the staff, and the head waiter spent all his time apologizing and urging patience. At the table next to mine, there had sat down an elderly gentleman whose striking garb seemed to suggest that he was a pilgrim, for he had on a long khaki cloak. It was rather like the one the local postman used to wear when I was a child in Rome, but much more elegant. The pilgrim had not taken it off, perhaps because he did not trust the cloakroom, or more likely because he was allergic to air-conditioning. Perhaps he would take it off in the open air – if he hadn't made a vow not to – because it was pretty hot on the Côte d'Azur, and would certainly be so in Rome.

He studied the menu with meticulous care, as though it were an ancient manuscript. Since the waiter appeared to be about to go away to deal with other customers and leave him to his meditation, he called him back in the kind of authoritarian tone which, in less democratic days, would have been described as worthy of a barracks. The poor waiter didn't bat an eyelid, and indeed I could hear that he was apologizing with professional humility. I don't know whether the pilgrim was speaking in such loud tones because he had acquired the habit through deafness, or whether he was gradually becoming enraged. At last he made his choice, and meanwhile asked for a half-bottle of Evian water *tout de suite*.

50

Bowing and scraping, the waiter hurried off, and was back with the water in a flash.

But the general subdued hubbub was immediately drowned out by a roar of anger. The pilgrim claimed he had not asked for the water to be ice cold, gave the waiter a dressing down, and asked to speak to whoever was in charge, in order to make a formal complaint. (No such person ever came.) At this point the waiter must have run out of patience, for he went on serving his other customers, ignoring the pilgrim's curses and calls, and indeed paying particular attention to my and other tables. What the pilgrim was expecting to receive from the kitchens I had not managed to catch; I know only that when we had already finished the table d'hôte (always a good idea when a restaurant is crowded, quite apart from the saving in money), the gentleman in the cloak had not been served with anything. But when we were served with coffee, the pilgrim lost all self-control. He leapt to his feet, grabbed his bag, and made for the door, uttering as he walked down the aisle extremely rude comments about hotel and restaurant workers in general and those of Nice in particular.

I saw him again in the plane, and felt curious, alas, to know who he was. It was Jacques Maritain. No, not another man of the same name, unfortunately, but the author of that *Humanisme intégral* which Monsignor Montini had taught us to regard as the best brief guide to life there is. I was dismayed at this discovery, and didn't have the courage to take advantage of our proximity to engage him in conversation, as I would have done with alacrity in other circumstances.

Thinking back on it after all these years – that is why I am setting it down on paper – there is nothing shocking about even the best balanced and self-controlled man taking it out on whoever happens to be within range, on a day when he is in a wretched temper. On the contrary, it is a sign of normality in a man. Perhaps the delay was causing him to miss some important appointment in Rome; and perhaps his irritability was also partly caused by the knowledge that, for the first time, he would not find his friend and admirer Giambattista Montini in Rome, for he had been 'promoted' Archbishop of Milan a few months earlier.

# 11
# Colonel Nasser

In July 1962 I accompanied the two Italian Defence Committees to certain African countries to assess the state of our war cemeteries there, and to solve certain related problems by making it clear for everyone to see that *all* Italian political parties, whether in government or in opposition, were as one on this matter. In this way we hoped to counteract any objections that it had been a 'fascist war' or the like.

For Cairo, there had simply been arranged some meetings with government ministers and the military authorities. These were held to our satisfaction, against the background of a city which was still very picturesque and rather chaotic, but with fewer beggars in the streets and less ostentation of wealth than I had seen in King Farouk's day.

The day before we left, I received an unexpected telephone message from Magistrati, the Italian Ambassador, to the effect that Nasser, who was not at that moment in Cairo, 'would be pleased' to see me. My mind immediately turned to those polite phrases so frequently used by politicians and, more especially, diplomats; but this was something different, because Nasser had sent his personal aircraft from Alexandria, and it was now waiting to pick us up. Magistrati apologized for not having had a chance to consult me, but explained that he could not easily have turned down the invitation. He had certainly done the right thing, and I thanked him, apologizing to my colleagues for abandoning our joint programme for a few hours.

Nasser received us at his residence by the sea on the outskirts of Alexandria. It was a very simple building, decorated in good taste, but quite without ostentation. The view, however, was

magnificent. As he pointed out the little bay in front of us, Nasser explained that he spent many hours swimming or rowing there, both for relaxation or meditation, and to ponder on events and intentions. He also confessed to us that he found the atmosphere here more conducive to communication with the other members of his family, 'for it's often difficult nowadays to make real contact with one's own children'.

Since the meeting had been arranged at short notice, there was no agenda. The Italian Ambassador, Counsellor Molaioni, and I had had no time during the flight to do more than exchange a few ideas, for we assumed that this was a courtesy invitation which would involve no more than a few minutes' conversation. As it turned out, however, Nasser kept us for the whole afternoon. We had an exchange of ideas which was quite free of the rigidity usually associated with official conversations and was, therefore, very frank and interesting. What is more, we were served every half-hour with an excellent cup of tea and a variety of delicious cakes which Nasser encouraged us to sample.

As a soldier himself, Nasser began by praising the Italian parliament for showing respect and honour towards those who had died for their country. He also mentioned the disadvantages suffered by our troops in Cyrenaica, in that they had had to make do with improvised trenches, whereas the Allies had whole under-ground cities in which to mount a defence, and then counter-attack when the time came. Mussolini had deceived himself (or had been deceived) in supposing that he would ride into Alexandria in triumph; and even if he had managed to capture Alexandria, he would still have been defeated in the long run. It was incredibly naïve of him to count on Egyptian hostility towards Great Britain as a means of taking the latter's place as a sort of 'patron' of the world of Islam.

Nasser certainly believed in Islam as a 'cement' which held together different peoples, but he felt that its authentic basis was essentially Muslim. He was surprised that the Western Powers – and the United States in particular – should interpret Egyptian initiatives in this area as having primarily a political significance or even as constituting subversive and pro-Soviet propaganda. In fact, the moderation and influence of the Egyptian people, together with the cultural potential of the University of Al-Azhar, meant that, if the inevitable resurgence of certain traditional values in Islamic culture were to have their epicentre outside Egypt, then the 'Arab factor' really would have a revolutionary dimension. For it would either take the form of a fanatical holy war which flouted the lessons of history, or else be used by extremist elements in search of personal power or a Marxist revolution.

There had recently been a political upheaval in Algeria. Ben Bella had fallen from favour, and had had to leave the country in great haste. Nasser was a friend of his, and valued his own role as mediator between the various Arab states which had gained their independence. He spoke very frankly about Algerian affairs, saying that there had been misunderstandings, but that at all costs a breakdown must be avoided, since it would harm not only the new state of Algeria but the whole Arab world; for it would demonstrate, so soon after independence had been gained, how immature the new states were, with all the consequences that might bring. He took the view, furthermore, that all the Algerian leaders, from Ben Khedda down, were honest men, and it should not be impossible for them to reach an agreement. As for Ben Bella, he had known him for many years, even before his arrest by the French, and had the highest regard for his patriotism and honesty. He hoped that no outsider would declare himself publicly for or against Ben Bella and the government. He hoped, in particular, that the King of Morocco and Bourguiba would support his attempt to bring about reconciliation and understanding, because otherwise the entire Arab cause would be seriously compromised. That the Algerian army should be somewhat difficult was in a sense understandable, but their political rectitude was guaranteed, and it was surely not surprising if these veterans of a long and bloody war of liberation wanted a say in the government of the country. There had been differences of approach and even of substance in the Revolutionary Committee, but they should not be exaggerated or generalized.

What struck me about Nasser was the calm and precise way he expressed himself, in a tone of voice which was determined and yet persuasive.

He went on to talk about the Cairo economic conference within the context of what he hoped would be world-wide policies in favour of underdeveloped countries; and he touched on his fear that power blocs such as the European Community might bring about an increase in disparities and a decrease in the willingness of individual nations to help Third World countries. When we explained that his fear was unjustified, he pointed out that his view was shared by countries such as Australia, New Zealand, and Canada, which, both as individual states and as members of the British Commonwealth, were in a much stronger position to withstand competition from the Common Market. We in our turn pointed out that it was hoped to enlarge the European Community by bringing in the United Kingdom, and to establish broad agreements with African states; while at the same time the EEC would rationalize its policies towards other countries, in a way which Egypt would be bound to approve.

A third topic of conversation was the Geneva Disarmament Conference, in which the United Arab Republic was involved. He told us that the subject of disagreement was the usual one, namely the relationship between disarmament and arms control. The Soviet Union seemed convinced that international control before disarmament was a disguised form of spying, and therefore rejected it. If one took due account of this view and the psychological attitude underlying it, Nasser said, it would take a great deal of effort to overcome the obstacles scattered along the way, and so achieve results. Egypt's natural position was to seek a kind of non-aligned autonomy within the world context.

By now I was beginning to become aware of Nasser's charisma as a statesman. He put his arguments calmly and in a way which showed the religious basis of his whole political credo. After he had sung the praises of the movement of non-aligned countries as providing a counterweight not *against* but *alongside* the two great East—West blocs, I asked him whether he thought the Soviet Union could supply arms to Egypt without making sure that, when it came to the crunch, they were used in an appropriate cause. He thought for a moment, and then replied:

'A poor nation like ours cannot refuse any assistance (especially when it comes to discouraging Israeli aggression), but you and the Soviets don't understand us sufficiently well. When the moment of decision arrives, we shall retain our full freedom of action.'

He then returned to the question of the Arab world, and made the general remark that *no one* had found it possible to protest at the precautionary measures he had had to take against those responsible for anti-religious revolutionary propaganda. He was evidently referring to the 'compulsory retirement' imposed on Egyptian communists, whether military or civilian.

Since the matter had struck me at the time, I mentioned to him that during the long briefing a few days earlier on the site of the Aswan Dam, the ministry official who was showing us round made not the least mention of the presence and assistance of the Russians, to the extent that a Russian engineer had complained to us about it. Nasser's reply was eloquent, though evasive:

> The Americans made a huge blunder in not building the dam themselves. For the sake of a few dollars [was it really such a small sum?] they wiped out the debt of gratitude which the Egyptian people owed them for having put a stop to the stupid Anglo-French attack. Unfortunately, where the Americans are concerned, matters have to be dealt with in separate compartments, and business apparently takes precedence over politics.

Our conversation then turned to Italy. He acknowledged the justification for setting up the Atlantic Alliance, and thought that while American military influence was paramount within it, the European experience of centuries was bound to have a restraining influence and to lend it direction. But there was an increasing risk of a Moscow–Washington crisis as armaments gradually increased. Hence his firm resolve to enhance the reputation of the non-aligned countries.

Nasser certainly did not think there was any possibility of Italy's joining this 'third force', but our position gave us a unique opportunity to be sympathetic and become involved in dialogue. This was especially true because of our physical proximity to the statesman who, more than any other, knew how to interpret the international needs of the moment, and was also able to foresee their likely developments. Marshal Tito was his idol, and he talked about him with immense enthusiasm and admiration. He was surprised that I had not yet met him, and advised me to arrange a meeting as soon as possible; he would mention the matter to Tito himself. In Nasser's view, Tito was a sincere, peace-loving man because he had known the horrors of war; and he had also displayed extraordinary courage in taking an independent line from the Communist bloc at a time when Stalin was extremely powerful and Soviet relations with China were very close.

I mentioned the positive role played by Italy in 1948, when the thwarting of the Popular Front had not only had good consequences at home, but had also allowed Tito to make his stand. Without wishing to show any disrespect for Marshal Tito, I expressed the opinion – which I still hold – that if a government headed by Togliatti and Nenni had existed on his western frontier, he would have had the greatest difficulty in establishing the independence of Yugoslav communism a mere matter of months after the Italian election of 18 April 1948.

Nasser showed that he had a good grasp of post-war events, and I was pleased that he praised De Gasperi's policy towards Yugoslavia of making a practical approach to overcoming the inevitable problems of the aftermath of the war and frontier controversies.

As regards relations between Italy and Egypt, we agreed that they were very good, and that after Prime Minister Fanfani's visit in 1959 important economic initiatives had been successfully set in motion. Nasser told us that he would very much like to see Italy, and in particular to enjoy a brief period of rest there. He had started to make arrangements for such a visit the year before, but events in Syria had required his attention. Fresh complex problems in North Africa and the Middle East were developing even as we spoke, and they did not encourage him to think about trips abroad. His expressions of respect for Italy went beyond the conventional, and he showed that he had a considerable knowledge of Italian problems.

It was now evening. Our host insisted on introducing us to his family, before accompanying us to our car with great cordiality and friendliness.

When Nasser died in September 1970, and I read that his body was accompanied by weeping crowds of his people, I was not in the least surprised.

# 12
# Lina Merlin

It was with genuine emotion (sometimes it can be a matter of social duty or courtesy) that in August 1979 I sent my condolences on the death of Lina Merlin – the only woman in the Italian parliament who succeeded in having her name attached to a law of very considerable importance.

She had retired from parliamentary life some years earlier, but I had kept up a friendly relationship with her, based partly on my admiration for her as a woman whose deep convictions had allowed her to overcome every obstacle and win the battle for the cause in which she believed and to which she had devoted herself, ignoring threats, criticisms (often barbed), and jibes.

She was born at Pozzonovo, near Padua, on 15 October 1887, and was therefore approaching sixty when I first met her at the Constituent Assembly, where she made her mark for liveliness, dedication, and a certain increasing stubbornness. She began raising objections, for example, because changes were not being made to the names of schools called after members of the royal family, and because books imbued with approval of fascism were not taken out of circulation. (This cost poor Bontempelli his seat in the Senate.) She was more constructive, however, in putting forward and defending sensible ideas on the family, trade union rights, and the economic contribution of the artisan class in Italy.

Every now and again she would take up her old role as victim of political persecution – with biting criticism of the police force, which in her view had not been satisfactorily reformed – or else as the militant Socialist, who would make stubborn demands for state control over the economy as well as for complete freedom in the organization and activities of trade unions.

On 18 April 1948, she was elected to the Senate, but she still frequented the Chamber of Deputies, with the specific aim of gaining support for and eliminating prejudices against *her* bill, whose purpose was to eliminate not prostitution, but the *exploitation* of prostitution and the brothels in which it took place. It grieved her that a woman should offer her body for money (fortunately there was less talk of male prostitution in those days), but that was not the point; what had to be done was to break the links between prostitutes and their 'protectors' – an inappropriate polite term used to refer to men who are more aptly described in a variety of different dialect terms (the literary term is 'pander').

She devoted herself full-time to this problem, and was able to turn to something else only in 1952, when she joined other members of parliament for the Polesine region in pushing through legislation to provide aid for the areas and communities there which had suffered from severe flooding. I remember her worrying about the children and (strange as it may seem to put the two together) the thousands of turkeys which had been fattened for export at Christmas to the American forces in Germany. The poor birds had taken refuge on patches of dry land, where they were safe from drowning but not from dying of cold or hunger. At all costs she wanted the turkeys brought to safety by military helicopter; and she was at least successful in having the helicopters drop them generous rations of food.

The year after this 'specialization' in disasters, she also became a member of the parliamentary committee for special aid to Calabria. She discovered just how poverty-stricken life could be down there, and she often used the poverty of her own Polesine region in the North to stress the absurdity of treating North and South in Italy as though they were separate but internally homogeneous entities.

In the second post-war parliament, Lina Merlin concentrated her efforts on ensuring that her bill on prostitution should not gather dust any longer; but it was only at the very last moment that she was successful. On 4 March 1958, the *Official Gazette* published Law No. 75 (dated 20 February and bearing the signatures of Zoli, Tambroni, Medici, and Gonella) on 'The Closing of Brothels'.

Angelina Merlin was known simply as Lina, or even as 'la Senatrice', but ordinary people often referred to her as 'la Merlin'. She decided it would be a good idea to ask her constituents to return her to the Chamber of Deputies, so that she could break down the barrier of stubborn hostility which was bound to surround her law, especially since there were fears of a medical nature (a possible resurgence of venereal diseases, which had almost disappeared thanks to improved drugs during recent decades). These produced doubts and objections even within her own party. She regretted that there were reservations in certain quarters of the Christian Democrat Party, even though the four signatories to the law were all Christian Democrats. She also attacked those who made use of more or less doctored pieces of historical research to show that troops of prostitutes had even followed the crusades for the liberation of the Holy Land; or that later on in the Papal States the Spanish Embassy's good offices had been used to maintain a *de facto* presence of accepted brothels in Rome.

I had always supported Lina Merlin in this debate, though I had no personal experience of the matter. (I belonged to a generation of young Catholics who wouldn't even accept the word *bordello* to mean brothel, since it just means 'confusion' in Northern Italy.) My support sprang from two fundamental points of hers: *almost* everywhere else in the world, legalized houses of ill repute (as they are sometimes called) no longer existed; and the number of such houses still open in Italy was very small – about two thousand girls being involved. At the very least, some other way of controlling prostitution had to be found. And I did not allow myself to be swayed by references to ecclesiastical history, however accurate or inaccurate they might be.

It was worrying, however, both that almost all the girls from the brothels turned down the rehabilitation offered by law, and that street-walkers almost certainly had a not disinterested guardian behind them, too. Then there was the difficulty of interpreting regulations on soliciting. If one or more of these girls stand along the main roads out of town, or at town crossroads, and wait for customers – perhaps at night and advertising themselves by lighting little fires (Fellini portrayed them very vividly in *Cabiria*) – is that soliciting or not? There was room here, in my view, for no end of psychological hypocrisy on the part of the law. Nor was it right to discriminate too strictly between street-walkers and those who operate in luxury hotels or suitably equipped homes of their own. It has been claimed in this connection that in Rome alone there are enough individual girl tenants in expensive flatlets to elect a member of parliament! (This is purely a matter of statistics, of course.)

None of us, however, could fail to be aware of the sincere concern for human welfare which had inspired Lina Merlin. If we did not support her we might well not be *democrats*, and we certainly would not be *Christians*.

When she settled in at the Chamber of Deputies again, however, Lina Merlin also wanted to play a more active part in public life, and she did so with such vigour that in 1961 she ended up by quarrelling with her own party. So she joined the Mixed Group and solemnly declared that she would not stand at the next election.

She worked hard in parliament. Apart from frequently commemorating well-known or almost unknown deceased persons (such as Gastone Costa, Celestino Ferrario, Pietro Bellora, Giovanni Ponti, and even Anita Garibaldi; that is, three Christian Democrats, a Socialist, and an . . . independent), she turned her attention to child welfare, railway workers who had been sacked by the fascists, the Teatro Massimo in Palermo and subsidies for opera performances abroad, a law to forbid the sacking of female workers who marry, provisions to assist deaf-mutes and stammerers, and even minor but highly technical matters such as 'the use of wire-reinforced glass in the skylights of factories and public buildings' and regulations to forbid the use of 'oestrogens as growth or sex neutralization factors in animals intended for human consumption'.

More impressive was her work in the Anti-Mafia Commission, where she paid particular attention to the links between Mafia and prostitution. She was unsuccessful, however, in a second attempt to get something abolished. She wanted to get rid of theatrical agencies, that is to say those intermediaries who operate as performers' representatives and obtain parts for them. However, it would have been unjust, in my opinion, if a second law bearing the name of Lina Merlin had unwittingly placed two very dissimilar activities on the same plane.

When I was Under-Secretary to the Prime Minister's Office, I had been involved in theatrical matters and had a fair knowledge of the subject. A senior civil servant, Nicola De Pirro, had explained to me that arrangements had already been made to abolish these agencies during the fascist period; but as a result of protests from performers, who were left to fend for themselves, a blind eye had been turned to the continuation of their activities. For if indeed singers of the stature of Ferruccio Tagliavini or Claudia Muzio had really no need to go knocking on theatre doors – in fact their agents could obtain a handsome fee for choosing La Scala rather than San Carlo, or vice versa – there were a multitude of minor performers who would have spent the whole year kicking their heels round the corner from the theatre, if some impresario had not acted on their behalf. When I talked to Lina Merlin about this, I realized that what she wanted to do was not just prevent performers from being financially exploited, but also close down those bogus agencies which were officially in order, but where girls were attracted by an engagement or an audition, and then pushed into being used in a quite different way.

This was the theme of one of her last speeches in parliament, delivered on 9 July 1962. She circulated it as a pamphlet entitled 'Behind the Scenes'. Not many of us were there to hear her, but I remember that she took to task the independent opera companies for their extravagant costs, and directors for their mania for the grandiose. She gave two examples. During the storm scene in *William Tell* at the Baths of Caracalla she had seen the ridiculous innovation of neon arrows, each one split into four parts. And in another major theatre, the ladies playing minor parts in *La Traviata* were proudly wearing genuine Burano lace on stage as well as expensive period fans. While she was at it, she also took to task the way music had degenerated and given rise to the 'howling style' of singing (wolves howl, and dogs howl when they become wolves again, she said, quoting Jack London). She went on to conclude that, if we remained indifferent to the danger that opera might die, we could be compared to the madman who damaged a masterpiece by Raphael, perhaps because he was convinced that only certain modern aberrations deserve the name of art. Poor Alberto Enrico Folchi, who was then Minister of Entertainment, assured Lina Merlin that he had absolutely no intention of seeing opera into its grave; but he avoided tackling the difficult question of agents and agencies.

Strangely, criticism of the Merlin law was echoed by magistrates. In their speeches at the inauguration of the judicial year, many state attorneys attributed to it an increase in crime rates, for which they supplied facts and figures; and a Florentine judge referred the whole matter to the Constitutional Court on the grounds that the law flouted the Italian constitution.

By now Lina Merlin was no longer a member of parliament, and she asked for my help in correcting the ideas that were in circulation. I willingly offered her space in my journal *Concretezza*, and every judge of the Constitutional Court was sent a copy of her article, entitled 'There is no going back' (16 February 1964). As the person who had proposed closing brothels in the first place, she now calmly set out her reply to all objections, supporting her case partly by reference to a convention adopted by the United Nations Assembly for the suppression of both the white slave trade and the exploitation of prostitution. Shortly before this, Pia Colini Lombardi, a member of the Chamber of Deputies, had in fact circulated a document in support of this important UN enactment, on behalf of the Italian delegation to the Twenty-Third Congress of the International Abolitionist Federation.

Lina Merlin's article was much commented on in the daily press. In it she wondered how it was that at no inauguration of the judicial year between 1860 and 1958 had any reference been made to the conflict between what was laid down in the Consolidation Act on the Police Force, and the situation as it really was in the areas of public hygiene, the protection of women and even of prostitutes' clients, 'while in these state-recognized brothels young people were being initiated into every kind of sexual depravity; and ill treatment, torment, and even crimes were being carried out without being reported, let alone punished'.

On 10 March 1964, she wrote to me from Milan to express her gratitude for my having published this 'SOS in the name of civilized society, which many people also call a Christian society'. Since Moro was Prime Minister at the time, and therefore had the right to make suggestions to the State Attorney for the meeting of the Constitutional Court on 18 March, she wanted him to re-read her speeches and those of other members of parliament (Senators Boggiano Pico, Congolani, Terracini, and Rizzo; and Deputies Riva and Tozzi Condivi) while the law was being discussed. 'Surely,' she wrote in conclusion, 'the judges should not accept the objections presented by some wretched little lawyer who represents a pimp.'

The judges did not accept the objections. She wrote to me, from Milan again, on 17 June to tell me about it:

> You are the first person I have told how happy and satisfied I am to have just received from the Secretary of the Constitutional Court a copy of their judgement, filed yesterday, on the constitutional legality of Law No. 75. Now it is the duty of those ministers who had proposed amendments to the law to withdraw their bill, or at least allow it to be shelved indefinitely, for it could be opposed on the same grounds used by the Constitutional Court to reject the claim that Law No. 75 was unconstitutional.
>
> If poor street-walkers are objectionable, why isn't a serious attempt made to rid Italy of the international gang of pimps? Have you read *Tempo Illustrato*? Its series of articles on the subject has been interrupted this week, though. Many thanks for your influential support. Yours sincerely . . .

On 3 March 1974, Lina Merlin dropped a bombshell in the Italian Left by announcing her opposition to divorce and by signing the petition for a referendum to repeal the divorce law. In doing so, she was taking up a position against a false modernity which 'encourages the break-up of the family, takes no account of the fate of children, and places women in a position of inferiority'.

The divorce law remained on the statute book because that is what the majority of Italians decided. But that did not make Lina Merlin abandon her beliefs. She went on living her life as she always had, in total intellectual independence, even though it cost her dear.

# 13
# John F. Kennedy

John Kennedy was a novelty as President of the United States, for he was the first one to be a Roman Catholic. The question of his Catholicism had even been discussed at the Democratic Party Convention, where Harry Truman, who was opposed to Kennedy, had said that what worried him was not the *possible* influence of the Pope but the *certain* influence of John's father (who had once been Ambassador in London, and whose multifarious activities had often aroused criticism).

Kennedy put together a very efficient government, largely made up of men who were young.

NATO meetings and direct contacts between Italy and the United States gave me the opportunity of getting to know his Defense Secretary, Robert McNamara, extremely well, and his Secretary of State (that is, Foreign Secretary), Dean Rusk, fairly well. We in Italy maintained our contacts with these two men even after a Republican victory caused them to leave the government. McNamara then spent two terms of office as President of the World Bank, where he confirmed the very real managerial skills which had already been apparent at the Pentagon, plus a keen sensitivity to the progress of underdeveloped countries. Rusk, on the other hand, became head of the University of Athens in Georgia. (Georgia is a state where place-names from the ancient classical world, such as Athens and Rome, have been revived; but when Georgia was called on to provide a President of the United States, he came from the obscure little town of Plains.)

Kennedy made a moving inaugural address ('My fellow citizens of the world, ask not what America will do for you, but what together we can do for the freedom of man'), and his foreign policy

was based on three main aims: to strengthen NATO, to improve inter-American relations by means of the 'Alliance for Progress' programme, and to re-establish friendly relations with African states. To provide psychological support for this last policy, he made good use in Congress of Andy Young, a disciple of Martin Luther King, whom Carter subsequently appointed Ambassador to the United Nations. Andy Young's occasionally undisciplined spontaneity in the minefield of the United Nations caused Washington embarrassment at times; but nowadays in particular there are many people in Washington who look back with nostalgia on 'the days of Andy'. In any case, he has recently and deservedly returned to the limelight by handsomely winning the mayoral election in Atlanta. He is a fascinating and intriguing personality, and he is well known even in Italy for having taken part in a congress at Bergamo on John XXIII's encyclical *Pacem in terris*; and more recently he took part in a peace rally at Rimini organized by the Comunione e Liberazione movement.

For the most part, Italy's support of the Atlantic Alliance was taken for granted, but there were a few who made it clear to us that they were worried about the strong opposition to the Atlantic Treaty existing in Italy. What would happen if conflict were ever, alas, to take place, and all those millions of Italian Communists and Socialists felt themselves to be linked to the potential enemy?

My own view was that we should let time sort things out, without any outside interference in Italian politics, and without seeking to gain the *partial* support or even the neutrality of those who were at present opposed to the Atlantic Treaty. What we had to do was slowly convince the *whole* of the Italian Left that NATO was an organization for peace, and that within it there was not even so much as a theoretical plan for attacking the Eastern bloc. It had to be shown that the whole orientation of NATO was simply to provide an adequate 'overall reply' if the Warsaw Pact countries were to mount an attack.

From the point of view of security, it seemed to me a waste of time to gain the support of the Socialists for NATO without that of the Communists. Indeed, it would have been a mistake, because it would have caused the extreme Left to dig in its heels. And if proof were needed of Italian common sense and willingness to support constitutional democracy, I could point to two convincing pieces of evidence. One was the undisturbed unloading of American arms at Leghorn, in spite of loud official protests from those who were opposed to them; and the other was the setting up at Gioia del Colle of missile ramps which could be seen for miles, while the opposition in parliament kept on asking whether rumours about their existence were true or not.

I would perhaps not have taken the trouble to write about these matters, but for the fact that in his book, *A Thousand Days: John F. Kennedy in the White House*, Arthur Schlesinger provides a detailed description of contacts made in Rome by American agents with the aim of bringing centre-left governments into being. The correct attitude, in my view, was to allow the Centre-Left to come into being as a natural convergence of basic party policies – especially as regards the Christian Democrat and Socialist parties – without pushing things too fast, and without oversimplifying the situation by seeing it solely in terms of the international political scene.   After the discussions held at Zevi's home, and the backing given by Ugo La Malfa, Washington had come to the conclusion that it had to support a broadening of the base of Italian government, to the extent that anyone who refused to join the crusade was assumed to be a reactionary and a clerical. Even Reinhardt, the US Ambassador in Rome, became involved, though I don't know whether it was a matter of personal conviction or whether he was simply acting on instructions.

When I was on a working trip to the United States, Dean Rusk spoke to me about the matter, clearly having been put up to it by some 'Italian expert', though he started by making it clear that this was just an exchange of ideas between friends and not an official approach. He took the view that the attitude I had adopted at the Christian Democrat Party congress might harm Italy's democratic progress, and act as an obstacle to the policies of Nenni, who was now regarded as utterly reliable since he had thrilled Americans by announcing that he was returning the Stalin Prize. I told him that the invasion of Hungary had certainly caused the Italian Left to rethink its position, but that it would be a mistake to force the issue without the Italian political parties getting together to work out in detail both a plan of operations and a series of strategic aims in relation to many matters, ranging from the economic to the institutional. Furthermore, to force the issue would serve no military purpose (the only one which could justify American interest in the problem), and ran the risk of causing the Social Democrats to feel that they were being undervalued and left on one side. I also pointed out that anyone who really wanted to make a contribution to the strengthening of democracy in Italy would have to work patiently at undoing the Communist breakaway of 1921 and reuniting all left-wing forces. At the moment, however, any such aim was certainly premature and impossible to achieve.

These matters came up again at a select lunch at the Villa Taverna on 2 July 1963 when Kennedy was on a state visit to Italy, but they were referred to in very general and ill-defined terms. I took the opportunity, however, of asking him whether, quite apart from his being a Catholic, he didn't think it strange that the United States had no diplomatic relations with the Vatican, unlike so many other countries who might be very 'lay' in their attitudes, or even Islamic. He replied that if he were elected for a second term of office, he would certainly solve the problem; but he didn't feel that he could tackle it now, because he wanted to avoid stirring up the very 'Catholic question' which he had worked so hard to avoid after his nomination.

Kennedy took the opportunity to express his interest in finding out about Italian policy towards the south of the country, and he told us how the families of early immigrants were now climbing high in American society, their children and grandchildren now providing many magistrates, university teachers, and managers of important companies. In the political arena, too, the Italians had done themselves proud, being present in considerable numbers in Congress and in state legislatures. He mentioned John Pastore of Rhode Island as a top expert on nuclear control, and pointed out that both Fiorello La Guardia and Vincent Impellitteri had been mayors of New York. And then, almost as though to have his own back for my bringing up the question of an American Ambassador to the Vatican, he pointed out that it was only in the hierarchy of the Catholic Church in America that the sons of Italians had so far failed to make their mark.

Kennedy was very proud of the fact that Americans of Italian origin – including the clergy – had almost all voted for him; and he mentioned that influential campaign assistance had been provided by men who had come from Italy for that purpose (including 'young' Salvatore Lima, the Mayor of Palermo).

I was favourably impressed at that same lunch by McGeorge Bundy, one of Kennedy's aides whom I had not encountered before, and who made a number of acute and well-informed observations on international politics.

I subsequently accompanied Kennedy on a visit to NATO headquarters at Bagnoli, and was delighted to be present when the people of Naples, who were packed for miles along the route

Kennedy took in an open car, gave him a tumultuous and spontaneous welcome.

John Kennedy had no chance to try for a second term as President, nor even to complete his first term of office, for he was assassinated four months later at Dallas while travelling in a festive motorcade with his wife Jacqueline and the Governor of Texas, John Connally. The murder remained shrouded in mystery; and it may just have been ghoulish boasting which led some Cuban refugees in the Dominican Republic to say in my hearing that the Dallas murder served the White House right for the useless loss of life at the Bay of Pigs – as though it were an act of judgement brought about by some medieval God.

On the initiative of the American Embassy, a memorial service for Kennedy was held in the church of St John Lateran in Rome. The mass was celebrated by Cardinal Spellman of New York in the presence of the Italian government and almost all the American bishops, who were in Rome for the Vatican Council. Cardinal Cushing of Boston, however, had immediately left for Washington, because he had very close ties with the Kennedy family.

In an article published in *Concretezza*, I had occasion to write: 'There can be so little doubt as to John F. Kennedy's great service to peace, that even Kruschev and Togliatti have been obliged to acknowledge it.'

# 14
# *Pietro Valdoni*

When he was elected to Rome city council as a Christian Democrat, Professor Valdoni's regular attendance and punctuality at the council chamber were such as had never been achieved by many worthy councillors who had a lot more spare time than he had. A journalist wrote that everything he did was well done.

Valdoni's behaviour during the 1966 election campaign was also extraordinary. He showed striking respect, in the first place, for the Rome electorate's political convictions. In his letter to the voters, he wrote: 'Should you decide to vote for the Christian Democrat Party, I shall be grateful if you will include my name amongst your preferences.' Moreover, he had visited some of the outlying Christian Democrat sections, where an illustrious and famous candidate such as he, received a most enthusiastic welcome (our enemies, said a young Christian Democrat from the Tufello district, will burst with rage).

It was indeed almost incredible how hard he worked at his profession and yet how he made himself available for other activities, whether it was working with Friuli-Venezia Giulia associations, being President of the Supreme Health Council, giving learned lectures, or accepting invitations to those Rome salons where what appeared to be no more than society gatherings were in fact serving the useful purpose of bringing together, *almost* by chance, important people with a variety of jobs and from a variety of origins.

One day I congratulated Valdoni on his multifarious activities. He replied that a man's productivity in life depends on how he organizes his time. But didn't all that time spent in the operating theatre, day after day, tire him out? All he would admit in that

connection was that at about eleven o'clock in the morning he would regularly drink a glass of water with a lot of sugar in it, thereby avoiding that sudden sleepiness which, at some hour of the day, all human beings feel to a greater or lesser extent, as a result of secretions from some gland or other. Ever since then I have treasured his valuable remedy, since it is an excellent substitute for that less scientific cure, the cold shower.

At an early hour in the morning he would already be in his university department, and would begin a series of operations, which might go on for as long as eight hours. Then, after a sandwich and a cup of coffee, he would move to the Sanatrix clinic and begin operating again until late in the evening. This was his typical timetable, though it might vary, with consultations, attendance at the more important congresses, and, during his period of office as a city councillor, his duties as a political representative.

During one of the many discussions on whether university professorships should be 'full-time' jobs, Aldo Moro (who was opposed to such a rigid system) asked me, as leader of the Christian Democrat parliamentary group, to use the case of Valdoni as strong evidence in support of his argument. I did so, with partial success, after being encouraged by a visit I paid to the University of California. Everybody there – from my guide, who was a professor of political economy who had spent a sabbatical year in Italy selling bowling-alleys, to all the other teachers I approached – told me that the idea of 'full-time' professorships was nonsense. But there had to be a strict check on the observance of teaching commitments, on keeping up to date with one's subject, and on giving individual attention to students at their request and without limitations. Anyone who failed to observe these rules could be sure that his contract would not be renewed the following year. (They don't have security of tenure or life appointments over there.) For the rest, if they devoted their hours or months of free time to a profession or to some other paid activity instead of playing golf or bridge, that was not a matter for criticism. On the contrary, contact with the *real* world enriched their experience and contributed to both their fields of activity. They went even further – and it must have been a well-known joke – for all the university teachers I spoke to (except for the bachelors) told me that if 'full-time' was introduced where they worked, they would pass their wives' bills on to me.

'Full-time' is a subject that Italian politicians and university professors like to bring up at frequent intervals, in order to acquire a following and show how righteous they apparently are. But every time a job falls vacant, a professor is sure to be proposed to fill it; and these applications are not just a formality. For if you look at who the chairmen of savings banks are, you will find that university professors are in a more or less overall majority. Evidently it is chic to talk about *full*-time and to practise *part*-time.

Professor Valdoni had been the uncontested number one in Italian surgery for some time, when he gained particular fame as a result of involvement in such celebrated cases as those of Palmiro Togliatti, John XXIII, and Paul VI.

When Togliatti was critically ill after the assassination attempt by Antonio Pallante, it was Valdoni's encouraging assessment of his case, on the afternoon of 14 July 1948, which calmed fears as to whether Togliatti would survive the fight for life which had been going on for some hours.

From that moment on he remained Togliatti's medical supervisor, alongside his personal physician, Mario Spallone. And when Togliatti had a cerebral haemorrhage in the Crimea, Valdoni rushed to his bedside at once, but, alas, no operation could save him this time.

How was Valdoni to carry out an examination of John XXIII without the patient being put into a state of alarm? The expedient devised was an audience for the committee of the College of Surgeons which was then holding a congress. However, the X-ray examinations spoke so clearly for themselves that no medical examination was necessary. Discussion centred on whether or not it was possible to carry out an operation, given the danger involved as a result of the advanced state of the tumour, the Pope's age, and his physical bulk.

It was claimed that the Vatican State Secretariat had opposed the operation, but Professor Gasbarrini told me that there was total medical agreement on not operating. However, when a medical bulletin was published in the Vatican newspaper *L'Osservatore romano*, the vague expression 'stomach trouble' had to be used as a compassionate terminological device to conceal from Pope John XXIII right to the end the extreme seriousness of his illness.

Pietro Valdoni returned to the Vatican during the pontificate of Paul VI in order to oversee the setting up of a makeshift (but beautifully equipped) operating theatre. Its purpose was to allow Valdoni, assisted by Professor Mario Arduino as urologist, a professor of clinical medicine, and a member of hospital staff, to carry out the most eminent of prostatectomies. Everything went very well, and the Pope remained a grateful admirer of Valdoni, as he explained in the most moving terms when Valdoni died.

One naturally wonders why Valdoni was elected to Rome city council only once. In 1971, I was one of those asked to press him to stand for election again (but he had already turned down a Christian Democrat offer to stand for the Senate in 1968), and I think I am right in suggesting that he was disappointed at the council's working practices. There were long delays in getting council meetings started; interminable speeches were devoted to saying obvious or irrational things; and it often happened that matters could not be voted on for lack of a quorum. He said he would think about it, but I did not bank on his agreeing. On 18 May 1971, he wrote to me:

> I regret having to say no to your suggestion. I have decided not to stand again at the local elections because I am over seventy-one, and also because now that I am off the permanent staff I cannot get assistants to help out while I am busy with the election campaign. In 1966 I was able to prepare for the election in good time, but that is not the case this time, and a brief preparation would not be satisfactory. Furthermore, the physical effort required is more than I can now manage. I have promised that I will do my best to persuade all my friends to keep the Christian Democrat vote as high as before. Please forgive my refusal. Your kindness towards me is something I still prize, as I have always done, and I hope it will continue.

There was nothing more I could do to persuade him. I wrote and thanked him in the following terms: 'I understand the reasons for your decision, and I hope we may collaborate in other ways (I have in mind possible contacts between you and the Christian Democrat parliamentary group on the difficult subject of health reform). Not to mention that the Christian Democrat Party owes you public thanks for your generous and exemplary work in the Rome city council.'

The following year I was pleased to accept an invitation as Prime Minister to attend a ceremony organized by the Rome Association of Triestini and Goriziani in honour of 'Pietro Valdoni, Trieste's ambassador to Italy and the world'. He was touched, and for the first time I could see in him some signs of tiredness.

In 1976 there was a rumour that Valdoni had cancer. His usual habit of openness was seen even here. Apparently he took his name off some X-ray plates and discussed them with his closest aides, agreeing as to the fatal gravity of the disease, and revealing only at the last moment that the lungs concerned were *his*.

His Christian faith was his support. In 1963, at the time of a tragic bereavement in the family, he had written to me saying, 'I am fortunate in that I can fill the gap in my life by working harder, and I am fortunate in believing in the Resurrection.'

He died in November 1976. Paride Stefanini – another great surgeon who was also to die of cancer – said of Valdoni that he was loved by his students 'because he didn't just teach surgery, he also taught standards of behaviour: how and in what way a man, or a surgeon, or an expert should devote himself to his country, to society, to his work, and to his teaching commitments. Valdoni never spared himself; he never spared himself for any reason whatsoever.'

And when Fiorenzo Angelini, the bishop responsible for the medical community in Rome, officiated at Valdoni's funeral, he said: 'What we are doing at this moment is not witnessing a death, but inheriting a call to life.'

A great crowd gathered to pay their last respects, from the President of the Republic, Giovanni Leone, to many ordinary people who owed it to Valdoni that they were still alive.

Valdoni was also a very attractive man. During the elections of ten years earlier, I heard a Pietralata girl say with a certain excitement: 'He looks like a film star. He reminds me of Walter Pidgeon, but he's more handsome.'

I happened to notice that this same young woman was present at the funeral that morning in the church of Santa Costanza. Like many other people there, her eyes were moist with tears of sincere sorrow.

# 15
# *Lyndon Johnson*

Lyndon Johnson automatically took possession of the White House on the tragic death of Kennedy, and it required some effort for him to demonstrate at international level those qualities which had given him a distinguished career in Congress but which, in accordance with established practice, had certainly not been used during his vice-presidency. In fact it was by accident that he became Kennedy's running partner, for Kennedy had offered to run on a joint ticket with him only because he was wrongly convinced that Johnson would turn the offer down.

When Johnson came to Italy as Vice-President in September 1962, I was amazed at his Texan exuberance. He paid little attention to the toast at the state banquet at the Villa Madama, and read his reply from prepared cards without the least involvement. He attempted to break through the boredom of protocol by suggesting that he should dance rather than stand and pretend to be interested in introductions to people he would never see again in his life. And as a gesture intended to get the dancing started, he lifted Linda Della Porta, the young wife of the Mayor of Rome, right off the ground. Alas, the gesture failed. The rules of protocol are rigid. For more than an hour, between coffee and a liqueur, he had to put up with a parade of guests.

General Vernon Walters had told him that I was about to go to the United States to visit some military bases, and he seemed interested in the fact that my itinerary included San Antonio. He suggested that if I wanted alcoholic drinks there, I should join a club. At the time the remark puzzled me, but I realized what he meant when I arrived in that attractive Texan city with its hundred canals, reminiscent of Venice. In those parts the sale of liquor was forbidden in public bars and permitted only in clubs. Consequently every bar had turned itself into a club, which one could join just by paying a few dollars. I was told that there were more than a thousand of these clubs in the town.

What really got me into Johnson's good books was a reference I made to the Space Research Center at Houston, which Johnson was very proud of. He even wrote a letter to thank me for my favourable passing reference to it, and renewed his good wishes for my trip to the United States.

I have no particular memories of Johnson's second term of office, and indeed there were no striking political events during either term. However, I did note in my diary, for 20 January 1965, a very beautiful remark of his: 'We have discovered that every child who is educated, every man who finds a job, and every sick person who is cured is like a candle added to an altar: it brightens the hopes of all the faithful.'

# 16

# Giovanni Leone

December 1971. It took twenty-three ballots to elect a President – two more than in the long election of 1964, which itself had seemed to constitute a hopefully unbeatable record.

Perhaps the way the election is carried out, with senators, deputies, and representatives of the regions voting together, has its effect and ought to be reconsidered. As President of the Chamber of Deputies, Pertini – whose ability and impartiality were amongst the few plus points in the whole affair – announced that work would begin at once on drawing up a new set of rules to govern the whole procedure.

Two ballots a day may be all very well in a Papal conclave (don't blame the Christian Democrats for making such a comparison; it was some thoroughly 'lay' politicians, who also brought up that hoary old rhetorical invitation to tear off the roof of the Chamber of Deputies – and as a matter of fact the Chamber would look much better without it), because the cardinals act as individuals, but we members of parliament work in groups and parties. In any case, history shows that it has sometimes taken a very long time to elect a Pope. It took 186 days to turn Cardinal Lambertini into Benedict XIV, and five years later it took as much as two years and three months to produce Celestine V (who, like De Nicola as President of the Republic, didn't stay long in the job). But that is not the problem.

When a particular candidate has been 'assessed' by the assembled senators and members of the Chamber of Deputies, it then has to be seen whether the secret ballot reflects the openly undertaken agreements. In my view, it is a waste of time to carry out the same identical voting ritual each morning and afternoon. It is better to

82

hold ballots less frequently, so that appropriate contacts and explanations can take place, both within political groups, and between groups which may possibly find common ground.

I certainly do not claim to have the necessary knowledge or skill to relate the whole story of events leading up to the election of Senator Giovanni Leone. I am bound in all modesty to admit that it was only some years after the previous presidential election in 1964 that I managed to put together all the pieces of the mosaic, especially as regards the reasons for the sudden appearance of Giulio Pastore as a candidate. His candidature appeared to be providing tactical support for an opposition candidate from within the Christian Democrat Party; but that was not in fact the case. Inevitably, therefore, certain aspects of what happened at the 1971 presidential election still escape me.

What I can do, however, is to sketch the outlines of these complex events of December 1971 with a certain degree of accuracy.

The Christian Democrat Party rejected the idea of early contacts with other parties to seek support for a short list of names, and went instead for a Christian Democrat president (without thereby seeking to browbeat or discriminate against other parties with similar ambitions). It was agreed that the party delegation authorized to negotiate could mention specific names only once the general assembly of Christian Democrat senators, members of the Chamber of Deputies, and regional councillors had met and chosen a candidate. This meeting was scheduled for a mere sixteen hours before the vote in the Chamber. It confirmed the idea of a single candidate, and discarded the suggestion that a first name should be put forward to sound out the situation, act as a standard bearer, or whatever you like to call it. For all that would achieve was to postpone the feared clash between our champion and that of the united Left; though, of course, it could conceivably happen that the *banderillero* would be so showered with votes that the *picadores* and the great *toreros* would never even enter the ring (if you will forgive my use of bullfighting terminology).

When the delegation came to the first party assembly on 8 December, it had very little to report. In our general review of the situation with the other parties, we had merely received confirmation of what everybody had known for several days:

(1) There would be a Socialist candidate supported by the whole of the parliamentary Left (Socialists, Proletarian Socialists, Communists, and the independent Left, plus subsequent support from Manifesto members of the Chamber of Deputies).

(2) Saragat would stand as the candidate of the Social Democrats.

(3) There would be a fair number of Liberals and members of the South Tyrol People's Party who would support the Christian Democrats (but the Liberals would vote for Malagodi in the meantime).

(4) A certain number of Republicans would similarly support the Christian Democrats, though they had a distinct preference for a candidate who might be a Christian Democrat but whose politics would not be of too bright a hue.

Contact with the extreme Right had, of course, been excluded, as a result of a formal vote taken by the National Council of the Christian Democrat Party.

The prospects were not too rosy, therefore, even if the failure to command sufficient support, from which all parties suffered, offered us the consolation of an uncertain outcome whether we looked to left or right.

The Christian Democrat Party chose Fanfani, whose position as principal candidate was more or less taken for granted. However, at the first ballot on 9 December, forty of Fanfani's Christian Democrat votes failed to appear: nine of the voters were absent, and thirty-one had taken advantage of the secret ballot to express their dissent. The scourge of 'rebels' had struck again, and little consolation was to be found in working out that there was a smaller proportion of them than in the past, and that similar tactics had been used by some of those who were supposed to vote for De Martino.

In the afternoon ballot, things were even worse; the number of clandestine dissidents went up by another fifteen. But they all toed the line in the third ballot.

It is important to establish the role played by these dissidents within the party. When we had our second round of conversations with the other delegations, and asked all the 'constitutional' parties to support Fanfani's candidature, while the Left refused outright, the Social Democrats said that they could not agree because of the lack of consistency in the Christian Democrat voting. After talking to Fanfani himself, however, they agreed to a test vote, which took place on 15 December, with Fanfani gaining 393 votes (94 per cent of the Christian Democrat vote). Let us look at the figures for this eleventh ballot. If we add to these 393 the 56 votes for Saragat, 48 for Malagodi, 12 Republican abstentions, and 5 blank voting papers from the South Tyrol, we get a total of 514 – which is more than the minimum required for election.

At this point the Social Democrats introduced a new argument, in addition to the one all parties put forward, that they wanted to be quite sure that no one was elected through the surreptitious support of neo-fascists and monarchists. They now said that the new president ought to be elected by more than a bare majority, and therefore it was necessary to seek some agreement between the two main blocs (the Christian Democrats and the Left).

This was the point at which Fanfani's candidature began to founder, in spite of a new round of negotiations which the Christian Democrat leaders and the party general assembly imposed upon us. Our well-founded expectation that we would obtain the votes of the Social Democrats and even the Republicans was fading to a worrying extent, and the Liberals were the only outsiders still willing to vote for a Christian Democrat candidate.

How could we find a way out of this impasse? If it was essential to achieve some agreement between the two blocs, it had to be between ourselves and the Socialists. But what kind of an agreement?

The Socialists insistently called on us to support their candidate, and we were willing to accept at once the repeated offer to drop De Martino in favour of the 'less colourful' Nenni (how times had changed!) or some other Socialist candidate whom the Christian Democrat Party would find acceptable and support. Obviously the Socialists had to obtain the agreement of their allies on the Left, but it was also true that a jointly backed Christian Democrat–Socialist candidate would immediately obtain enough votes (424 plus 104) to be successful; so it was a question of finding someone of sufficient standing in government circles. Was this just an academic exercise, in view of the pre-established left-wing front? Perhaps. But it is also true that you don't invent a 'constitutional range' of parties and reject it at the same time.

La Malfa broke a lance in public on behalf of Nenni's candidature. The Christian Democrat Party's room for manoeuvre was becoming increasingly restricted.

When it was discovered that, as things were, we Christian Democrats were unwilling to vote for a non-Christian Democrat candidate (an attitude confirmed by the party leaders), the Socialists and the other parties of the Left made a counter-offer which can be summed up more or less as follows: we are willing to back down on a Socialist or other non-Christian Democrat candidate, provided that the Christian Democrat Party replaces Fanfani by another candidate whose reputation as a progressive Catholic, and whose career in high public office, will allow voters of the Left to understand why we have abandoned De Martino and Nenni in order to elect a Christian Democrat.

Anyone who is accustomed to assessing other people's difficulties as well as his own will acknowledge that the Left was not behaving irresponsibly. And he must also acknowledge that they did not have recourse to some underhand manoeuvre to disunite the Christian Democrat groups. Negotiations remained the responsibility of the parties, and this was an enormous improvement on any other kind of negotiation. But the Socialists made the mistake of thinking that the required characteristics – which they had set out in a thoroughly normal way – could all be found in one single Christian Democrat. By placing this over-ambitious mantle on Aldo Moro, they effectively undermined his position, although it was not their intention to do so. It ill suited him, and caused a number of Christian Democrats to react against what they saw as a Christian Democrat being *imposed from outside*.

Since the Social Democrats confirmed that they wanted the successful candidate to be elected by *a large majority*, however, and declared that they did not wish to express an opinion on proposed candidates (except to say that Fanfani would not do) until *after* Christian Democrats and Socialists had reached an agreement, we Christian Democrats were effectively being made to play the Socialist game. The situation became that much more difficult, moreover, when on 18 December, Saragat dropped his challenging bombshell by withdrawing his candidature and calling on the 1,008 electors in the Chamber of Deputies to give a large majority to a president who would be the right one both to serve Italy at such a difficult period and to put an end to this tense electoral struggle.

But that was not the last twist to the story. Since the Social Democrats realized that they would have to explain themselves, and since the Socialists were insisting on the straight choice of Nenni or Moro, the former party now aligned themselves with the Republicans (who had taken this line all along) by saying that they would vote for a Christian Democrat provided his name was not Fanfani or Moro. Let it be quite clear, incidentally, that there was nothing personal in all this; it was just a question of making political judgements as to the repercussions which, rightly or wrongly, a particular choice would have on public opinion. Indeed, there was nothing but praise on all sides for De Martino, Fanfani, and Moro as individuals, precisely from people who regretted that they could not vote for them.

Just before a general meeting of Christian Democrats held to sort this problem out, the Social Democrats and Republicans suddenly found themselves in alliance with the Liberals, and now abandoned their insistence on a *large majority*, offering to vote with us for a Christian Democrat candidate who, the Liberals suggested, might be any one of Leone, Rumor, or Taviani.

This late offering of one from three was opposed on the Left by insistence on the candidature of Moro. But the Christian Democrat groups decided by a majority to go for one from three, and since Rumor and Taviani had in the meantime withdrawn, Leone was the only one remaining.

The Christian Democrats had voted by secret ballot after a lively debate, during which the members from Liguria had announced that they would set up an independent regional Christian Democrat constitution (on the lines of Strauss's Bavarian Christian Democrats) if Moro became President. I cannot give numbers, as we promised not to, but I can say that Leone was top of the ballot, with a majority that was more than slight but less than substantial.

1964–1971: *multa renascentur quae iam cecidere*. Leone's strength evidently lay not only in his personal qualities, but also in his non-involvement in any factions or pressure groups.

Our invitation to the Left to vote for Leone was turned down (once again for political reasons which had no *personal* implications). There was then a moment of hesitation, because the Republicans seemed to be tempted again by the prospect of Nenni appearing as an unofficial candidate on the Left; but when La Malfa added the weight of the Republican Party to the support for Leone on the night of 22 December, the latter agreed to stand; and so Christian Democrats, Social Democrats, Liberals, Republicans, and the South Tyrol People's Party decided to vote for him in the twenty-second ballot in the late evening of 23 December. He failed to gain the necessary majority by one vote, while the new Socialist candidate, Nenni, obtained about as many votes as De Martino.

It would have been quite absurd and incomprehensible for us to plunge back into complicated negotiations, and at the ballot held on the morning of Christmas Eve, Life Senator Giovanni Leone received 518 votes, thereby becoming the sixth President of the Italian Republic.

President Leone seemed to have all the necessary qualities to exert a general appeal as a candidate rather than an appeal to this or that group within the electorate. If that was indeed the case, and though there might be understandable arguments about him for the first few days, one would have expected to witness a release of tension and an objective recognition of the new President's ability to calm Italian anxieties. That was true, however, only of the early years of his presidency.

When the election result was announced, I caused surprise amongst those sitting beside me in my seat as leader of the Christian Democrat group, by smiling. I could not help remembering the telephone calls I used to receive, between 1945 and 1953, every time there was a cabinet crisis, asking me to tell De Gasperi that *Professor* Giovanni Leone would prefer not to be considered for ministerial or under-secretarial posts, because he would never abandon the *real world* of the university and the Law Courts. I don't deny that, the first time this happened, I thought it an ingenious way of bringing himself to De Gasperi's attention, but I soon learned that was not the case. Besides, De Gasperi knew him well, both as Secretary of the Christian Democrat Party for the city of Naples in 1944, and as a member of the Constituent Assembly, where, to use De Gasperi's words to me, he had valued Leone's qualities as a 'pragmatic professor'.

He had been appointed to a university chair as a brilliant young man, and had then gone the usual round of Italian universities: from Camerino to Messina, and from there to Bari, Naples, and Rome, all the while pursuing his research and updating his highly regarded manual on criminal and trial law.

His work in parliament did not prevent him from pursuing his career in teaching and the law, so he accepted appointment as Vice-President of the Chamber of Deputies, and then as President when Gronchi became President of the Republic. (Since the counting of the votes had been televised it had brought Leone great publicity, and his Neapolitan accent was charmingly to the fore, especially when he used the phrase 'schede *bianghe*'.)

During his eight years in these two positions, he showed considerable skill in organizing and directing the Chamber's business, as well as a great capacity for hard work. While in his seat as President of the Chamber, he could often be seen correcting the proofs of his academic books; but if some member of parliament wandered off the subject in a speech, he was deluding himself if he thought that Leone would not notice. There would be a prompt reaction and, often by means of some pungent but good-natured piece of irony, matters were put right. Nor did he lack firmness if required. That had become clear in 1952 during the difficult discussions on amendments to the electoral law. Since Gronchi was ill, Leone regularly took his place, and at the very beginning of the debate he had been obliged to make his presence felt, as a result of a serious incident which is worth relating. During a lively discussion on procedure, a member of the Chamber named Lizzadri had rashly come out with the remark:

'Now it's Gonella interpreting procedure instead of the President of the Chamber!'

He thereby aroused the immediate and thoroughly justified ire of the said President, who burst out, 'I won't tolerate this. I am expelling you from the Chamber!'

Lizzadri gave some feeble excuse which could scarcely be heard amidst the inevitable uproar and exchanges of rude remarks, and then the matter of his expulsion was put to the vote and passed; but Lizzadri did not leave the Chamber. So, at 4.45 p.m., Leone adjourned the session. Two hours went by before Lizzadri left the Chamber, and only after another hour was spent in diplomatic consultations was it possible to resume the session. Nenni opened proceedings by making a speech of pacification and, as leader of the parliamentary group to which Lizzadri belonged, suggested that his protégé had succumbed to the overheated atmosphere, and asked that he be given the opportunity to provide a calm explanation of what had happened.

Leone first gave Lizzadri permission to re-enter the Chamber and make a brief explanatory speech (this was really a roundabout way of asking him to apologize), and then asked the Chamber to turn the previously imposed punishment into a simple reprimand. The Chamber approved.

That was the sort of man Leone was, and we witnessed his great strength of character during the tense days of the Tambroni government.

On 30 June, news reached the Chamber of the first incidents in Genoa resulting from the famous MSI congress. Members of parliament began to get excited, and a heated atmosphere developed, which was to lead to the most dramatic sessions over which Leone presided throughout his eight years in office.

On 1 July, there was some excitement over parliamentary questions put to Spataro as Minister of the Interior. Leone managed to keep order, and firmly stated, 'I shall see that this session, like all others, is carried on calmly and soberly.' But it was impossible to maintain order on 6 July, when there took place in the Chamber an angry tumult which must be rated one of the ugliest incidents in the whole history of the Italian parliament.

At about 8 p.m. news reached the Chamber that a member of parliament had been injured during riots in Rome. Left-wing

members came down on to the floor of the Chamber and started a
fight, with the result that Li Causi, who was standing in as
President, was obliged to suspend proceedings.

A couple of hours later Leone tried to resume the session. He
expressed his great regret that some members had been the victims
of unparliamentary behaviour, and promised that he would ask for
a thorough investigation to be made, in order to identify those
responsible. However, there was no hope of maintaining order in a
Chamber where Giancarlo Pajetta was greeted with rapturous
applause when he shouted: 'Long live the members of parliament
who are fighting alongside the people and are battling in the
squares!' and uttered such slogans as 'Down with the government!
Out with the government!'

Within a few minutes the floor of the Chamber was again invaded
by the occupants of the benches on the left, and a particularly
serious affray developed, very much at the expense of the Chamber
officials who tried to form a barrier between the two sides and
found themselves the victims of physical violence without, of
course, being able to hit back.

Once again Leone suspended proceedings, and it was after
midnight before they could be resumed. Here is his appeal, which
succeeded in calming things down somewhat (without his having
to punish individuals), and allowed proceedings to reach a conclusion without further complications:

> The very serious incident which took place this evening cannot be
> allowed to pass by without my saying how strongly and seriously I
> deplore it. Not only was physical violence used, but an attack was
> made on the benches where members of the government were
> sitting ready to discuss quite different matters.
>
> I must praise and thank the Chamber officials who unselfishly
> carried out a task which it was not their duty to perform. Two of
> them, Ricci and Loffredi, have been injured. Loffredi has been taken
> to hospital.
>
> My expression of disapproval must not be an end in itself. It must
> also be taken as a warning that incidents of that kind must not be
> allowed to happen again. . . . I ask the Chamber to listen to its
> President in silence, especially when he is addressing it gravely but
> also calmly. . . . If such episodes were to recur, my duty as President
> would oblige me to impose serious penalties and to bring those
> responsible to public attention.

The next day, unfortunately, there were riots in Reggio Emilia,
and three people were killed. In spite of Leone's call for calm in the

Chamber, there were repeated shouts of 'murderers' from the benches on the left again. During the fierce debate that followed, a strange phenomenon occurred. There were loud shots of 'Long live parliament' from both the Left and the Centre-Right; but the shouts came in alternate waves. First one group and then the other would rise to their feet, shouting and clapping, thereby demonstrating how different was the meaning given to the expression on different sides of the Chamber.

Leone was keeping an expert eye on the situation, and succeeded in arousing applause which was general (at last!), when he in his turn proposed the same cry, 'Long live parliament', in what was now a tolerant, democratic atmosphere. As for the outbursts of individuals, Leone made his way with consummate skill through the crossfire of insults, continually calming down one person or another with appropriate calls to order. And if a fresh outburst occurred, instead of adjourning proceedings, he managed to suppress it by demonstrating that it had arisen from a misinterpretation of a quite innocent interjection (a matter between Cossiga and Pajetta, let us say), and by calling the Communists to order as a group.

After an opportune speech by Ruggero Villa had led to an enthusiastic demonstration of support for the forces of law and order ('Long live the police! Long live the Carabinieri!' was the cry in the centre and on the right, as members leapt to their feet), the Prime Minister made a brief, calm statement which brought those two unfortunate and tempestuous days to an end.

For a few days, while those 'points of convergence' were being established which would lead to the formation of a new government headed by Fanfani, the atmosphere remained tense, but no serious incidents occurred. A full discussion of the political situation in Italy was developing in the Chamber, stemming from a number of parliamentary questions. Finally, on 19 July, Tambroni resigned as Prime Minister.

When it proved difficult to form a government after the 1963 elections, Leone was asked to head a government for the summer. He agreed to do so purely out of a sense of responsibility, because he knew very well that the regular prime ministers would soon take over again, as indeed they did in November. Five years later (June to November 1968) he was given the same summer task, but in the meantime President Saragat had made him a senator for life, thereby compensating him to some extent for the end of his reign in the Chamber of Deputies.

Anyone who supposed that Leone's brief summer governments were devoted to bathing or other recreational activities would be quite wrong. There was a book published in 1964 called *Five Months in the Prime Minister's Office*, which shows that the opposite is true. During both summers the papers were full of praise for Leone's self-sacrifice. He was called 'The Cincinnatus of the Christian Democrat Party', 'The Breakdown Van of the Centre-Left', and 'The Joker in the Italian Political Pack'. Jokers are very useful in a lot of games.

As a party man, Leone is the son of his father, who held an important position in the Popular Party; but he has never been an organization man. It is true that he was Secretary of the Christian Democrat Party for the City of Naples, but that was in the very early days, before the party organization really came into being. Leone always refused to become involved in it. Indeed, he wrote an article in *La Stampa* in 1965 which did not please any political party. 'Party organizations are expensive,' he wrote. 'Who is going to produce the large sums required?'

It was precisely these qualities ('a president outside the political rough-and-tumble') which led to his reaching the highest position in the state, for it seems that a non-aligned person is more acceptable there.

Leone might well have become President earlier than he did, for during the difficult presidential election of 1962, when Segni was elected, everybody had a chance to observe his impartiality and his outstanding political integrity. He was sure he could take over from Segni as candidate, and win; but it was he who got Segni out of trouble, when he could simply have used a little ostentatious impartiality, as the person in charge of election proceedings, to spoil Segni's chances by postponing a ballot to the following day – especially since some hint of that kind had come from the President's Palace. Segni had had difficulty in gaining momentum, having achieved the following votes in the first seven ballots: 330, 340, 341, 354, 396, 399, 389. The minimum number of votes required for victory was 428, and by means of an exceptional effort it proved possible during the afternoon of 6 May 1962 to boost Segni's vote to the barely insufficient figure of 424 (against 337 for Saragat and 20 for the outgoing President, Gronchi). On the crest of this wave, Leone immediately arranged for the next ballot to take place, and it was here that Gronchi's last-ditch supporters finally laid down their arms. Segni was elected President with 443 votes. A postponement of the ballot to the next day would certainly have given Gronchi's supporters time to arrange for all the candidates to be dropped, and for Giovanni Leone, President of the Chamber of Deputies, to be elected as candidate *super partes*.

While this was going on, I was away at a meeting of the Atlantic Council in Athens (where I was also representing Segni, the Foreign Minister), and I had not followed all the ramifications of the nine ballots. This caused me to receive something of a reprimand from Leone, when I wrote an account of the election in *Concretezza*. In it I made a few ironical comments about the 'third man', who had been left at the starting-gate.

Here is the text of the letter I received from Leone, together with my reply and his acknowledgement:

Dear Giulio,

I had awaited the appearance of *Concretezza* in the (naïve!) hope that your honesty and your outstanding ability to describe events would make you feel it necessary to point out how I had behaved. Instead of which, I find that when the article you signed speaks of the third man, it even indulges in irony by remarking: 'But what a lot of third men there were!' and by suggesting that it was not felt necessary to judge my behaviour in the 'Zanzariera'.

I know you were in Athens on the last day; but I imagine you will have been informed on your return that on the Saturday night massive support had converged on a particular third man, and that this was the same third man who had given his friends clear and precise instructions to vote for Segni in the Christian Democrat Group and in the election proper. He had also avoided all contact with friends in his own group and delegations from other groups, in spite of the various requests he had received. What I mean is that if (while doing my duty, of course) I had allowed reluctant voters to hand in blank voting papers in the eighth ballot, the third man would certainly have appeared on the scene at once; and (let me no longer hide behind generic phrases) that third man would have been me.

To my great delight (as many television viewers could tell from my expression), I found that Segni was very close to success in the eighth ballot, and that is when I made the mistake – as everybody has pointed out and as I myself recognize – of immediately arranging for another ballot. You yourself had asked Cortese to inform me that that was what you wanted; and I have to point out that Cortese in the event failed to reach me and therefore asked Piermani to pass the message on. But Piermani did not manage to inform me in time. You see, then, that the decision to hold a ninth ballot immediately was not even affected by your wishes: it sprang from my own spontaneous and unselfish impulse.

Would it have been so difficult for you to say a few words about my behaviour – without making much of it, obliquely perhaps, but at least in one way or another? Or did you feel, perhaps, that in the jungle of political life, the emergence of a disinterested gentleman was to be considered such an improbable event as to be better concealed? To show you the extent to which other people have acknowledged the facts of the case, let me draw your attention to: (1) a piece by Baldacci – a man with whom I have never had any contact – on page 9 in the 13 May issue of the magazine *ABC*; (2) the 17 May issue of *Vita*, page 16, first column; (3) the 20 May issue of *Settimana INCOM*, page 9, second and third columns; and (4) an ADN note, which I enclose. (Naturally I had no prior knowledge of these testimonies.)

I apologize for letting off steam.

Yours sincerely,<br>G. Leone

Rome. 16 May 1962

Dear Leone,

I hasten to answer your letter, and begin by thanking you three times over: for the affection which you continue to show me, for the consideration and attention which you give my little magazine, and finally – and this is very unusual in our cases – for the fact that, having something to reproach me with, you do so to me in person.

As I wrote in the article, I have not been able to piece together in full detail what happened at the recent presidential election, because there are some very serious matters still to be investigated. However, I have almost completed my inquiries into these matters, and find that they mean making a very serious criticism of certain behaviour.

I was unaware of the change of opinion which you refer to as having occurred on the Saturday night (I was in Greece from Friday morning until Sunday afternoon), and I have to acknowledge that neither previously nor then did you ask anyone to say anything in your support. From this I had concluded that you were in that same frame of mind which you showed when, at moments of government crisis, you sometimes appeared on the scene simply to say that you did not want a government post. My reference to the superfluity of 'third men' did not imply a criticism of anyone, especially since most of them had supposedly been drawn into the affair not of their own volition but as a result of the cunning and frankly diabolical machinations which others had introduced into the whole painful proceedings.

When I write a final assessment of the election, I shall emphasize that point, and I shall lay particular stress on your impartiality – which is, in any case, well known.

As for me, even in the particular international circle from which I had come, I had been able to observe the deep impression made by the use of the two hundred Communist votes to mount an attack on Segni, and I saw this as the most important aspect of the final stages leading to the happy outcome. That was the crux of my article.

I send you my warmest greetings for the present . . . and the future.

Yours sincerely
Giulio Andreotti

Rome. 17 May 1962

My dear Giulio,

First of all, I am glad that you noticed and appreciated the friendly nature of the feelings which induced me to write to you after reading your magazine, of which I am a regular reader.

I think that you will make many discoveries if you make a full investigation, and some of them will be quite disconcerting.

Although I have always remained on the sidelines, I too have been made aware of a number of things, and I may well talk to you about them.

With thanks.
Yours sincerely,
G. Leone

Rome. 18 May 1962

An even more bitter experience, not solely or even principally for Leone as an individual, but rather for the Christian Democrat Party as a whole, was the presidential election of December 1964, made necessary by President Segni's removal from the scene, after he was struck down by paralysis and an incurable illness. The election took nine days and sixteen humiliating ballots.

The Christian Democrat Party had chosen Giovanni Leone as its candidate, and to be successful it was necessary for him to win 642 votes in one of the first three ballots or 482 in a subsequent one. Leone's progress was as follows: 319, 304, 298, 290, 294, 278, 313, 312, 305, 299, 382, 401, 393, 406, 386. At this point, that is to say after the fifteenth ballot, Leone withdrew – in some indignation – the candidature which the Christian Democrat Party had awarded him in a secret ballot; but *for the time being* he expressed no opinion on the matter.

In order to curtail the activities of 'rebels', the Christian Democrat Party now decided not to involve its battalions in the vote, and when the results of the sixteenth ballot were announced, there were 349 votes for Nenni, 39 for De Marsanich, and 36 for Malagugini, with 368 abstentions.

95

It was the evening of Christmas Day and nerves were on edge, all the more so because members of parliament were far from their homes on a day which is a family festival even for non-believers.

In the end, Nenni withdrew; and on 28 December, Saragat was elected with 646 votes.

A careful and impartial historian of Giovanni Leone's period of almost seven years as President of the Republic cannot help but judge with approval a whole series of his actions and attitudes. And when he turns his attention to the comments that were expressed about them, he will find that approval suddenly turned to harsh criticism, sometimes from the same groups or individuals and in relation to the same events.

Take, for example, Leone's detailed message to parliament in October 1975. In it, he paid particular attention to the crisis that was threatening Italy, and suggested that parliament needed to take urgent measures to combat it. Except for trade union reservations about the way strikes ought to be regulated, and for a certain dislike of unnecessarily complicated suggestions about the *way* parliament should consider messages from the President, its reception was anything but hostile. I remember in particular a statement by Natta that the Communist Party took upon itself to examine all the matters raised, even though they might not accept the diagnosis offered. And Leone also gave a considerable impetus to the consideration of possible amendments to the Italian constitution.

As Head of State, Leone was also very active in undertaking visits abroad, and in offering hospitality at the President's Palace to sovereigns and presidents of different political backgrounds.

It was in legal matters, however, that he really stood out. I recall, for example, a lecture he gave on 2 October 1973 at the Institut de France in Rome on comparative developments in Italian and French law, which produced the warmest congratulations from the French government and from 'difficult' universities north of the Alps. Leone's university background was something he obviously held dear, and his habit of approaching problems from a juridical standpoint caused him at times to seem to undervalue their political aspect – and for purist politicians the political aspect is practically the only thing that counts.

Every Head of State has his own personality and temperament. The first criticisms of Leone resulted from the (very Neapolitan) habit he was noticed to have of warding off the evil eye by openly extending the index and little fingers of his right hand. Perhaps it is the case that this gesture has lost its ritual significance, just as telling the beads on an Islamic rosary no longer has a religious meaning for many Muslims, but is a mechanical activity which enables them to concentrate while carrying on a conversation. Indeed, that austere President of the Senate, Giuseppe Paratore, used to keep in his jacket pocket a horn-shaped piece of coral as big as a fountain-pen, and he often 'used' it to protect himself against persons or circumstances which were potentially threatening. (When he died, his widow gave it to me as a memento, but I don't actually carry it on my person, perhaps because, as a good Roman, I am inclined to adopt an ironical attitude to the evil eye.)

You have to take Leone as he is. When he attended football matches, you couldn't stop him shouting his support, and some of the words he used were less than polite. Indeed, when the Light Blues of Naples were in action, he used to call on more or less unheard-of saints to support them, because, he said, important saints are like lawyers with too many cases; they haven't time to give them proper attention and so neglect them.

There was a story, too, in Christian Democrat circles, about an open-air political meeting near Caserta during the heat of the 1948 election campaign. Togliatti had threatened to 'kick the posterior' of De Gasperi, only to be followed on the platform by Leone, who began by assuring his audience that he would do likewise to Togliatti and his sister (but the language he used was nearer the knuckle than that).

To my mind, many of the upright gentlemen who were scandalized at Giovanni Leone's earthy approach were motivated by fairly obvious hypocrisy. Surely it is better to give vent to a certain exuberance than hide it under a very stiff exterior, thereby displaying a bogus personality and a purely formal righteousness.

Leone's legal scrupulousness was seen at its most sensitive during the weeks of the Moro tragedy. Perhaps his anxiety over Moro's fate was rendered that much more intense by certain special factors; not only had they occupied equivalent chairs at the universities of Bari and Naples, but Leone also remembered the ballot within the various Christian Democrat groups which had resulted in his being preferred to his friend and colleague. Every day Leone urged us to seek possible ways out, though he shared our firm determination to face up to the terrorist attack.

On a number of occasions, by day and night, Leone telephoned Cossiga or me to be brought up to date on developments, and he would curse the impenetrable wall we were faced with. When the

Moro family turned to him in an understandable – but impractical – attempt to by-pass the government, Leone was heart-broken. But we always had his full support. He was always ready, pen in hand, to sign anything that might be of use. The very touching public message which he addressed to the Moro family at the time was typical.

I had occasion to admire his sense of justice in a quite different sphere, when he made a sharp distinction between his decisions as President and the resentment which he legitimately felt at the way he had been treated in the past. He was not exactly well disposed towards those responsible for setting a shameful trap to discredit him on the eve of the selection of candidates for the presidential election, but he was not averse to letting matters ride and finding a more than honourable way out for the actual perpetrator, who perhaps was unaware of what had so shamefully been plotted (at whose request?) within the organization he headed. I am referring to the maiden voyage of the yacht *Tiziana* in April 1971, with the Leone family on board, as well as members of the government and personalities from the world of culture and finance. At Corfu, a man disguised as an officer had secretly come on board – letting it be understood that he was on the track of Soviet spies – and had taken still and cine photographs of guests, including Giovanni Leone in the act of playing the guitar and singing at the top of his voice. The man had then written a report which included a few malicious comments, but in which he had to acknowledge that he had not been able to discover anything disreputable.

The anti-Leone campaign, which specifically aimed to force him to resign before the last six months of his term as President, came into being quite suddenly. It is still not clear whether it was a personal attack launched by an individual, or a key move towards checkmating the Christian Democrats and making room for another party to take their place.

Even a few 'boot-lickers', who at an early stage had sung the praises of President Leone for opening the doors of the ex-Papal palace to an influx of young people, now indulged in supercilious prose to criticize the fact that, in the same halls where Pius IX and Victor Emmanuel II held gloomy court, brilliant young men could be found at some reception not on the official list. In their search for the utmost in offensiveness, they barely drew the line at calling into question the renowned beauty of Leone's wife Vittoria, and they didn't even spare Leone's brother, accusing him of trading in favours – though the accusation was rejected by the courts, which gave judgement against the slanderers and imposed an all-too-insufficient monetary penalty.

There was talk of a 'parallel foreign policy' which the Foreign Ministry had to demonstrate to be false. Then Leone was accused of tax evasion during his past career as a lawyer, but it was easy to show that his declarations of income were a lot more truthful than those of lawyer colleagues with a host of criminal cases on their books. His long-standing friendship with Professor Lefevre was used in a vain attempt to involve him in the Lockheed scandal, by associating him with the sought-after and mysterious person code-named 'Antelope Cobbler'.

I am in a position to recount an episode involving Professor Lefevre, which happened when I was Minister of Industry in one of Leone's governments. Lefevre was at that time chairman of an oil company which had moved from the Trastevere district of Rome to the Fregene area, and he came to seek permission to enlarge the refinery, for a number of technical reasons. Since the proximity of the beach at Fregene made this undesirable, I refused permission and was not swayed by his further insistence. Yet I received not a word of reprimand or of support for Lefevre from Leone, although he was Prime Minister at the time.

The attacks on Leone showed no signs of abating, however, although certain accusations fell quite flat. The report that one of his sons had passed an oral examination at university with flying colours but without being asked a single question was shown to be completely false. Others present at the time had, on the contrary, been surprised at the severity of the examiner, who had failed young Leone at a time when failures and withdrawals were very rare.

What happened at this time sadly reflects the truth of the saying that if you throw enough mud some of it sticks.

I advised the President's Palace – and perhaps I was wrong to do so – not to descend to daily denials and arguments, as Nino Valentino, the head of the press office, wanted. My view is that a President must not get involved in public debate and that, except where the interests of the state are involved, he must save statements and appropriate reactions for after his term of office. I suggested that this should be said clearly and with unflinching dignity, and that the slippery path invitingly indicated by *agents provocateurs* should be avoided. When I consulted the various political parties, moreover, they all approved of this policy, with the single exception of La Malfa, who had been one of the founder members of the Leone-for-President campaign, but was now stoutly asserting that he should resign.

I have tried hard to find an explanation for what happened next. On 9 June, Italians voted in four referendums; and in two cases the results were surprising. The Radical appeal to reject the law on the public financing of political parties was itself rejected, but only by a narrow margin (56 to 44 per cent of the vote), in spite of the fact that all the other parties supported the law, and that in almost all the large cities there was a majority against repealing it. Were fourteen million Italians really against the parties? In the case of the Reale anti-terrorist law, it was unpleasant to find that seven million Italians (of whom two and a half million lived in the South) could,. in a sense, be considered to be on the side of terrorism. It was a misleading interpretation, but one which could easily catch on.

After the announcement of the result, Berlinguer complained loudly that the other parties had dragged their feet, thereby leaving the Communists *exposed*. Now, I think it was partly this resentment, but principally the fear of Radical and Socialist competition, and the failure to influence public opinion in the large cities, which suggested tough action to restore credibility to the Communist Party.

On 15 June, Berlinguer telephoned me to give me advance notice that it had been decided to join the demand for President Leone's resignation; and when I asked for a delay so that the situation could be carefully examined and discussed, he told me that Paolo Bufalini had already gone to the President's Palace to give the news. He was to make it clear, however, that this was simply a tactical political move, and that the Communist Party did not necessarily accept as justified the specific charges in the campaign against Leone.

The Socialist announcement that they, too, were no longer prepared to defend Leone must, I think, be related to the decision taken at Communist headquarters; and it was certainly not possible to contemplate a debate and vote in parliament on the matter.

Could I threaten to resign? All I would probably achieve was to add fuel to the anti-Christian Democrat fire, and add one crisis to another. Nor do I think the Christian Democrat Party failed to provide an opportunity for the Communists and Socialists to abandon the demand that they had made so abruptly.

To complete the picture, I should mention that it had been announced on 15 June that the President would broadcast a message on television that evening, and that the text had been sent by an aide to the headquarters of the Christian Democrat and Communist parties, for advance information. (I don't know whether it was sent to any other parties.) It may be that this advance information had the effect of precipitating events slightly, by causing action to be taken to avoid the appearance or reality of a clash of attitudes.

Zaccagnini and I went to see Leone, to inform him that his position was now no longer tenable. It was one of the most unpleasant moments of my life, for I was conscious both of the inevitability and of the profound injustice of it all.

A few hours later, I received Leone's official letter of resignation: 'Dear Prime Minister, I have to tell you that I have today resigned as President of the Republic. I therefore take the liberty of sending you the Deed of Resignation, signed by me. Yours faithfully, Giovanni Leone.'

Five days later, the Senate took note that Leone had returned to its ranks, but this time it was as ex-Head of State, in accordance with Article 59 of the Constitution.

People were generally stunned at what had happened. Even the anti-Leone lobby did not sing too many hymns of victory. Arturo Carlo Jemolo wrote to Leone to express his solidarity, and to say that once again he would not vote for the Christian Democrat Party (thereby attributing to our party greater power and responsibility than it really had).

Leone retired to a life of isolation at Le Rughe, and it is only recently that he has been seen in society again, except for attending concerts at the Accademia di Santa Cecilia as well as the more important sessions of parliament. It was a heavy blow to him and his family, and he has endured it in proud and solitary silence.

Whenever magistrates denounce the slanderers, there is always some political commentator on call who will say that the ex-President is having his 'revenge'.

I am still convinced, however, that even in the cut-throat conditions of public life, the truth will come out in the end. It is a championship in which there is always a return match.

# 17
# General Perón

It was early on in my career in government (I had recently been appointed Under-Secretary to De Gasperi) that I found myself having to make arrival and hospitality arrangements for Evita Perón on a state visit to Rome. There was a striking contrast between her vivacious beauty and femininity on the one hand, and her self-confidence in setting out and arguing her political ideas. Putting into operation the programme which had been prepared for the imposing wife of the President of Argentina was fraught with difficulty, for she was consistently two or three hours late for her appointments, thereby throwing those responsible for Foreign Office protocol into a fearful tizzy. Even when it came to a formal reception at the Villa Aldobrandini, she arrived at a time by which she should already have left, thereby putting the *corps diplomatique* into something of an ill humour. Fortunately, they took it out on the Argentinian Ambassador, Ocampos Jimenez, rather than on her.

A few years later, in 1952, Evita died, and General Perón was obliged to go into exile in Spain.

Italy continued to maintain excellent relations with her sister nation (half the Argentinians have Italian blood), and I myself had occasion to go there twice: firstly when Argentina celebrated one hundred and fifty years of independence, and on another occasion to visit the armed forces. This gave me the opportunity of meeting two presidents of Italian origin: Frondizi and Ilia. Frondizi later came on an official visit to Italy, and I was given the task of taking him to Milan for a lecture at the Chamber of Commerce, followed by a rather good lunch at the private residence of Guido and Mariuccia Zerilli Marimò. Another Argentinian Head of State,

General Aramburu, came to Rome several times on official visits. He was a very intelligent man, and was always liked by those who met him. Unfortunately he was killed by terrorists, who kept his body hidden for a long time.

As though by tacit agreement, there was no mention of Perón in official conversations, and he appeared to have been completely forgotten by the entire population. But appearances can be misleading, and as soon as one entered into an Argentinian's confidence, there were sighs of nostalgia and expressions of admiration for General Perón. The exception, however, were economic experts, who found it difficult to understand how General Perón and his wife had managed to get through Argentina's substantial reserves by selling corn and meat left, right, and centre during the war years.

What happened in Argentina was part of a cyclical pattern of history. When inflation soared and left- and right-wing terrorism spread, the country abolished political parties and put power into the hands of the military. But the peso failed to bounce back, industry failed to take off, and acts of violence continued to occur. (I recall one police chief who had boasted to me that anyone who wanted to kill him had better get him with his first shot, because he would have no time to fire a second. In the event, he was blown to pieces by a shell, while trying to take a few hours' recreation in a motor boat.)

This was the point at which it was said that military government must be set aside, democratic political parties re-established, and a general election held.

During this lengthy, if temporary, period of constitutional government, Perón sent out feelers from his home in Madrid to find out whether he could make a brief trip to Italy as a tourist. The Argentinian Embassy in Rome was very much opposed to the idea, but as Italian Prime Minister at the time, I saw no reason why he should be prevented from coming. I hit upon a compromise, however, by receiving him in my private office in parliament rather than at the official prime ministerial offices at the Palazzo Chigi. Perón was accompanied by his wife Isabelita, whom he had married after several years as a widower. She was physically very petite, having nothing of the striking presence of Evita; and, at any rate during that meeting, she betrayed no sign of any particular interest in matters of politics.

General Perón was showing his age, but declared with a certain pride that if the Argentinian people called him back as a result of a general election, he would accept the duty of devoting his last years to restoring his shattered country.

The Argentinian people did call him back. The supporters of Perón achieved a landslide victory, and Perón returned in triumph, after a brief interregnum with Campora as President. Campora was a dentist who was much embarrassed by the extreme left-wing tendencies of his children, with the result that he was sent away from Buenos Aires as Ambassador to Mexico.

Through the Italian Embassy in Buenos Aires, Perón let the Italian government know that he would appreciate it if I were sent as Italian representative at the 'handing over of power', that is to say at his official installation as President. When I arrived in Argentina, I was struck by the large number of election posters still in position, showing a photo-montage of Juan Perón with Evita on one side and Isabelita on the other. The latter had been appointed Vice-President of the Republic. Perón had chosen his wife for the position because there were numerous candidates, and he wanted to avoid discontenting Left or Right. Rumour had it that she was much under the influence of Lopez Rega, a powerful minister and counsellor.

After the ceremony at Casa Rosada, Perón addressed the crowd in Plaza de Mayo, but their tremendous enthusiasm gradually waned as they were invited to return to barracks and abandon the use of violence. The *montoneros* seemed less than thrilled at the prospect of behaving themselves. Just to be on the safe side, the new President had made his speech from behind a transparent bullet-proof screen.

When it was my turn to shake his hand, he thanked me again for the welcome he had received in Rome in 1972, and invited me to his house for that evening. I assumed it was a reception and asked the Italian Ambassador to come with me, but we were greatly surprised to find that the only other people at the General's residence were Isabelita and Signor Gelli, whom I knew as managing director of the Permaflex mattress company at Frosinone. At first I thought it was someone who resembled him, but it really was Gelli; and while Perón was very polite to us, his deference towards Gelli amounted almost to grovelling. Perhaps, I mused, they were comrades from old army days in Italy; for when Perón had been military attaché in Rome, he had insisted on spending a certain amount of time with the Italian alpine troops. No reference was made to aprons, masonic lodges, or the Great Architect of the Universe. Perón recalled with emotion the time he had spent in Italy, and once again expressed his gratitude for the friendly way he had been received by me as Prime Minister. His interpretation of those days as the turning-point leading to his return to power seemed to me over-rhetorical and exaggerated. He said he wanted to do something for the Italian people, and told me he had arranged a meeting for the next day, at which his ministers, the Italian Ambassador, and I would examine some mutually advantageous projects.

Pride of place amongst the objects decorating his drawing-room was held by his Italian alpine hat. Whether he had put it on show for our benefit or whether it was in its normal place I cannot say. But that his heart beat still with the Italian alpine troops was brought home to me in a comic way at the meeting in the Casa Rosada – which he insisted on chairing himself. This was a matter of some significance, for it was only the second day of his presidency, and he must have had a very full diary. He began by saying that Argentina needed to sign productive agreements with Italy in areas where there was a potential mutual advantage, and he cited the fishing industry, using a rather quaint turn of phrase.

'Ours is the only country', he said, 'where the fish die of old age.'

He invited the ministers present to begin work immediately on a mixed project involving setting up a fishing fleet, canning, trading, and so on. But at this point he suddenly dropped his talk of business affairs to ask me whether the Italian alpine troops still sang 'that wonderful song'. Could he mean 'La Montanara'? He made a grimace of annoyance at his failure to remember the words, and returned to the subject of development programmes, setting out his basic ideas for putting Argentina on its feet again – something that military governments were quite unable to do. (But hadn't he been a colonel when he began his political career?)

Suddenly there is another interruption. President Perón rises to his feet, his eyes sparkling with joy. He has remembered the words of the alpine song, and with stentorian voice starts singing a ribald Italian drinking song: 'Osteria numero uno . . .'.

His ministers stare at him in curiosity. The Italian Ambassador sits bolt upright in his chair. As a lower-class Roman I could join in and turn the solo into a chorus; but I feel I would rather not.

Perón sat down with an air of satisfaction. I don't suppose the council chamber of the Argentinian cabinet has ever known, before or since, another such non-political intermezzo. As we left the meeting, His Excellency Lopez Rega, who according to popular rumour was capable of working magic, took me to say my farewells to Isabelita, who was already at work in her vice-presidential office. She told me of her intention that her first official visit should be to Italy. Whether she had in mind a repeat performance of Evita's journey, or whether she was referring to a state visit with the General, I cannot say. In the latter case, we would have to take all necessary precautions to ensure that the General did not confuse the Italian national anthem with a vulgar drinking song.

It was not long before Perón died, however, and although Isabelita did in fact go on a presidential visit to Rome, she was afterwards removed from office and placed under arrest. Lopez Rega left the country by 'magical' means and, although in fact alive and well, apparently had his own obituary published, thereby solving any problems pending with the judicial authorities in Argentina.

The military came back to power, the value of the peso shot down, economic plans became no more than good intentions, and the fish continued to die of old age.

When General Videla came to Rome in 1978 for the enthronement of the new Pope, he told me that his task was to put right fifty years of mistakes made by his predecessors. I took the liberty of suggesting that he should be careful about making statements like that, for they seemed to me unjustified at least as regards the presidents I had known. What's more, I added, his successors would express exactly the same opinion of him.

# 18
# *The Shah of Persia*

Perhaps it is because I am hopeless at dancing and have never frequented dance halls, even as a spectator, that I have a vivid memory of the Shah of Persia's arrival in Rome one evening, after being put to headlong and hurried flight by the revolt which Mossadeq had stirred up.

Two hours after landing at Fiumicino airport, he had deposited his luggage – such as it was – at the Grand Hotel, and was already taking the floor at the Belvedere delle Rose with his magnificent wife Soraya. They held the stage until four o'clock in the morning, while the Peacock Throne in Tehran trembled at this first sinister creak.

Later on, when I was commenting on Pope Pius IX's ostentatious calm on the day Italian troops took Rome from him (he invented a word-game to show the Papal Curia and the people of Rome how calm he was), it crossed my mind that perhaps the Shah of Persia had wanted his behaviour to demonstrate to his subjects how much he trusted them. He certainly could not have done so by means of a word-game; and Pius IX would certainly have been prevented by his age, his aches and pains, and his priestly celibacy from visiting some nineteenth-century equivalent of a *palais de danse*. Not even just the once, to cheer up and calm down his Roman subjects on the eve of what was presumably the semi-final stage of his pontificate.

I obtained a second unfortunate impression of the Shah when I met him again in Venice, where he had gone on his own (Soraya had by now been repudiated) to see the film festival. His welcome at San Nicolò al Lido airport (Tessera had not yet been built) had been arranged to have a certain solemn splendour even though it was a private occasion (that is, no music or flags). The Shah, however,

showed little sign of appreciating it; for, as soon as he had been introduced to the authorities, he turned to the prefect and asked him point-blank to provide him with a lady for the night.

Poor Gregorio Notarianni was so taken aback that he came up with an astonishing reply. It satisfied that illustrious guest, but certainly not the official referred to in it, nor any of the rest of us (and thank heavens Lina Merlin was not there). What he said was, 'That's a job for the Chief of Police.'

How the matter ended I cannot say (though I am sure, of course, that no official got involved), because after the film show I took my leave and returned to Rome; but I confess that I was somewhat disconcerted by this striking non-observance of the saying that *noblesse oblige*.

Fifteen years or so went by, and I had almost forgotten the Venice affair, when the Iranian Ambassador came to the Ministry of Defence to ask me whether we could devote a quite informal half-day to the Shah, who wanted to obtain from our General Staff a detailed run-down of the military situation in the Mediterranean and adjacent areas. We naturally agreed, and so I had occasion, on 24 February 1964, to spend an afternoon with a quite different Shah. There was something almost monastic about him, even if it was high-society monasticism, and his one preoccupation was to safeguard peace. His remarks were very much to the point; he paid close attention to the survey provided by General Aldo Rossi and his aides (especially General Galatieri di Genola); and the information which the Shah provided about his own country's military potential and plans for development filled our officers with understandable envy.

I asked him an apparently irrelevant question. How did he think the thousands of students who attended foreign universities in both Western and socialist countries would readapt to life in Iran? Only a few days earlier, an Iranian who had just graduated in architecture at Milan had told me how deeply worried he was about the psychological trauma which almost every returning Iranian suffered, whether they had absorbed revolutionary Marxist ideas, or were scandalized at a materialism which they called capitalist and so took refuge in some kind of anti-modern fundamentalism. (Perhaps this latter attitude is a key to understanding the appeal of Khomeini.)

The Shah answered me politely, making it quite clear, at the same time, that my question had nothing to do with the security matters we were discussing. The education system was being greatly developed, he said, not just by means of bursaries for study abroad (many of which were paid for by the state) but also through a capillary extension of its network, which now covered the whole nation. This was evidence of the way the Iranian people had become a really modern nation, freeing themselves of prejudices and age-old accretions and dealing a heavy blow to illiteracy.

Ten years later, a political crisis occurred in Iran, largely thanks to Ayatollah Khomeini. After a long period of exile in Iraq, he had fled to Paris and from there was delivering thunderous attacks on the Shah, assisted by a substantial group of Iranian business men and intellectuals who had been victims of the terrible Savak – the imperial political police. Strangely enough, it was President Carter who unwittingly pushed the Shah over the precipice. As an act of friendship towards the Shah and his new wife Farah Dhiba, he was spending the New Year with them, and in a public speech he turned to his favourite subject: human rights – thereby arousing a well-orchestrated outburst of criticism of the Savak, who apparently didn't bother themselves with niceties of conduct and weren't issued with kid gloves.

A popular uprising went on for weeks. The army opposed it less and less; and the Muslim clergy fomented it, for they were horrified at the open neglect of the duties of Ramadan and the wholesale disregard of Islamic prohibitionism. So the Shah and his family, under pressure from a ferocious mob, left their country and began an odyssey of flight and exile, which was made still more painful by a tumour which rapidly overcame the dethroned Emperor's resistance.

A powerful military machine – on land, at sea, and in the air – had in this way demonstrated all its very costly uselessness.

# 19
# *Hiro Hito*

'Andreotti – you're a shit!'

Even though it was the Emperor of Japan who described me in this way one autumn evening in 1964, I was a little taken aback. Coppini, the Italian Ambassador in Tokyo, made desperate signs to me, for fear that I might make a scene, but then relaxed when he saw me smile. The Emperor went on to ask after my health and that of my family, and questioned me about the weather in Italy at that time of the year and my plane journey to Tokyo. After this standard diplomatic opening, our conversation turned to the organization of the previous Olympic Games in Rome, which Hiro Hito warmly praised as offering a helpful model to the Japanese Olympic Committee.

Not much was said about politics. He recalled with pleasure a trip to Italy made in his youth, and ended with another exciting remark: he assured me as Emperor, though there were still more than fifty hours to go, that there would be bright sunshine during the opening ceremony of the Games on the Saturday, to be closely followed by heavy rain in the late afternoon.

When he said goodbye to me, the Emperor warmly thanked the Italian armed forces for sending two military expeditions to Japan on the occasion of the Games, in the form of the *Andrea Doria* and a party of cadets from the Air Force Academy. He gave personal instructions that our cadets should be made especially welcome.

Once we had taken leave of the imperial presence, Coppini hastened to explain to me that the expression which sounded in Italian like 'you're a shit' was in fact a Japanese courtesy term used after a person's surname rather like *san*, which means 'Mr'. (I was addressed as Andreotti-*san* in my hotel.) He apologized for not warning me in advance (but he did warn the Minister of Tourism,

Achille Corona, who arrived shortly afterwards). I was reminded with amusement of the bill sponsored by Nenni after the war to abolish the title 'excellency'. The Italian Ambassador also informed me that the local weather-forecasting service was extremely efficient, and that the tiniest cloud formations were accurately forecast days ahead of their appearance.

I had come to Tokyo not as a member of the Italian government, but as a result of a personal invitation, in my capacity as ex-President of the Italian Olympics of four years earlier. A substantial Japanese delegation had been present throughout the work of preparation for the Games, and with military precision they had recorded and filmed, made notes, and asked questions. They had even come to a meeting with the local mussel growers in Naples about clearing an area of the sea required for races – in which, as it turned out, King Constantine of Greece gained some success, as a kind of compensation for the subsequent loss of his kingdom.

The Japanese are exquisitely polite. I had been greeted at Tokyo airport by no less than four ex-ambassadors to Rome, who were all smiles, bows, and courtesies, as well as by Daigoro Yasukawa, the President of the Eighteenth Olympic Games, who was delighted to have been informed that I was the bearer of an Italian decoration for him.

The Olympic Games went remarkably smoothly, with events televised at all the venues so that, apart from anything else, the journalists could follow all the events in the comfort of their hotels. It was absolutely forbidden, however, for seats to be left empty in the stands, and so squads of students armed with gay little flags were always at the ready to fill any vacant places.

The Emperor had already welcomed the members of the International Olympic Committee (informing them collectively that they, too, were shits!), and now declared the Games open, staying to watch a firework display in full daylight (with amazing cascades of black and coral pink). He left the stand just in time to avoid the downpour which he had forecast.

I shall never forget the rest of that week in Japan, quite apart from the Olympic Games. Amongst other things, I learned some surprising details about the Japanese industrial system, which arouses such fear amongst competitors throughout the world. When I visited a Toshiba factory (producing 40,000 black-and-white television sets a month and 4,000 colour sets), two basic points were put to me. (1) Factories must be worked to maximum capacity, regardless of market analyses and complicated forecasts for the future; what you don't sell at home you export to Hong Kong or elsewhere. (2) It is a mistake to use skilled workers, because the work has to be very basic, with simple movements, and workers can be moved from one department to another every six months to prevent monotony from causing fatigue. I asked whether such a system was viable on a world scale, and was assured that it was – for at least ten years. Then Chinese markets would open up.

Nine years later I returned to Japan as Italian Prime Minister to meet Premier Tanaka and Foreign Minister Ohira.

The audience held at the Imperial Palace on 24 April 1973 was quite charming. Hiro Hito and the Empress welcomed my wife and me very warmly. They kept us in conversation for a long while, and asked amongst other things about the subject of my conversations at the White House (I had gone to Japan straight from Washington). The Emperor does not play an active part in Japanese politics, but neither is he just a remote figurehead. He succeeds remarkably well in striking a balance between the limitations imposed by his official position and his consciousness of the real importance of events.

The lunch in our honour was held in the Great Hall of the palace. Its largest wall is made entirely of glass, and hence gives one the impression of being right inside the splendid garden, through which a long queue of silent and watchful visitors slowly made its way. The menu was European: consommé ambassadeur, soles et crevettes frites, filet de boeuf à l'incision, salade de Saison, pouding poire, dessert.

Hiro Hito made me a gift of two vases decorated with chrysanthemums, which are a symbol of joy and glory in Japan. Fortunately I am not superstitious, and so my mind did not turn to the melancholy association with funerals which they have in Italy.

The Emperor accompanied us to the gate when we left, and was bowed to by the small passing crowd of Japanese tourists. I am told that before the war no Japanese citizen was allowed to look the Emperor in the face. All that was abruptly changed by the bomb at Hiroshima, the military defeat, and the forthright activities of General MacArthur; but they saved the monarchy. In Italy, the Allied Command made no attempt to do anything of the sort.

The Emperor no longer wears sumptuous silk robes. Instead, he wears the black jacket and grey striped trousers of a city business man; but he has a solidly established position within the new Japanese order of things. His family is respected, and the future of his dynasty is assured.

As a foreign guest I was profoundly impressed.

I was also struck by the way industry has progressed. When I visited the Nippon Electric Company, headed by my old friend Koji Koba Yashi, I found that special skills are no longer frowned on there, that trade unions are losing their decorative role, and that strikes are beginning to crop up. (Some time ago the workers on the underground railway downed tools for the first time; the public crowds were so taken aback and so enraged that they destroyed the central station.) But the most striking innovation is the introduction of original Japanese models. The imitation of European and American models is a thing of the past. Here at NEC, for example, they have devised and perfected a very advanced automatic postal system. We can expect competition to become increasingly tough.

June 1979. It was Tokyo's turn to host the summit meeting of the seven most industrialized nations. Attached to our invitations was an extremely precise timetable, detailing our arrival times, how long the sessions would last, and when we should come down from our rooms to the hotel foyer and climb into the bullet-proof limousines which were to take us from the New Otani Hotel (where all the delegations were staying) to the nearby conference building. Mrs Thatcher was supposed to leave two minutes and fifteen seconds before me, but she was a few moments late, thereby causing complicated problems of protocol, for it was not clear whether I should be sent off all the same, or whether the pre-arranged order should be adhered to.

Forlani, Pandolfi, and I went from the airport to the hotel by helicopter, and as soon as we entered the foyer we were faced with an impressive array of policemen and policewomen. The latter carry a regulation shoulder-bag, which presumably does not contain rouge and things like that. What is more, they inform us that they are all judo experts, so they can break the back of any would-be attacker with smiles on their faces. Security is paramount, and even when a team of hotel barbers comes to shave me (a procedure which is rather like a surgical operation without an anaesthetic), two security men keep an eye on them. Jimmy Carter, I suppose, will have been surrounded by a regiment of them.

There is to be a dinner at Court during the two days of the summit. The Emperor receives us one by one (Giscard d'Estaing, Carter, Schmidt, me, Mrs Thatcher, Clark, and Ohira) and – thanks to the amazing efficiency of his records and his civil servants – tells me that he is glad to see me for the third time and asks after my wife.

The Empress is not feeling very well. She comes to greet us only

115

when aperitifs are being served, and apologizes for not being present at the banquet. First, however, she poses with us for the official photograph, which is taken only after a sort of mini-procession and a ceremony which reminds me of that delightful ritual associated with taking tea.

My place at table was between two princesses, one of whom had been a pupil at a Catholic school in Europe, and was very keen on the periodical old girls' reunions. The other displayed a real understanding of Italian art, and talked to me admiringly of a certain artisan goldsmith from Rome (Virgilio Mortet) who had recently had an exhibition in Tokyo of tiny flower sculptures, inspired by a particularly productive visit to Japan.

Once again the menu was Western. (Premier Ohira, however, had offered us a typical Japanese lunch, involving those knees-bend-knees-stretch gymnastics that make one's tiniest bones creak.)

There was also some typical Japanese after-dinner entertainment, involving ten minutes of Bugaku dancing by a single male dancer, upholstered, one might almost say, in an enormous wild animal costume. The musical accompaniment had a very slow rhythm, reminiscent of the drumbeat used just before the condemned are executed. I remembered that on my previous visit to Japan I had spent an evening at the theatre in the expert company of a Jesuit who knew all about Kabuki, Noh, and other types of Japanese theatre. Now, in the Imperial Palace, I could have done with this knowledgeable priest's explanations, but unfortunately I couldn't go and consult him because I had learned that in the meantime he had left not only his chair at the Sophia University but the Company of Jesus as well.

That night the Imperial Palace was floodlit in an ingenious way, which threw into high relief the most attractive parts of the garden, showing up both the blossom on the cherry trees and the extraordinarily beautiful play of the dark-coloured stones.

We left for Italy without delay, stopping off at Moscow to exchange impressions of the summit and the almost simultaneous meeting of Comecon. Kosygin arranged for me to see the room where Stalin worked. Could this be a sign that he was being rehabilitated?

We went for a brief trip to see both the Olympic village in its advanced state of construction, and an Italian exhibition of rather frivolous goods. It was interesting to observe how much the people of Moscow admired Valentino dresses. Let us hope that they don't equate fashion goods and luxuries with 'Western civilization'!

# 20
# *Richard Nixon*

In 1960, Richard Nixon had been Kennedy's opponent in the presidential election, and was defeated by a mere handful of votes. It was even said that if he had asked for a recount in a few States the result would have been different. Kennedy, however, does not seem to have been grateful for his failure to do so, because when Nixon was the Republican candidate for Governor of California two years later, a message went out from the White House to the Californians inviting them to 'bury' the man who had been 'slaughtered' in the presidential election. The Californians did as they were told, and so Brown, the Democratic candidate, was elected; but anyone who thought that Nixon was now out for the count was sadly mistaken. Six years later Nixon became President, defeating his opponent by a substantial margin.

What is more, the American people so appreciated what he achieved in his four years in office that he was triumphantly re-elected in 1972, thereby causing jealousy and resentment within the Republican Party, whose success in the congressional elections failed to match the personal achievement of the President. In fact it was almost as though Nixon's Democratic opponent, McGovern, had been chosen to make his task easier.

I made an official call on Nixon in April 1973, and gained a very favourable impression of him from our conversations. In particular, he showed great respect for internal Italian politics, and did not put questions either about Italian parliamentary groupings or about the prospects of abandoning a very difficult coalition formula. (Unfortunately, the very narrow majority enjoyed by the Italian government encouraged the activities of 'rebels', with disastrous results for the budget, apart from anything else.) Both in his

speeches (on my arrival and at dinner) and in conversation, he paid almost exclusive attention to international politics, setting out his own point of view and asking quite frankly for comments and objections.

I was not surprised that he should confirm the existence of good relations with Moscow. The previous October, Kosygin had told me he approved of Nixon, expressing satisfaction at his easy re-election, in that – within their different political and social frameworks – the United States and the Soviet Union enjoyed frank and fruitful relations. It was precisely because of these good relations that Nixon had been able to adopt the policy of extending a friendly hand to China, for he thought it absurd that Peking should be denied membership of the club of influential nations, and he did not accept the attitude of those who could see overtures to China only as a way of getting at the Soviet Union.

Nixon also thought Japan a country of great importance, and expressed surprise that we in Europe paid so little attention to our relations with Tokyo. He was right. Japanese competition was very tough, and it was practically impossible to penetrate their home market; but the problem needed to be seen in a wider context, keeping in mind that the most pessimistic view of the future looked to an anti-Western Tokyo–Peking axis.

Before leaving the United States, I was guest of honour at a social evening at the White House at which we were entertained by Frank Sinatra, who had now been readmitted to polite society after a period in quarantine.

Nixon's undoing was Watergate – simply because he did not have the sense to declare immediately that he had nothing to do with this stupid piece of electoral espionage organized by an over-zealous aide. Out of undeserved generosity, Nixon failed to disown him and have him punished. The inquiry which led to Nixon's obligatory exit from the White House was led by two men of Italian origin: Judge Sirica and Peter Rodino, the latter being Chairman of the House Judiciary Committee. Nixon was saved from personal prosecution by a 'pardon' from his successor as President, Gerald Ford. Ford had not been elected Vice-President in 1972, but had been appointed by Congress to replace Spiro Agnew when the latter was obliged to resign over a tax scandal.

Nixon's popularity dropped like a stone, and in particular the principal newspapers showed no mercy in destroying his reputation, without worrying in the least about the possible damage that might do to the United States. I have certainly no wish to underestimate the gravity of the offence of trying to cover up a crime and, even worse, lying to the nation; but it seemed to me both ungenerous and unjust not to acknowledge Nixon's achievements during his six years in the White House. When I happened to be in the United States in 1975, I paid a private call on him at his home in San Clemente, where he was living in total isolation, much troubled, moreover, by poor health.

# 21
# *Georges Pompidou*

Georges Pompidou, President of the French Republic, died in the spring of 1974. Some hours after the sad announcement of his death, I was at Paris airport and noticed with melancholy curiosity that the latest issue of *France Dimanche* had an enormous headline which read: 'Is Pompidou about to go?'

The (apparently) famous astrologer Madame Soleil had looked into the destiny of Pompidou. He was born under the sign of Cancer (a sadly ironical coincidence) with an ascendant in Leo. She concluded: 'It is certain that whatever happens to him, he will choose the best path to follow, both for himself and for France.'

Perhaps some similar episode led to the coining of the less than complimentary Italian saying 'to hell with the astrologer'. However, I don't doubt that, after catching such a crab, our professional lady of the horoscope will have been more careful and less widely read. But let us leave her to her stars and note the general dismay at the death of Pompidou and at the news that for some time he had been silently suffering extreme pain, caused by a deadly disease whose exact nature it was discreetly decided not to reveal even after his death.

That statesmen can be seriously ill must evidently not be admitted. First of all it was said that President Pompidou had a kind of influenza; and when everyone was amazed to see how bloated he looked in pictures and on television, the explanation given was that he was taking large doses of cortisone. Thus there began a see–saw of worrying rumours and encouraging reports. It was said that the influenza kept recurring; that signs of weakness were to be attributed to overwork; that his doctors promised he would be perfectly all right again if only he would agree to a brief period of complete rest.

A few days before his death, two ministers had declared that by June the President would be back on form again.

Furthermore, Pompidou continued to chair a cabinet meeting every Wednesday, undertook tiring state visits, and received foreign ambassadors; and he had recently both caused and solved a government crisis.

When his end came, therefore, it caused not only the grief which it would have caused anyway, but an additional sense of distress at its suddenness.

During the 'reign' of Pompidou's illustrious predecessor, frequent anxious questions were asked as to what would happen after de Gaulle. In particular, while almost the whole world applauded France's constitutional reform and praised the effect it would have on the efficiency of the state administration and on the formation of a parliamentary majority, there were those who asked in apprehension (and since I did so in writing, I can reveal that I was one of them without running the risk of being accused of hindsight) whether this efficient mechanism was not being offered on a plate, in the near or distant future, to those who wanted to organize an alliance between Marxism and part of the radical bourgeoisie or, alternatively, a totalitarian right-wing coalition.

When General de Gaulle was buried in the little cemetery at Colombey-les-Deux-Eglises, Pompidou took over the reins of power with such comparative ease that many were able to argue that questions and doubts about the Gaullist constitution were quite ill founded, since it was now demonstrating how well it worked even after de Gaulle's death. But perhaps a few people are beginning to have second thoughts today.

President Pompidou's term of office was characterized by a kind of 'novelty within continuity'. This is not surprising when one reflects on his long experience of faithful service to de Gaulle, and his having had to put up with sudden dismissal from the post of Prime Minister. One has to keep in mind certain rather independent declarations of political intent which he made at that very period, when he was on holiday in Rome as a guest at the Palazzo Farnese.

So, in due course, he became President of France. After winning the presidential election (by only a narrow margin over Alain Poher, although the Communists withdrew their candidate at the second ballot and switched their support to Pompidou), he began to tone down the tougher obstinacies of Gaullist policy by almost imperceptible degrees. De Gaulle's 'No' to British entry into the Common Market was withdrawn, and on the home front the 'hard man' Debré was to some extent pushed out of the way. These were the characteristic signs of innovation in his policies. There were also clear indications of Pompidou's open-mindedness at the Italo-French talks at Lucca in the summer of 1972; and at the European summit in October of the same year it was allowed full rein on the question of good relations between Europe and the United States.

Later on one had the impression that he was retreating, and commentators interpreted this as caused by the pressure of internal politics. The shadow of Mitterrand and the Popular Front made it advisable to adopt remedies which were 'substantial' if not 'extreme'.

For many years, de Gaulle had thought he could be sure of maintaining peace amongst his local fellow nations by keeping his distance from NATO and the United States and holding out a friendly hand to Moscow (the old-style governments which preceded him had tried to achieve the same result by weakening European solidarity, as Mendès-France did, in the troubled waters of Indo-China). The end result, however, was to bring Moscow and Washington appreciably closer together, which is certainly not what de Gaulle wanted. A similar result had followed from the policy of creating a special friendly relationship between France and West Germany; for it led, again contrary to intentions, to the direct re-establishment of friendly relations between the West Germans and the Russians and East Europeans.

Was it one of the basic aims of the Pompidou government to seek to establish a special line to the Kremlin and thereby deprive Mitterrand of a trump-card? There are a few strong clues to suggest that this was indeed the case. There had recently been an additional reason for cooling relations with the United States; the French government wanted to be more pro-Arab – a move which was completely in line with their supplying Mirages and other materials for the Middle East war.

All this counts for little or nothing to the statesman who now lies in a simple tomb alongside all the other inhabitants of the cemetery at Orvilliers. But it has a great deal of importance for the immediate and middle-term future of France, Europe, and the world.

In the new race for the presidency, the French Left had an initial advantage (not an overwhelming one, but not a negligible one either), in that it had long since decided on its strategy and chosen its champion. Furthermore, the Popular Front does not arouse much apprehension amongst the French, since they tried it on another occasion, and having done so, dropped it smartly. Mitterrand, moreover, was a cultured man with a following even in circles which were anything but of the extreme Left. A friend told me he had met and been impressed by him in earlier days at the home of the Comte de Paris. What he did not tell me, though, was whether his recollection of their meeting on this social occasion would cause him to vote for Mitterrand.

As for the other camps, since the usual hopeless candidates had appeared on the extreme Right and Left, attention was turned to the Gaullist choice (they suddenly plumped for Chaban-Delmas), to the optimistic candidature of Edgar Faure, and to the independent candidature of that forceful personality, Giscard d'Estaing.

The ex-President of the National Assembly was in a sense in the same position as Pompidou, because he too had made an . . . early exit as Prime Minister; and there was a vague feeling that his parliamentary group was putting him forward as a candidate in order to get its revenge. Furthermore, the deputy who was also Mayor of Bordeaux had had to protect his rear against polemical pamphleteers who were trying to implicate him in wine adulteration scandals and other frauds of which the great wine-makers of the region were accused. And to complete the picture, it must be mentioned that Pompidou circles had not been untainted by scandal, since the row about Parisian plans for La Villette had been dragged in. In the battle for the presidency it had evidently been the case for some time that there were no holds barred.

Chaban-Delmas could make use of the fact that he was popular and had outstanding personal qualities which could be used in television broadcasts to the voters. Faure was President of the National Assembly, and the card up his sleeve was the support he would get from the Gaullists in the second ballot, together with that of all the other voters who were opposed to Mitterrand's Left. Whereas Mitterrand obviously hoped to gain from the quarrels between his rivals and from cracks in the Gaullist front – in which case the Gaullists themselves would live to regret not having seized the chance of concentrating all their hopes on Pierre Mesmer.

In the end it was the outsider Valéry Giscard d'Estaing who made it. But for Mitterrand it was a useful dress rehearsal.

# 22
# Idi Amin

It makes one feel rather uncomfortable to hear prayers being said at a funeral for a person who has the same name as oneself. At least, that is how I felt about it. In the evening after the funeral, I was attending a meeting of Christian Democrat parliamentary group leaders to devise a suitable way of honouring the memory of our colleague Giulio Pastore. The words '. . . for the late Giulio' were still ringing in my ears when an attendant came to say that a Negro bishop wished to see me.

The person concerned was Monsignor Cipriano Kihangire, Bishop of Gulu. He was in Italy for medical treatment, as a guest of Monsignor Enrico Manfredini, and had come to ask me for assistance for his severely poverty-stricken flock. It was an odd coincidence that he should arrive at that moment; and the cost of building a nursery school at Kitgum seemed very small compared with any other project. That is how the Giulio Pastore nursery school came into being.

Uganda is a country where Catholics and other Christians are in roughly equal numbers, but where a small Muslim minority (about 2 per cent of the population) acquired a position of power after Idi Amin had sent his predecessor, Milton Obote, into exile at Dar-es-Salaam, and acquired dictatorial powers for himself. It was not clear whether Amin's Muslim religion sprang from inner conviction – for early in his political career he had been on friendly terms with Israel – or whether it was intended to attract the welcome attentions of the Libyan government. At any rate, after expelling the Indians, who apparently had an almost total monopoly of trade, and after breaking off relations with the United States, he ordered the residence permits of Catholic missionaries to be withdrawn.

But he was out in his calculations, because the withdrawal of permits meant that both the school and hospital systems of Uganda would be in dire straits within a matter of days. And the reaction of the authorities and the people was so prompt and vigorous that His Excellency was obliged to go into reverse, starting by replacing (perhaps with physical violence?) the unfortunate minister who had proposed the move. Face had to be saved, however, and the solution was found in an Italo-Ugandan agreement for scientific and technical co-operation, which would give those same people (doctors, and male and female members of religious orders), who had up to now been classed as missionaries, a new justification for residing in Uganda. Since the Kitgum nursery school was now ready, I was invited to go and officially open it, and at the same time sign the Italo-Ugandan agreement.

My trip to Uganda in January 1974 was unforgettable. Amin had wanted it to coincide with the anniversary of Ugandan independence, and wanted me to be present at the various picturesque anniversary ceremonies – perhaps because it suited him to have a delegation from Western Europe present.

My first meeting with this gigantic man was very cordial. He talked about the contribution of the Italian missionaries (especially those belonging to the congregations founded by Comboni) to the development of Uganda in such glowing terms that no one could have believed they were in the presence of the man who had tried to throw them out. He wanted me to see other Catholic institutions besides those at Gulu and Kitgum, and for this purpose he put his personal helicopter at my disposal, together with its Neapolitan pilot, Colonel Dante Cafiero, who 'held both the keys to his heart'. He also asked me to spend a few hours at the University of Kampala – the oldest university in Africa and the pride and joy of Ugandans.

Amin had been heavyweight boxing champion of Uganda, while Princess Bagaya, who held the post of Deputy Minister at the Foreign Ministry, had just been crowned Miss Uganda. Amin had at first shown a very high regard for her, but at a certain point he was struck by a suspicion that she was trying to take his sceptre from him, so to get rid of her he invented a sordid story of an affair at Orly airport. She, however, was held by a London court to have been defamed, and Amin was sentenced to pay what I suppose were symbolic damages.

As a boxer, he was extremely proud of having laid out 'the great Italian champion Serra'. I confess I had never heard of Serra, but I took great care not to let him know that, though I was much afraid that he might ask me something about Serra's boxing career.

When I returned to Rome, I asked for information, and learned that there had indeed been a boxer named Armando Serra (born in 1912 or 1916), and that he had had a modest career as an amateur, with three victories in 1946: one against Gilardoni and two against Deiana. But there was no trace of a fight with Amin (in any case Serra was a middleweight), and I didn't waste time on further investigation.

But to return to my visit to Uganda. There was a football match between an Iraqi team and a local team. The locals lost, so Amin took the field himself to ensure that Uganda would get its revenge in the tug of war. The Iraqis won that too, to the considerable and evident annoyance of President Amin. There was also a minor incident during the military parade, which was linked to a gymnastics display: a military helicopter, which was supposed to deposit Amin at the culminating point of the show, landed a few minutes early, causing people to flee in all directions and raising an embarrassing cloud of dust. At the reception for the delegations, however, there were some beautiful folk performances. Amin passed from table to table making affable remarks and asking for comments. At the closing dinner, a small choir from Guinea Bissau used an anything–but–unbiased song to express the conviction that, apart from Amin and their own leader Macias, there were no statesmen worthy of respect anywhere in the world. Yet that was nothing compared to the judgement passed on white men in another song; the ideas expressed were of such a kind that one would have expected them, on any other occasion, to make a Negro blush.

It had been arranged that the official opening of the Kitgum nursery school should have an attractive ceremony with some very catchy songs, accompanied by rudimentary wind and stringed instruments. At the celebration of mass, when it came to the exchange of symbols of peace, hundreds of people came and shook our hands with great cordiality. Before we set off for home I was offered traditional gifts: a bow and arrows to defend me from my enemies, some small wooden objects, a forest drum, and some dried pumpkins for keeping water cool in the house. An old lady wanted me to accept the crochet hook she was using, apologizing for having nothing else to offer. It was important that a guest should be given a great many souvenirs of the families he had visited in the town.

I gained an understanding of the sense of tradition in that part of Africa nowhere better than at the leper hospital at Morolem (where I met Giovanni Battista Cesana, a bishop from Lombardy who had handed over his diocese to a native and stayed in Africa to serve the lepers as a humble assistant parish priest). Outside the hospital itself, where young Italian nuns complemented the medical treatment with their extraordinary capacity for making people cheerful, some hundreds of families were camping. They were waiting for relatives to complete their treatment and were living in the meantime on millet and fruit. I thought the treatment was a sort of first aid, but I was told these families might remain waiting for as long as two or three years.

I was thrilled when I learned that some of the pavilions in this leper hospital had been donated by the pupils of the Liceo Virgilio, the school which my children attended, in Rome.

I suspect that it was without precedent when an Italian honour was bestowed at the Equator, amidst the joyous celebrations of a gaily dressed crowd which somehow felt that it too was being honoured.

The recipient of the honour was Luigi Molinaro, a missionary who had been born eight-six years earlier at Volpino, outside Verona. For sixty-two years he had chosen to live in Africa, where he had taken on many different roles, from explorer to compiler of a grammar of the Madi language, and from teacher-priest to historian of the unknown traditions of a region which includes the peoples of Uganda and Sudan.

Amongst the most moved of those present was Cipriano Kihangire, a Ugandan whom Father Molinaro had baptized as long ago as 1918, and whose solemn figure now wore the robes of Bishop of Gulu. But the local Protestant pastor and Muslim *cadi* were also sharing the common rejoicing with obvious satisfaction.

When I took my leave of Amin (but not of the minister who had signed the agreement with me, because, I was informed, during the intervening few days he had ended up in the Nile on suspicion of spying for the Russians) he expressed a keen desire to be invited to Italy, partly in order to meet the Pope.

He came in September of the following year, and in proposing a toast at the lunch which Leone gave him at Castelporziano, he said:

> The numerous hospitals and schools built in Uganda thanks to the work of Italian missionaries bear witness to your contribution to our progress. It is my desire that the various Italian missions, as well as

economic and technical experts, should soon reach all the provinces of Uganda – a country which is physically similar to yours and which can offer you an interesting opportunity to provide economic aid and assistance.

The next day, the Vatican newspaper *L'Osservatore romano* reported that 'The Holy Father received in audience HE Alhajji Field Marshal Idi Amin Dada, VC, DSO, MC, President of the Republic of Uganda, and his retinue'. Also reported was Paul VI's speech in which he had expressed 'Our respect, esteem, and love' for Uganda.

Before Amin went on to Turin, a dinner was given in his honour by the President of the Senate, Giovanni Spagnoli, two of whose sons had for years been voluntarily serving the Ugandan people as Catholic doctors.

Things were not going well in Uganda. Friction had been increased by tribal differences, and the army (especially the contingent of faithful Sudanese soldiers) was accused of persecution, with torture chambers and the frequent disappearance of men and women. Relations with neighbouring countries were also very strained, especially Tanzania, because Obote was the guest of Julius Nyerere, and Amin considered him to be the rallying-point for the guerrilla war.

The Human Rights Commission in Geneva condemned what was going on – though no African country voted for the motion – and the world press paid more and more attention to Uganda. London kept its political (but not commercial) distance, and unlike all the other Commonwealth leaders, Amin was not invited to Queen Elizabeth's jubilee celebrations. Some said he would go just the same, but it turned out to be no more than a press rumour. Amin took his revenge by opening a charity fund to help Britain solve its energy problems.

Difficulties over residence permits for Italian missionaries came up again, partly because it is unfortunately the case that, when things are going badly, you look for scapegoats amongst foreigners. In March 1977, Amin played down the difficulties to the Italian Ambassador (Eugenio Rubino had now taken over from Renzo Falaschi), and jokingly said he was still using the rifle I had given him. He wanted me to know that he had tried it out that very morning, not on an acolyte, as a Ugandan king was supposed to have done in the last century, but on guinea fowl, seven of which had been downed with a single shot.

It was about this time that Associated Press issued a news-flash, according to which Amin, when talking about Charles Ofumbi, the late Minister of the Interior (who had died in mysterious circumstances along with another minister and an Anglican archbishop, Jarrai Lusum), had said reprovingly that Ofumbi ill-treated Christian missionaries.

Meanwhile, guerrilla activity was slowly turning into war, for the skirmishes between Tanzania and Uganda were now occurring every day. Amin was still trying to give an impression of normality, though he had to admit that conditions were appalling in certain provinces such as Karamoja, for which a charity appeal was started by the Archbishop of Bologna, Monsignor Manfredini, and that well-known deacon, Vittorio Pastori. The work of the charity is still developing. On 3 May 1978, Amin broadcast a message to the Red Brigades in Italy, asking them to release Aldo Moro.

The situation in Uganda rapidly deteriorated. Amin was defeated by Nyerere's army, and he too had to go into exile. He lived in Libya for some time and then moved to Saudi Arabia.

Elections were held, but were criticized for the obvious lack of secrecy, in that there were separate ballot boxes for the different parties. The result was a small majority for Obote over the democratic list of Paul Semogerere, a member of the international Christian Democrat movement.

Obote has taken up the reins of government in Uganda again, and experts in African affairs hope that Julius Nyerere (a Catholic) will be successful in helping Obote (a Protestant) and Semogerere (a Catholic) to find a way of settling their differences.

There are a few who say that Amin has not yet given up hope of stepping in if the two quarrelling parties wear each other out.

# 23
# Gerald Ford

Those Republicans who thought it would do their party good to join the anti-Nixon chorus were disappointed at the results of the 1976 presidential election, in which Jimmy Carter, Governor of the state of Georgia, had a clear victory over Ford in a skilfully created climate of renewal and expiation.

An analysis of mass psychology in the United States would reveal a striking alternation of collective euphoria and depression, the latter being intensified in recent years by defeat in Vietnam. One man who saw quite clearly that this would happen was Cardinal Spellman. On his return from a Christmas visit to the troops fighting in Vietnam, he told me one day that the deepest emotions of the American people would be disturbed and disorientated for a long time. Until now, Americans had felt that they had an almost religious mission to bring freedom to the whole world. All sorts of sacrifices were accepted by American families as a duty placed upon them, so to speak, by God. Huge resources of men and materials had been devoted to the achievement of victory in two world wars; the burden of ensuring the defence of Europe by keeping three hundred thousand troops there for an indefinite period had been shouldered; and Korea had been at least partly saved. But now that the failure of their intervention in Vietnam was apparent, protests against the war itself and the manner in which it was being fought rapidly increased in number. When the Stars and Stripes came down in Saigon, Spellman said, a long period would begin during which Americans would be an easy prey to every kind of emotion.

I don't know whether the disturbances of 1968, sparked off at the University of California, can be explained in this way; but it certainly accounts for the climate of self-chastisement in which the long debate over Watergate took place.

Carter was the life-raft, as it were, which Americans grasped in an attempt to purge themselves of Nixon's sin, and there was a certain appropriateness in this, since he has a genuine reputation as a man of religious vision. (He is a devout Baptist, and once told me that at the close of every day he and his wife read a chapter of the Bible together.) Four years later, more or less the same flag was successfully raised by Ronald Reagan, from an equivalent but opposite political position.

But let me return to Ford. Had it not been for the disastrous state of Italy in 1976, I probably would not have had occasion to meet him. I had taken over from Moro as Prime Minister, at a time when public finance was in chaos and the lira was subject to international speculation of a kind which threatened to ruin Italy in a matter of weeks. I felt it necessary, nevertheless, to go and seek a concrete gesture of solidarity from the United States. It was not financial help I was asking for – it was only right that any such help should go to the underdeveloped countries – but a monetary guarantee which would end the depredations of speculators and give us time to operate a strict recovery programme, which was considered vital by political parties, trade unions, and government alike.

At that point the early November election had already taken place, but the new American administration had not yet taken up office. The experts in protocol claimed that it was not the done thing to go and call on the outgoing President; and I was advised not to do so for the additional reason that if I didn't also meet the incoming President I would lose face. (But, to my considerable annoyance, these same pundits then claimed that it was also not done for the incoming President to become involved in international relations before his inauguration at the end of January.) I insisted on the visit, however, and John Volpe, the US Ambassador in Rome, actively supported me.

Just to make Italy's situation even more critical, another oil price increase was being threatened. On 3 December, I had met President Giscard d'Estaing of France at Migliarino, and he maintained that if there was an increase of 10 per cent France would also be in grave difficulties. Together, therefore, we proposed a special summit meeting of the industrialized nations, which was of additional interest to me, because it would allow me to correct the negative impression created by the already famous joint declaration of Puerto Rico.

Two days later I left for Washington, somewhat consoled by an article in the *Corriere della Sera* by Professor Modigliani, in which the Italian government's efforts were given praise. This was a good visiting card in certain American circles, and as soon as Ford spoke to me I realized that his press office had drawn his attention to the article, because he praised our plans in more or less the same terms.

For my part, I began by pointing out that the pessimistic forecast made at Puerto Rico was unfounded, that Italy had closed ranks – in a sort of internal political truce – and that we reckoned we could overcome our difficulties on the basis of this common platform.

Ford asked me whether the Communists also supported the modernization of the Italian armed forces in accordance with the collective undertakings of the Atlantic Alliance. It was a perfectly fair question, and even suggested a friendly attitude on Ford's part, because it gave me the opportunity to answer the question in the affirmative. I said that the Communists had not opposed the special law for the Navy and would behave similarly in relation to the Army and Air Force.

The United States, too, was worried about another increase in the price of oil, but Ford was realistic in his belief that OPEC would insist on 10 per cent (the rumoured rate of increase). He had personally contacted the King of Saudi Arabia, the Shah of Persia, and the President of Venezuela, and had suggested to them that it was in their economic interest not to plunge the Western nations into debt, and to support aid to the developing countries; but he was not confident that they would change their minds. He suggested that Italy should try to influence states such as Iraq, with whom the United States did not have direct relations.

Prospects were gloomy, because for Italy a 10 per cent increase meant 700 million dollars a year. I mentioned an idea I had already brought up at the European Council at The Hague, namely that a six-month moratorium should be requested; but Ford did not think that would be acceptable to the producer countries. Still less did he like the idea of price differentials according to whether the purchasers themselves sold goods or services to the oil-producing countries.

I spoke frankly to President Ford about the conditions imposed by the International Monetary Fund for opening a credit line – something we needed before we could ask for a loan from the European Community as well. We were being asked to guarantee that the government programme would be approved by both houses of parliament within a matter of weeks, and that the trade unions would promise to adopt an attitude of non-belligerence if not actually of support. This showed that those who criticized the new political situation in Italy, in which the Communists had ceased to be in opposition, were either ignorant of the realities of Italian political life, or else resigned to (if not actually happy at) an Italian economic collapse. My message was addressed to Ford, but the intended recipients were those who really had the power to help us but usually gave us plenty of advice and no assistance. Perhaps they would now understand.

President Ford was very sympathetic, and promised me that he would issue instructions to the Treasury to give us the help we needed, though the very particular situation of the American government made any assistance more difficult to obtain. He had also arranged that, in spite of our heavy programme of talks, my aides and I would have contacts not only with the 'transition team' but also with the Chairman of the Federal Reserve Board and other influential people in the world of finance and trade unions. Vice-President Nelson Rockefeller and Robert McNamara, both of whom were old friends of mine, did a great deal to smooth our path – not forgetting the American press, which is usually ill informed on Italian affairs and takes little interest in them. Twelve Senators from the two political parties came to a breakfast at Blair House, and this produced a conversation in which our problems were explained. I was also able to discuss them with Cyrus Vance (backed as the likely new Secretary of State), who had come specially from New York, and Walter Mondale, the Vice-President elect. It looked, therefore, as though my journey was going to serve some purpose, in spite of the gloomy forecasts of my advisers. But I needed results that would help the lira.

Ford seemed well disposed towards Italy, but equally if not more important were John Volpe's courageous efforts in persuading the Treasury Secretary, Bill Simon, to overcome any misgivings he may have felt and to agree on the communiqué I needed to keep foreign speculators at bay. We also obtained an important credit line to allow us to embark on our Plan for Energy, which is unfortunately still in its infancy.

There was an emotional moment at the official reception at the White House when the star of the evening, the southern singer Tony Orlando, referred to Ford's unsuccessful election campaign. I noticed that the President was overcome with emotion for a moment, and tightly squeezed his wife's hand.

Before I left the United States, I had a long talk with Henry Kissinger, and an exchange of ideas with the top officials of the Foreign Affairs Council and the Brookings Institution, who were working out Carter's government programme.

Kissinger was very doubtful about the possibility of a basic change of attitude in European Communist parties, and expressed the opinion that their burying the hatchet with the middle classes and the political movements which they had traditionally opposed was no more than a tactical manoeuvre. With touching sincerity, however, he wished the Italian government success in its activities, recognizing not only that we had regained a good deal of ground since Puerto Rico, but also that Italian attitudes to America had much improved since Nixon's visit to Rome, when the atmosphere had been very tense.

It was no coincidence that the official communiqué at the end of my visit recognized 'the importance of the growing consensus amongst Italians over the government's economic programme'.

# 24
# Vittorio Cini

Ninety-two is a ripe old age, but Vittorio Cini's mind and body seemed to have been unaffected by the advancing years. So the news of his death on 18 September 1977 took me by surprise, as a sort of unnatural event. Just a few months earlier I had visited him in his little house in Rome, made out of a perfect restoration of the little temple of Herodes Atticus on the Appia Pignatelli. He was then in fine fettle, and full of ideas for the Foundation in Venice which he had set up in memory of his son Giorgio, who had died in a tragic air accident in 1949.

In his archaeological jewel of a house on the Appian Way, I had been struck by a witty little picture hanging in a prominent position in the hall. It showed a family tree with many ramifications but only three names: Adam and Eve at one end, and Vittorio Cini at the other.

Soon after I became Under-Secretary to the Prime Minister's Office in 1947, I found that amongst the many problems I had to sort out was that of the Universal Exhibition Agency, which had been created to organize a great international exhibition in 1942. For obvious reasons, the agency had not done what it was supposed to, and there had been left on its books an assortment of half-finished buildings. The agency's administrator was Leonardo Severi, a highly distinguished administrative magistrate who had also been Minister of National Education in Badoglio's first government. Every month he sent a report to the Prime Minister's Office in which the only item on the credit side was a decrease in the quantity of marble slabs and other valuable materials stolen during the preceding month. However slight the fall, Severi drew attention to it as a small achievement. Another cloud on the horizon

was that the land which had at the appropriate time been expropriated would revert to its owners, since the compulsory purchase by the state was rendered null by the fact that the exhibition never materialized.

The man who chanced to give me an idea for solving this problem was Monsignor Giovanni Urbani, who had years earlier been adviser to the Venice branch of the Catholic student movement. (His flock consisted of the female members, while the male members were in the care of Don Sandro Gottardi, now Archbishop of Trento.)

'Ask Vittorio Cini's advice. He knows all about the E42 and will surely be able to suggest a way out.'

Apart from this particular pressing problem, I confess that I was intrigued at the prospect of meeting Cini, because there had been a rumour in 1943 that, before the Fascist Grand Council put paid to fascism in July of that year, Cini and Alfredo de Marsico had put Mussolini with his back to the wall at a cabinet meeting. Cini had been one of the organizers of the exhibition, and he came to see me several times, accompanied by Virgilio Testa, his closest aide of exhibition times and a man who, having successfully appealed against being purged as a fascist, was to be reinstated as Secretary-General to the Commune of Rome. Vittorio Cini, on the other hand, had been left untouched by the heavy reckoning imposed on members of the royal Senate (to which he had belonged since 1934). Testa was both a legal expert and a town planner, and I remember how in our three-cornered discussions he could rapidly find practical application for ingenious ideas put forward by Cini.

That is how there came into being the idea of creating a model district which would pay for itself through the sale of large buildings as office blocks and of small sites for luxury detached houses surrounded by obligatory green areas. This overall plan undoubtedly served a public purpose, and it afforded protection against the claims of former owners; for it was only the *type* of use that was changing, and therefore the rights already exercised by the state were not undermined. E42 was crossed out, and the acronym EUR was put in its place, to describe a more modern and rational gateway to the city of Rome.

De Gasperi approved the plan. Testa was appointed administrator (and Counsellor of State as well, much to the delight of members of the local authority, who knew what a stern taskmaster he was, and were afraid he would return to his old job). A certain number of private individuals bought back at twenty thousand or more lire per square metre sites for which they had been paid forty centesimi ten years earlier. There were no more thefts to report.

When he spoke of his past involvement in government, Cini did not use those justificatory circumlocutions that were fashionable at the time. Factors which had brought him to Mussolini's attention were: his reputation as a financier and as the man responsible for important industrial developments in Venice, and land reclamation work; extraordinary munificent undertakings at Ferrara and Monselice; and, not least, the fact that he was a 'self-made man'. In 1935, Mussolini had congratulated him on a speech he had made in the Senate on the budget of the corporations, though Cini had thought it might get him into trouble. He had in fact begun by declaring:

'I shall not speak about the crisis (too much has been said already), for I wish to avoid repetitions and clichés. If I refer to it at all, it is merely to emphasize that it is in the first place a *political* crisis, secondly a *spiritual* crisis, and only thirdly a *technical* crisis.'

He had gone on to suggest that, in combating the slump in prices, it was necessary to take due acccount of competition at home, which ought not to be blunted by the enforced creation of corporations:

> This tendency is accentuated by extreme believers in the corporative system, who see corporations as the instrument which will lead us from private management to state socialism. It is difficult to tell whether there are many such people, or whether they simply make a lot of noise, for they alone are left to shout, while we entrepreneurs as a group find it more convenient to stand on the sidelines, reserving the right to take offence and complain later on. The members of this group of extremists are sufferers from collectivist nostalgia, people who can't leave things alone, and professional revolutionaries, who seek only to destroy, never to create. At the very moment when comrade Stalin puts on his evening dress, perhaps to attend the State Ball on the anniversary of the Russian Revolution, certain *camerati* tend to present themselves in shirt sleeves and attempt to pass off as corporationist what is really contraband of a distinctly Bolshevik flavour.

By early 1943, the railways had been seriously damaged by air raids; the postal and telegraph network was in such financial difficulty that any modernization programme had had to be abandoned; and the merchant navy was under constant threat and unable to carry out its tasks. This was the moment when Italy turned to Count Cini as Minister of Communications. (The King had made him Count of Monselice in recognition of his long and dedicated work there.) When he presented his ministerial budget, he spoke both of important tasks to be carried out and of small economies to be made. Methane had to be developed, as did river navigation; the administration had to get rid of post-office jobs which were useless and too expensive, and unnecessary telegrams had to be curtailed.

He managed to balance the books in his ministry, and his almost meticulous care in his ministerial work, while bearing witness to his dedication, did not by any means indicate that he was not fully aware of what had been irreparably destroyed in Italian society. As I have already pointed out, he made this clear in the cabinet; and he consequently tendered his resignation – which was neither accepted nor rejected. By now everything was falling apart.

He was arrested by the Germans and ended up in the terrible concentration camp at Dachau, from which he managed to escape and make his way to Switzerland. After the Liberation, he set to work again, intending to make an active contribution to post-war reconstruction in Venice and in the many other cities to which his interests had spread in the course of time.

His son was killed when piloting a light aircraft over the Côte d'Azur and making signs of greeting to his friend Merle Oberon. While the dreadful news did not succeed in destroying Vittorio Cini, it completely transformed his character and caused him to alter his way of life profoundly.

It was then that he undertook the improvement and restoration of the island of San Giorgio Maggiore, making it the home of the cultural and social activities of the Cini Foundation, which he created in memory of Giorgio.

The Cini Foundation is divided into three centres, of which two (the Naval Centre and the Arts and Crafts Centre) are devoted to the vocational training of young people, whereas the third has scientific and cultural aims. This is the Centre for Culture and Civilization, which includes the School of San Giorgio for the Study of Venetian Culture. The latter consists of four institutes for specialized and advanced study, one of which is an Art History Institute with a large specialized library and a very rich collection of art photographs, not to mention valuable collections of old drawings, illuminated manuscripts dating from the twelfth to the fourteenth centuries, and *incunabula*. The Foundation's art activities are also carried on in the form of publications, lectures, classes, conferences, and debates, which make it not only a splendid home for collections and materials for the study of history, but also an active and lively contributor to contemporary culture.

After shouldering the enormous burden of bringing about the rebirth of the island of San Giorgio, Vittorio Cini regularly provided funds to balance the budgets of the various activities. He was justifiably worried, however, that the whole operation might collapse after his death, as often happens in the case of personal activities, even though they may for a time have considerable dimensions. He therefore sought the assistance of some outstanding personalities – Vittore Branca and Bruno Visentini were just two of them – and tried to attract the attention of the state to the Foundation, in the hope of obtaining the kind of aid which he had never wanted to ask for during his lifetime.

I noticed how moved he was when Pope John XXIII gave a solemn audience to the Foundation on the occasion of its tenth anniversary, and recalled in his speech how he used to climb up into the belfry of San Giorgio 'as though to bless from up there the promising activities of the Cini Foundation'.

He was very grateful, too, for any act of friendship towards the Foundation, however small. He came to see me in delight when he learned that I was giving to the Salesian school on the island a copy of a small statue of Don Bosco, which the ninety-year-old sculptor Pietro Canonico had completed for me shortly before he died. He was happy, Canonico told me at the hospital where I had gone to thank him, that he had at last succeeded in representing Don Bosco as he had known him as a child, and better than in the large statue which he had sculpted many years earlier for St Peter's in Rome.

The other great tragedy in Cini's life, after the death of his son, was the Vajont disaster of 9 October 1963. The dam built by SADE (an electrical company of which Cini was Chairman) had held, but the tidal wave (300 million cubic metres of water) created by the huge landslide had poured down into the valley, destroying Longarone, seriously damaging Erto and Casso, and bringing death and despair to many families. What depressed him was not so much the grim prospect of criminal responsibility, but rather the anguish of the villages and the risk of unjustly losing his reputation as an upright and careful business man. There was, naturally, a long and acrimonious debate about the affair. Parliament set up a Committee of Inquiry, headed by Leopoldo Rubinacci and including senators and members of the Chamber of Deputies who had personal expertise in the field. In its final report, however, the committee went no further than to say that it could not provide a definitive explanation of the causes of the disaster, since certain of the salient characteristics of what had happened seemed to be inexplicable. It was impossible to reach 'certain and definitive conclusions as to the causes of the catastrophe'.

There remained a suspicion that there had been defects in design or supervision, or other reprehensible or criminal shortcomings, and the matter was left to be dealt with in the courts, with reports by experts and counter-experts. To make matters more complicated, SADE had been taken over by the Montecatini company, which had itself merged with Edison; and as a result of the nationalization law the dam had become the property of the state, and was under the electricity authority, ENEL.

The state was therefore in the position of being both principal accuser and co-accused.

Cini maintained that those who had suffered in the disaster should be compensated at once, both on humanitarian grounds and also to avoid civil disputes. He also told me that, when SADE shares were valued at the time of the take-over, a substantial fund had been set aside for this purpose. The Chairman of Montedison (Valerio), however, on the advice of his lawyers (especially Cesare Tumedei, who opposed compensation payments, because he always considered them as indicating an admission of guilt), dug in his heels for a long time, in spite of ENEL's disagreement.

At Count Cini's funeral, the Patriarch of Venice, Albino Luciani, said that since Cini had left a written statement that only the praises of God should be sung in church, he could not sing Cini's praises. But the future Pope had no hesitation in saying that with Cini he had always felt like a child before his father, whose behest must always be obeyed.

On the anniversary of his death, I willingly accepted an invitation from Visentini to go and speak about Cini at the Foundation, and be present at the unveiling of a plaque which aptly stated: 'If you seek his monument, look around you.'

Robert Bresson was also there with André Cayatte (who had won a Golden Lion that year for his film *Le Passage du Rhin*). Bresson paid a touching tribute to Cini: 'St George may be a fictitious saint, as André Malraux claims, but the island of San Giorgio Maggiore is absolutely real.'

Venice – and not just Venice – owes its particular *reality* to Vittorio Cini for all time.

# 25

# *Indira Gandhi*

Although I was very busy as Minister of Defence at the time, I nevertheless accepted an invitation in December 1964 to go to Bombay to address the International Eucharist Conference and give a lecture at Bombay University. I don't deny that I had a special reason for going. The Italian security service had accepted the task of discreetly assisting the local security services in looking after the personal safety of the Pope, since there had been some worrying rumours in circulation as to the hostile intentions of certain pro-Pakistani and pro-Portuguese groups (the Goa affair had happened quite recently). It was not a bad idea, therefore, that I too should be there to provide in my turn any necessary support for the little band of Italians commanded by General Viggiani. He wore civilian clothes and never left Paul VI's side for a moment, with the result that he too did a complete circuit of the Via Crucis behind the Pope in the great oval arena where large public ceremonies were held. Members of the diplomatic corps were curious to know the identity of the fourth person, immediately behind the two torch-bearers and the Pope – who was himself bent beneath the weight of a large wooden cross. I told the Belgian Ambassador that he was a volunteer Cyrenian in case Paul VI should get too tired, but he didn't seem convinced.

Fortunately everything went off without incident, except for an explosion which was strangely reminiscent of the Via Rasella bomb in Rome in 1944 (both involved road-sweeping equipment); but no one was hurt, and it was not even clear whether it was an abortive terrorist attack or something else.

People in authority and ordinary members of the public had gathered in Bombay from all parts of India, wearing their local

costumes. Among them were the 'head hunters', who presented me with a tie, with joking references to the preparatory rites for decapitation. But I don't believe they can have been very fashionable any more, for their spokesman was a young Salesian, and Don Bosco's methods surely don't involve the use of the executioner's axe.

I had an official meeting with my opposite number, the Indian Minister of Defence, Y. B. Chavan; but then the Italian Ambassador, Justo Giusti del Giardino, invited the Minister of Information, Mrs Indira Gandhi, to lunch. He thought she had a great future ahead of her. So that is how I made the acquaintance of Pandit Nehru's daughter, and I was able to appreciate the depth of her reasoning powers and her sound knowledge of European affairs.

She spoke very frankly about difficulties which had arisen over the fact that such a special occasion as the Pope's visit included Bombay but not Delhi. At first it had been thought that the state welcome might be offered by the Vice-President, but since he was a Muslim there was a risk of intensifying thereby the hostility of Hindus and others. (The Indian Communist Party, for example, was openly critical of the government for its handling of the food crisis, or at least that is what it claimed.)

Indian religious leaders had called for calm, and this, together with the intelligent work of Cardinal Valerian Gracias, had lowered the temperature. In order to be in Bombay, President Radhakrishnan had put off an eye operation due to be carried out in London at that particular period.

Mrs Gandhi was frank enough to stress the considerable psychological advantage to India of the Pope's visit. The Portuguese press was in fact alone in expressing disapproval, on the grounds that the visit might be interpreted as involving implicit approval of the recent annexation of Goa. But that was yet another reason why the Indian government should feel satisfied.

Mrs Gandhi maintained that amongst the various political movements in India there were certain local parties, such as the right-wing Hindu Maha Sabha, to whose pronouncements one should not pay too much attention. She thought their attack on the mass conversions to Catholicism which the Eucharistic Conference was supposedly trying to bring about was mere propaganda, and did not spring from genuine apprehension. And their claim that they would oppose any distribution of charity to non-Christians was empty words.

As for the Communists, she had no doubt that, if things continued to go well, their leader would at least greet the Pope at the airport on his arrival and departure. That is exactly what happened.

Indira Gandhi was much struck by the intellectual side of the Pope and his sincere respect for all cultures. She considered India's guest not so much the influential leader of a church of world-wide importance, but rather as one of those international personalities who 'belong to the world', over and above any special position they may hold.

She also expressed strong approval of Cardinal Agagianian, who had preceded the Pope as Papal Legate. She was much struck by the variety of 'characters' amongst the leaders of the Church of Rome.

The forecast made by the Italian Ambassador, Giusti del Giardino, proved to be accurate. Indira Gandhi soon achieved a majority in the Congress and became Prime Minister.

It was in that capacity that I met her in Rome during my own premiership in 1973. She was on her way to the United States, and had asked for a meeting to be arranged. For her convenience it took place at Fiumicino airport. The principal subject of our conversation was the role of non-aligned countries both in mitigating the USA–USSR polarization in world affairs, and in at last bringing into being an effective policy of aid to developing countries.

The death of Nasser had deprived the movement of one of its leaders; and there was no hiding the fact that Marshal Tito was a very old man. It seemed clear to me that Mrs Gandhi saw herself as the leader required, since the leadership had to be entrusted to a great people and a state that was *really* non-aligned.

Her conversation included several critical references to the attitude of certain Western countries, including Italy, to non-alignment, which they interpreted as being a policy of convenience, and more anti-West than anti-East. There might be certain individual non-aligned countries whose position was less than absolutely clear, but most of them – and certainly the movement as such – were utterly convinced of the historical mission of non-alignment.

I took it from what she said that even the Indian nuclear programme – apart from its scientific and technological side, which I, as Minister of Industry, would be able to appreciate at the conference of the International Atomic Energy Agency in Vienna – was to be seen as belonging to an area of freedom from Great Power influence.

It was here at Fiumicino that I learned that Mrs Gandhi had family links with Italy, because one of her sons had married an

Italian girl and was living in Turin. She had a long telephone conversation with him from the VIP lounge at the airport (and I did not bother to withdraw, because it was obvious that I did not understand her language at all).

Later on there were hard times for Mrs Gandhi and her party. In 1977 they suddenly lost their majority – after a period during which, it has to be admitted, there had been a severely repressive regime – and were also accused of electoral malpractices. But this was no more than a temporary period of . . . very busy rest. Less than three years later, she gained a two-thirds majority in parliament and took over the reins of government again. After the death of Tito, she had a silent battle with Fidel Castro for the leadership of the non-aligned countries, and even succeeded in arranging for their last congress – due to be held in Baghdad – to be moved to Delhi, because of the continuing war between Iraq and Iran (both non-aligned countries, which shows that non-alignment is not in itself sufficient to bring friendship and harmony).

Mrs Gandhi made a brilliant opening speech, as she had previously done at the FAO in Rome in 1981. And she summoned all the world's heads of state and government to go to New York for an informal meeting during the annual UN assembly in the autumn of 1983.

Politics is not everything. A few years ago Indira Gandhi suffered the tragic loss of her son Sanjay, who had embarked on a political career, and had recently followed his mother through thick and thin. I contacted her on this occasion, and was able to observe that there are moments in life which no oriental impassiveness or political detachment can cope with, even though there is a kind of understandable reserve which makes one try not to let one's grief or joy show through.

# 26
# *Aldo Moro*

In the autumn of 1938, Aldo Moro, who was then President of FUCI (the Catholic student movement), summoned me to its very modest head office in Largo Cavalleggeri in Rome. Little did I realize then that our lives would henceforward run on almost parallel lines, in spite of our great differences of temperament. We had already met at a few earlier student movement meetings (I had joined as soon as I left school, and had attended congresses at Florence and Genoa, at the latter of which I played an active part in a protest against the newly published race laws), but I felt that Moro had not noticed my contributions either at the congresses or at the club premises in Piazza S. Agostino. As a matter of fact, now that he had taken over from Giovanni Ambrosetti as national president of FUCI, he rarely went there. I was now very surprised to find, therefore, that I was being offered the editorship of the journal *Azione Fucina*; and I rashly accepted.

We thus worked together for a few years in the same tiny premises (I lay emphasis on the size for the benefit of those who will insist that in those days Catholic Action was too big for its boots), supervising the journal's framework and collaborating on the organization of various FUCI events. Aldo nearly always wrote the leading article, thereby causing serious problems for the printers, since he would completely revise it once or even more than once at the proof stage. Though his prose style was somewhat pompous, his ideas came across with great clarity. His search for stylistic perfection led him to make much use of adjectives and adverbs, as could also be observed in his speeches at congresses, study groups, and area conferences, thereby giving an impression of a deep understanding of the matters concerned, and a high cultural level.

150

One very problematical issue of *Azione Fucina* was the one that came out in June 1940, immediately after Italy's declaration of war. We had kept to the Vatican line of praising 'non-belligerence', and we suddenly found ourselves on the horns of a dilemma: were we to bow to our civil masters even if they were behaving irresponsibly, or should we continue to come out in praise of peace and condemn this fresh 'useless massacre'? There were endless discussions on the matter, involving Aldo and our ecclesiastical advisers Monsignor Guido Anichini, Don Emilio Guano, and Don Franco Costa (known to us as 'the arm' and 'the minds'). In the end we agreed that, as long as members of FUCI were risking their lives on the battle-fronts with the rest of Italy's youth, it would be unfair to dissociate ourselves from the nation's desire to avoid losses and defeat. We did not wave any flags, and we did not cease to write of the need for peace, but we had to keep in mind that this war was not just fascism's tragedy but first and foremost Italy's. Not that FUCI felt the least sympathy for fascism; and the feeling was reciprocated.

Here's a strange thing. In the middle of that very month of June 1940, we were about to publish an extract from a draft speech by Gabriele D'Annunzio in which he rejected the idea of declaring war against France. Somehow or other a Lombard member of FUCI had got this from the Vittoriale, and we were enormously proud of our journalistic scoop. Even after the publication of the Mussolini–D'Annunzio correspondence, it was not very clear to me whether D'Annunzio had been asked to write the speech in order to make it appear that this was official policy, or whether Mussolini had really meant to keep out of the war, until he was suddenly persuaded to join in for fear that Hitler might win on his own.

Our first issue after the declaration of war placed a certain emphasis on the King's and Mussolini's proclamations, but after that we managed to keep a reasonable balance and, with a couple of exceptions, just managed to steer clear of the eagle-eyed censor. I had asked Don Sergio Pignedoli, a navy chaplain serving at sea, to write our 'Letter to the Armed Forces', but I was also happy to publish letter from members of FUCI. Our first encounter with the censor resulted from an article written by Giorgio Bachelet from the Russian front, in which he praised the sympathetic and humane behaviour of the ordinary Soviet people towards Italian soldiers. Down they came on us like a ton of bricks! We had praised the enemy! The issue was confiscated, and we were given a severe warning.

Our second crime consisted of expressing admiration, in an article signed by Sergio Pignedoli, for Italian sailors, who were doing their wartime duty without harbouring feelings of hatred for the enemy. By pure coincidence, the article was published on the very day that Mussolini called on Italians to hate the British for at least three generations. There was a total clash of attitudes here, and publication of our journal was suspended. Only after a whole month of diplomatic negotiations (involving the State Secretariat and the Italian Ambassador to the Holy See) were we given another warning and allowed to resume publication.

When I became Under-Secretary to the Prime Minister's Office, I was astonished to learn from Giorgio Nelson Page that the measures taken against *Azione Fucina* had been authorized by Mussolini in person. He showed me a file in which Sergio Pignedoli's article had been blue-pencilled with a specific order to stop publication, signed 'M.'.

I was not sure whether to feel flattered that we had merited such attention, or to attribute the disastrous outcome of the war to the fact that the Commander-in-Chief of the Armed Forces – who also happened to be the Head of Government and heaven knows what else besides – had wasted his time on things like that.

Then came the moment when Moro received his call-up papers and had to leave Rome. I, on the other hand, was lucky enough to be refused acceptance on an officer cadet training course on grounds of 'anaemia and poor general health', though I had at first found my rejection both humiliating and worrying. I was therefore posted as a medical orderly to the College of Legal Medicine, where I was taken under the wing of Lieutenant-General Alfredo Bucciante, the head of the college. He gave me some legal research to do on the source of special pension rights, and left me all the free time I needed for my FUCI work. And, what was almost miraculous, I found myself exempted from wearing uniform and sleeping in barracks. There had been an apocalyptic invasion of bedbugs in the barracks, and I might have carried this veritable Egyptian plague with me if I had had to commute from barracks to college offices. Evidence of the risk involved was there for all to see, and it quickly led the General to grant me this double exemption.

By writing to Aldo Moro and going to see him occasionally, I managed to persuade him to stay on as President of FUCI for a while. Later, I agreed to act as 'regent', partly in the hope that the war would soon come to an end. Alas, that was not to be; so Moro submitted his firm resignation, and suggested to Pius XII, with the approval of Monsignor Montini, that I should be appointed his successor.

During our meetings, we had often talked about 'after the war' and the complicated problems that would arise for Catholics as for everyone else. I was struck by Moro's lack of interest in direct political commitment (it was almost an allergy), but I attributed it partly to his current sense of responsibility towards FUCI (apart from our journal's censorship problems, the Special Tribunal was investigating certain members accused of subversive activities, and the police were also looking into us), and partly to his lack of sympathy for those responsible for reorganizing the Christian Democrat Party. I, on the other hand, was beginning to collaborate with them, and Montini and his 'Superior' certainly didn't disapprove.

When Rome was liberated and politics ceased to be a clandestine activity, I resigned as President of FUCI, and my place was taken by Ivo Murgia. Moro had turned his full attention to his university career (philosophy of law and criminal law). He listened with respect to my own decisions, but I remember that he spoke eloquently of the priority to be given to one's professional duty, and he criticized my having been obliged to interrupt my legal work because of the burden of my responsibilities to FUCI.

It was in 1946 that Moro embarked on a political career with the Christian Democrats; and by coincidence it was I who was sent by the Apulian headquarters to draw up the list of candidates for the election to the Constituent Assembly in the Bari–Foggia constituency. I got the impression that Moro agreed to stand largely because he was told to by his close friend Archbishop Marcello Mimmi.

He was successful in the election, and took an active part in the work of the Constituent Assembly, where he struck up a close political friendship with Giorgio La Pira, Giuseppe Dossetti, and Amintore Fanfani. This soon led to the formation of an organized group within the Christian Democrat Party in effective opposition to the whole band of ex-members of the Partito Popolare and other 'elders'. It was this group which, in 1948, managed to torpedo Sforza's candidature for the presidency of the Republic, thereby causing great displeasure to De Gasperi. Nevertheless, De Gasperi was intelligent and unbiased enough always to invite the *professorini* to buckle down to work alongside everybody else. Sometimes he managed to persuade them to his way of thinking, but on a few occasions their team spirit proved very strong. Thus when Fanfani

154

turned down the job of Minister of Labour, Moro refused to stay on as Under-Secretary for Foreign Affairs, giving 'group discipline' as his reason for doing so, rather than his poor health, which was well known. He had in fact suffered a severe attack of arthritis, which he overcame thanks to intensive cortisone treatment, but this had a certain effect on his heart, to the extent that for fifteen years he never travelled by plane.

Shortly before De Gasperi's death, the Christian Democrat Party had been almost totally taken over by the Chiesa Nuova group (so called because the unmarried members and those without families in Rome lodged together at the convent of the Portuguese nuns in Via della Chiesa Nuova), and after his death the leadership of the Christian Democrat group in the Chamber of Deputies was given to Moro, with Fanfani as Party Secretary.

There was a great deal of tension within the Christian Democrat Party, partly because the architects of the great election victory of 1948 were ill disposed to being downgraded or, worse still, pushed aside. The result was that a very heterogeneous group of Christian Democrats ended up by gathering round Guido Gonella and Giovanni Gronchi (the latter had failed even to gather enough signatures to make up a list at the 1954 Naples congress, and had lost the battle to introduce proportional representation into the party's internal elections). This survival committee, so to speak, put me forward as a rival to Moro for the leadership of the parliamentary party.

I explained to Moro that there was nothing personal about my standing against him, and I did not accept his invitation to withdraw my candidature, for I saw myself as an uncontroversial link between the old and the new. (What does 'new' mean, anyway? The Chiesa Nuova of the Portuguese nuns – who were at school with my mother – has been called a 'new' church for nearly five centuries!)

I was defeated by twenty votes or so (though some friends of mine complained that a certain number of votes against me had been mysteriously added on), but this did not prevent me from remaining on cordial terms with Moro, especially since the opposition were already showing signs that their solidarity was under stress.

After De Gasperi's government had fallen in February 1953, and Pella had been got rid of in February 1954, a four-party coalition had been reconstituted; and when it came to the presidential election of 1955, an attempt was made to assist and preserve the coalition by not putting forward a Christian Democrat candidate. It is true that this was not an official decision, and that Scelba and Fanfani both supported the candidature of Cesare Merzagora, who was a true independent but had twice been elected to the Senate as a Christian Democrat in the extremely safe Vimercate constituency.

I was personally in favour of the re-election of Einaudi, because that would not only have rewarded his personal integrity and prestige, but would also have avoided otherwise inevitable ruptures within the Christian Democrat parliamentary group. When my wife and I were invited to a private dinner with President Einaudi and his wife at the President's Palace, I received confirmation that Einaudi was very keen on re-election and that his wife Ida was equally enthusiastic.

I then wrote an article in *Oggi* in which I refuted objections to an elderly president, pointing out how many good popes had been elected in the twilight of their lives. It is only a pity that I could not at that time take John XXIII as an example.

When the Christian Democrat groups met at Palazzo Barberini, Gonella, I, and some other friends vainly supported Einaudi's candidature, and were even able to announce that Gronchi supported him (though Gronchi was already the candidate of the Left). But the concentrated fire of the Party Secretary, Prime Minister Scelba, and the two group leaders, Moro and Ceschi, was too much for us, and Merzagora's candidature easily won the day – thereby doing him a great disservice.

They say in Rome that when there is a papal election, the man who goes into the conclave as Pope comes out a cardinal. You can imagine, then, how Merzagora came out of the presidential election, for while he was backed by the Christian Democrats as a 'lay' candidate, he was thought of by the 'lay' parties as a Christian Democrat (at least in a minor way), and his position was made worse by his being the involuntary cause of offence being given to Einaudi.

Gronchi won the race for the presidency with ridiculous ease, and shortly afterwards Segni took over from Scelba as Prime Minister, thereby setting in motion the gradual break-up of the big Chiesa Nuova group. Moro could be seen to be gradually drifting away from Fanfani and acquiring more power than him. This happened at the Florence congress, thanks to the deciding votes of the little independent band of my friends in the Primavera group. But anyone who thought they had now put a stop to the swing towards centre-left governments (attributed to Fanfani) was sadly mistaken, because Moro raised a standard whose colours were similar but much brighter. At the Naples congress, I expressed my own attitude in a parody of an advertising slogan used by a particular brand of detergent: 'I thought the Centre-Left was the one led by Fanfani, until I encountered the one led by Moro.'

In my opinion, the new understanding between Nenni's Socialists and the Christian Democrats was a very shaky edifice. I thought it a mistake to build from the top downwards rather than from the outside inwards; and there was no solid political programme – except for the costly business of nationalizing the electricity industry, over which the state already had full authority free of charge, in that it controlled the building of power-stations, and price tariffs. It also seemed to me offensive to Saragat and his Social Democrats. They were certainly not overjoyed to hear the enthusiastic toasts to the 'historic alliance' of Socialists and Christian Democrats which had already partly taken place in 1947.

My fears were indeed justified, for the new alliance was contemporaneously and authoritatively described both as *isolating* the Communists and as *an approach* to the Communists.

I had decided not to accept a post in the new government, but Moro was most insistent that I should remain as Minister of Defence, so that the new direction in Italian politics should not be misinterpreted by other countries as a cause for alarm. Two years later, however, by which time any such fear had been allayed, I received a telegram from Moro when I was in Washington for a NATO meeting, to the effect that he needed the Social Democrat Tremelloni as Minister of Defence, but wanted me to remain in government. I moved to the Ministry of Industry, where one job to be done was that of reorganizing the Nuclear Energy Committee (CNEN), which had been put in disarray by the unjust persecution of Professor Felice Ippolito. When my predecessor, Senator Lami Starnuti, handed over to me, he told me quite frankly that he had made a point of never setting foot in the offices of CNEN, although as Minister of Industry he was its chairman. I, on the contrary, felt that energy was a vitally important area, so I went there every week, in an attempt to set the committee in motion again, for its programme of work was almost completely paralysed. I also tried to push forward a project for a nuclear-powered ship, since it would be very handy if oil became more expensive – a likely event, even if one could not yet guess the extent of a price increase. Italy, however, is a country where there is a great deal of talk about innovation and even revolution, but where it is difficult to conduct negotiations, and still more to reach decisions when that magic ingredient 'a precedent' is missing.

I had accepted the Ministry of Industry (Moro had given me the option of that or Education) partly because it meant that I would be a member of the Supreme Defence Council and so retain links with an area of government in which I had had ministerial responsibility for seven consecutive years – not without some success, both on the international scene and at home. I felt that, amongst other things, I could help avoid possible damage from a personality clash between the Army Chief of Staff and the Defence Chief of Staff. General Di Lorenzo had been appointed to the former post against my advice. I thought he should have been left to continue his excellent work as Commandant of the Carabinieri, rather than appointed to a position for which he was unsuited. I had suggested to President Saragat first General Vedovato and then General Ciglieri, and I had asked Moro not to insist on Di Lorenzo. Saragat had explicitly turned down the Di Lorenzo idea, but suddenly changed his mind, saying he was convinced that it would be particularly useful to have an engineer at the head of the army (Di Lorenzo was a *marine* engineer!). Since my objections were based purely on the question of personality, however, I felt bound to accept the joint opinion of the Prime Minister and the President of the Republic. I just hoped that my long experience as a politician would enable me to cool down any heat generated betweeen General Aloia and General Di Lorenzo. If I had known that I would be leaving the Ministry of Defence, I would have made sure that the previous Defence Chief of Staff, General Aldo Rossi, stayed in that post. Unfortunately, the manoeuvre to upset my plans for filling senior positions was successful. (I had been given advance warning of this by General Viggiani, the head of military intelligence.) The result was years of quarrels and a serious lack of harmony, which certainly did not do the Italian armed forces any good.

When I left the Ministry of Industry in late 1968, I willingly devoted myself to parliamentary activities, and was elected President of the Christian Democrat parliamentary group. This time there was no clash with Moro, for he had now become quite separated from the old *doroteo* group, and we were totally agreed on a number of foreign policy ideas. For the second time since the days of FUCI I found myself in a post which Moro had previously held with distinction. In 1970 I was asked to form a government, but failed, because the Social Democrats opposed me. They suspected me of pro-Socialist sympathies, because of the working friendship that had developed in the Chamber of Deputies between me and Luigi Bertoldi, the leader of the Socialist Party group. In 1972 I was again asked to form a government, and this time I succeeded. It was a one-party government which operated in an almost caretaker capacity because of the common conviction – of which President Leone was aware – that we would have to have an early election and then start all over again. Moro stayed on as Foreign Minister (he had taken up the post in succession to Pietro Nenni in Rumor's one-party government which resulted from the second split between Social Democrats and Socialists), and during those few months in which I was Prime Minister we worked hard together.

In view of the previous centre-left crisis, it seemed sensible, after the election, that I should invite the Liberals to join the coalition, too, but the Socialists announced that they would not sit at the same table as the Liberals even for preliminary discussions, so I was forced to form a government without the Socialists.

We were exposed to fierce attacks from the Left and were subject to the weekly activities of 'rebels'. In spite of our small majority, we lasted for almost a year, thanks to the close collaboration of Arnaldo Forlani, who was then Secretary of the Christian Democrat Party. Moro had decided not to remain in the government in spite of appeals from me, because he felt he was too closely associated with the centre-left formula, and he wanted a free hand to work towards its revival. He gave me valuable advice from outside government, however, and helped me to convince the Christian Democrat Party that it would be valuable for Italy to have a consultative agreement with the Soviet Union, in addition to its relations within the Western Alliance; and indeed this agreement came in for praise during my subsequent visits to Washington and Tokyo.

It was this very widening of horizons, however, and the prospect that our grasp of the situation would be strengthened, which aroused a sudden bitter attack on the government. The move was welcomed in certain quarters of the Christian Democrat Party, and a joint plot, known as the Palazzo Giustiniani plot, was hatched, to replace Forlani and me with Fanfani and Rumor.

I returned to the ranks of the Chamber, so to speak; but Moro suggested that I should take his place as President of the Chamber Foreign Affairs Committee. That was stage three in our parallel careers.

The improvised agreement between Christian Democrats and Socialists did not last for long, however, and some Christian

Democrats felt impeded in their activities by the aftermath of party congresses. Consequently there was a cabinet crisis after a few months, and Rumor personally invited me to return to the cabinet as Minister of Defence; and I cannot deny that I saw in the invitation a way of having my own back for the earlier sly manoeuvres against me. When I took over from Tanassi, I stated publicly that never again must SIFAR (the military intelligence service) or other services be allowed to deviate from their proper function, and if ever military commanders were asked to do something outside their proper sphere of action, they should refuse to obey, wherever the orders came from.

I have never found myself in a comfortable ministry (perhaps I would not be offered one), and I was soon at grips with two affairs involving General Vito Miceli, whom my predecessor had appointed head of the military intelligence service SID, as the old SIFAR was now called. A SID investigation, headed by General Maletti, into the neo-fascist movement led by Prince Valerio Borghese had thrown up evidence that General Miceli had had certain direct contacts with Prince Borghese. With the full approval of General Miceli himself, the whole dossier was passed to the State Prosecutor's Office in Rome. At the subsequent trial, various people were found guilty, but General Miceli was acquitted.

The Giannettini affair was more serious and more delicate. I was informed one day that the Milan magistrates investigating the Piazza Fontana bomb outrage were about to suspend their investigation on the formal grounds that the Ministry of Defence was failing to collaborate by refusing to say whether Guido Giannettini was or was not an intelligence service informer. Now, it is perfectly obvious that sources of information must be protected. But when there is a legal investigation going on in which it is actually being insinuated that violence has been perpetrated by the state, no cover can be respected. Therefore, in order to get things done quickly and avoid an impasse with the Milan magistrates, I took the opportunity of stating in an interview that Giannettini was indeed an informer. In this way it was possible to reopen the dialogue between the Ministry and Judges D'Ambrosio and Alessandrini. I am sure that if my predecessor had been properly approached, there would have been no refusal to collaborate.

Unfortunately it turned out that there had been serious misdemeanours by SID in connection with Giannettini. I had been informed in a written note that, after a warrant for his arrest had been issued, no further contacts had been made with him, and that in any case he was abroad. But Giannettini himself declared that these contacts had continued, and that payments had been made to him personally at Orly airport. This forced me to cancel the appointment of General Miceli (who had in the meantime been replaced as head of SID by Admiral Casardi) as Commander of the Milan Army Corps, and to set up a disciplinary investigation. Furthermore, another magistrate, who was investigating another fascist-type movement, accused General Miceli of committing certain offences, and arranged for him to be arrested. I do not know whether it is true that Moro wrote him a letter of support (when I asked him, he neither confirmed nor denied it), but his reaction to my detailed report on what had happened was to say curtly, 'You have harmed a good man.'

Miceli was subsequently elected to the Chamber of Deputies as a member of the right-wing Movimento Sociale Italiano, and in his first speech in the Chamber he made a violent attack on me, revealing – to the amazement of all those present – that he had advised the President of the Republic not to ask me to form a government. However, even before being invited to form a government, I had been summarily ousted as Minister of Defence for the second time. Every possible means of discrediting me had first been used, including an anonymous letter which accused me, believe it or not, of allowing Judge Tamburino access to SID offices in the exercise of his duty. It was beyond my comprehension why the President of the Chamber of Deputies should hasten to forward the letter to the Committee of Inquiry, which rapidly carried out an investigation and exonerated me by 18 votes to 2 (the two MSI members). There were other greater and smaller dirty tricks played on me subsequently, and behind all of them I could feel the influence of the SID affair of 1974.

Even after this second enforced retirement from my defence post, I was asked to remain in the cabinet, and in a sense my arm was being twisted, because I was told that if I did not agree, Forlani would refuse to take my place as Minister of Defence in the Moro cabinet. On the one hand I felt justified displeasure at what was a mistaken and unjustified surrender (not to the armed forces as such, but to certain military personnel whom I had been obliged to dismiss and punish – without any personal animosity on my part), and on the other there was the prospect of bringing to an end a lean period in Forlani's career (the trouble had begun at Palazzo Giustiniani). I therefore had no real choice: I accepted the Ministry of the Budget with responsibility for Special Aid to Southern Italy.

On the afternoon when I made up my mind, I didn't manage to contact Moro, and subsequently learned that he had gone to ground in a cinema. He was grateful, at any rate, for my acceptance. This was the beginning of the period of my most fruitful collaboration with Moro. He much appreciated both my acceptance of the superior position of La Malfa (as Deputy Prime Minister), even on matters relating to my ministry, and my making no protest over several speeches touching on financial matters within my ministerial competence, which were prepared by Nino Andreatta at Moro's request and delivered by Moro himself in parliament – where I first learned of their existence. This was no time for indulging one's personal pride or carping about the rules. The fact remained, however, that Italy's finances were in a bad way.

Moro was not very keen on economic problems. He considered them thorns in his flesh which had to be endured. When Rumor handed over the reins of government to Moro, he had been obliged to tell Moro that Italy was as deep in debt as it was possible to be, to the extent that the German banks had asked for Italy's gold reserves to be used as security for a loan. And in spite of every effort, matters were continuing to get worse. When I went to see Moro, however, he preferred to discuss general subjects, such as the prospects for social progress, rather than Italy's monetary and budget problems. I recall that on more than one occasion, while commenting on the disastrous result of the divorce referendum, he took time to cast his mind back over history and deplore the tardiness with which Catholics face up to the implications of a changing world. And he pointed out the paradox that those in favour of divorce ('the ones who want to regularize their position') were the people who least believed in the family as an institution.

In December 1975, the Socialists caused a government crisis, apparently as a result of a misunderstanding. Moro was deeply hurt at this, partly because Francesco De Martino was not so much Secretary of the Socialist Party as a close friend whom he had known since university days. This was an unforgivable offence. So Moro put together a Christian Democrat–Republican alliance, under the eternal illusion that an early general election would have a beneficial effect.

The election did not allow the Communists to realize their hope of overtaking the Christian Democrats, but it did appreciably increase their parliamentary strength, making it that much less likely that the Socialists would come out of opposition again.

This was the situation when Moro went to Puerto Rico for the industrialized nations' summit, at the beginning of which there took place the famous lunch for four (Ford, Schmidt, Callaghan, and Giscard d'Estaing), at which extremely pessimistic conclusions were drawn about the future of democracy in Italy – conclusions which were subsequently made public in a statement by Chancellor Schmidt. Was this a diplomatic affront to Moro, apart from anything else? It has recently come to light, in a book by Ducci, a former Italian Ambassador in London, that Moro had been invited to this working lunch, but had preferred to stay with his aides and study the papers for the summit, not having had the time to examine them before his departure, because of the Italian general election.

By the time he returned to Rome, he had firmly made up his mind to resign, and it was he who insisted on my heading a government of reconciliation, in an attempt to avert financial disaster. He talked to me with unusual warmth, recalling our friendship of FUCI days and promising me his whole-hearted, fraternal support.

Moro had much appreciated the fact that when I became Minister of the Budget I chose as my Chief of Cabinet Tullio Ancora, who had been a discreet and loyal assistant of his, as well as a personal friend. I had made my choice partly in the knowledge that Moro would be pleased, but principally because I was aware of Ancora's good qualities, for I had been so impressed by his work as an official of the Chamber of Deputies that I had myself put his name forward and had him appointed Counsellor of State.

I think it is largely due to Dr Ancora if my relationship with Moro during these last years was closer and more friendly than previously. I am not an easy-going, extrovert person, but Aldo Moro's introversion was more marked than mine. Ever since our days in FUCI, when our spirited nature as students caused us to carry out with cheerful irresponsibility what were really no less than acts of vandalism (such as throwing our beds out into the courtyard of the Cestello seminary in Florence, in whose uncomfortable dormitories we were guests during a congress), Moro's seriousness had caused him to stand out in splendid isolation. He even wore a jacket and tie on social occasions, and would never abandon a group in conversation if the subject was thoroughly serious.

I was surprised when I heard that he was marrying Noretta Chiavarelli, for she had always been involved in our group escapades. Indeed, there were some personal practical jokes of hers which became famous in the chronicles of FUCI. There was an occasion at Camaldoli, for example, when a young graduate who was new to our gatherings put his shoes outside his cell door at night, as though he were in a hotel and they would be cleaned for him. She hid the shoes and forgot to put them back in the morning, so the poor wretch had to hire a car and go down to Bibbiena without any shoes on to buy himself another pair. Only in the afternoon did Noretta remember her strange joke and return the shoes to the young man whose feet were their rightful owners.

I reminded Moro of those years at the very time when he persuaded me to take over from him as Prime Minister. This was the fourth time I had stepped into Moro's shoes, the previous three being the presidency of FUCI, the leadership of the Christian Democrat group in parliament, and the chairmanship of the Foreign Affairs Committee.

Craxi had now taken over from De Martino as Secretary of the Socialist Party. The Socialists declared that they would not dissociate themselves from the Communist line; the Social Democrats said they would do likewise in relation to the Socialists and the Christian Democrat leadership – having first gone through the motions of reviving the Centre-Left – was forced to take stock of the fact that it requires two parties to make a marriage, even in politics. So it was to me that President Leone gave the problem of sorting things out. That is how I came to head a so-called 'government of no no-confidence', with Communist abstention rather than opposition for the first time since 1947.

What happened subsequently is a matter of public knowledge, and I myself have contributed to an understanding of the vicissitudes of what was one of the most difficult periods of government in Italy, by the publication of my diaries. The Communists wanted more involvement in government than mere abstention, and Moro had fought hard to prevent this from upsetting the political balance achieved in July 1976, which was producing good results. Inflation had been halved, currency reserves had been built up again, the balance of payments was back in surplus, and employment had increased. We tried to work out with Moro a formula for a *parliamentary* majority, on the clear understanding that there would be no commitment for the future involved, and that the common progress being achieved in parliament witih the Communists and everybody else should lead to a more relaxed future in which there would be greater mutual respect between the parties. Meanwhile, we had to use Pandolfi's three-year plan to demonstrate that we were capable of introducing solid structural improvements rather than just efficient first aid. Right until the last moment, I tried to get Moro to agree to lead the government, but he remained firmly convinced that his job was to protect our rear by means of the great prestige he had regained, especially within the Christian Democrat Party. The only thing he insisted on was that the government which the Communists would now vote for should have the same make-up as the one which had enjoyed their abstention two years earlier. Perhaps in doing so he had in mind a provisional plan to make absolutely clear that any request for changes put forward by the Communists would be resisted. And it took some effort on my part to prevent there being any additional ministers or under-secretaries, for, rightly or wrongly, that would have been considered a provocation.

This was a period when Moro paid particular attention to personal relationships, especially with young members of parliament; whereas one could see in him a certain intolerance of those who worked against his views in an underhand way, and refused to accept a frank dialogue. We obviously saw a great deal of each other, and this gave me a better chance to understand some less obvious aspects of his personality which had puzzled me when I had first noticed them.

He would stick to his friends, for example, through thick and thin, but he was fairly merciless towards anyone who behaved badly towards him or, worse still, betrayed him.

An example of the first quality was the affair of the appointment of a man of somewhat doubtful reputation as Chairman of the Cogne company. A complaint was made to me about the matter by that great Trieste patriot, Guglielmo Reiss Romoli, who has since died, alas, but at that time held a high position in the public telephone holding company. When I mentioned the matter to Moro, however, he simply shrugged his shoulders in annoyance. Reiss Romoli then approached Ugo La Malfa with a copy of the man's less than spotless criminal record; but Moro's reaction was that it was just a question of personal jealousy, and he scolded La Malfa for exhibiting a document he had no right to possess. And shortly afterwards Moro provided another entry for this particular man's curriculum vitae by having him appointed President of the Vittoriale degli Italiani, the D'Annunzio state museum. I have never met the person in question, and I therefore make no personal judgement; I have mentioned the matter simply as a typical case of Moro's tendency to remain totally firm in the defence of those whom he fully trusted.

As for his attitude towards those who abandoned their political allegiance to him, I will simply recall two episodes. One is the case of the bitter invective which he directed at his former group allies Taviani and Piccoli at a congress; and the other is his harsh criticism of the Socialists, right up to the time of his kidnapping, for having put his government in crisis in late 1975 and early 1976. This is another piece of the jigsaw puzzle which is missing from the accounts of those who greatly emphasize the existence of a special relationship between Moro and the Socialists during his captivity.

Moro was kidnapped on 16 March, on his way to the Chamber of Deputies for the formal presentation of the government which he had worked so hard to bring into being. For me, it was the most dramatic event in my whole life. On the one hand I was distraught at the murder of his escort and fearful for Aldo's own fate, while on the other it was my duty to maintain cool control of the situation, without knowing what the terrorists who had carried out this incredible crime planned to do in the following hours and days.

In my diaries for the years 1976–9, I have published the chronicle of those terrible fifty-five days leading to the discovery of Moro's body only a matter of yards from the headquarters of the Christian Democrats and the Communists.

My hope is that judicial proceedings will be so assisted by revelations from criminals who have agreed to give evidence, and by the work of the special Parliamentary Committee of Inquiry, that it will be possible to shed more light on the affair than has so far been possible.

That the state could not adhere to any request for what was unacceptably called 'an exchange of prisoners' is beyond doubt. And our conscience is clear, for each of us as politicians had, and still has, a duty to remain steadfast in his conduct.

It has also been shown beyond doubt that the government tried everything it possibly could, directly or indirectly, to solve the problem. Indeed, I can affirm quite categorically that more was done than is generally known.

There remains the mystery of the many letters written by Aldo Moro during his captivity, for they run counter to the thoughts and actions of his entire political life. Alongside the letters, the Red Brigades tried also to have accepted as genuine a memorandum full of insults, malicious comments, and self-criticism of an anti-Christian Democrat kind. Even Noretta Moro – who, heaven knows, has been severely critical of all of us, and has declared

Aldo's letters from captivity to be genuine – declared in the Assize Court that this memorandum was a forgery.

My own memory of Aldo Moro is firmly linked to the moving prayer said by Pope Paul VI at the funeral mass in St John Lateran. The man who celebrated mass and said that prayer was not just the Pope; he was our old spiritual adviser of FUCI days.

My relationship with Aldo has its beginning and its ending in FUCI. It was a very sad ending.

# 27
# *Jimmy Carter*

Less than a week after the new administration had taken office, Carter sent his Vice-President, Walter Mondale, to Europe. Mondale arrived in Rome on 28 January 1977, together with a first–class team of aides (David Aaron, Mainard Glitman, David Clift, Richard Cooper, and Fred Bergsten), and we were able to discuss further the matters which had come up at our December meeting at Blair House. Before flying off again, Mondale made some very favourable comments about the current situation in Italy, and five days later wrote me a personal letter in which he said he had reported to Carter both the spirit and the substance of our conversations, which had created an opportunity 'to develop an increasing co-operation between our two governments from now on'.

The first European head of government to visit Carter was James Callaghan, who reported back at the European Council meeting of 25 March to the effect that 'He won't be an easy travelling companion, but we shall travel a long way together.' In May we both met him in London at a summit of the industrialized nations and a meeting of the NATO Council. During the four days we worked together, I was struck by two of Carter's qualities: his determination to gain control of the economic situation by effecting a drastic reduction in oil imports by 1984 (was he already planning two terms of office?); and his great caution over the use of nuclear energy, which developed into outright hostility to plans to build breeder reactors, in which the nuclear fuel is reproduced by the reactor itself. Having once worked under Admiral Rickover, he had an almost morbid fear of the military application of that particular nuclear technology. And since it was only too easy to object that countries which did not produce uranium would be at a

disadvantage, he suggested that there might be a uranium pool to prevent speculative profiteering. He also urged that research into alternatives to both oil and nuclear energy should be speeded up, and announced that the United States budget would earmark special sums for this purpose; but since I knew something about solar energy, I reckoned that, at least in that area, his forecasts were unrealistic.

At bilateral conversations held in the US Embassy in London, Carter insisted that I should visit Washington before the summer holidays. I went there at the end of July, and by a coincidence my reception was even more cordial than it might otherwise have been. As I emerged from talks at the Elysée Palace a week earlier, I had said in answer to some questions from French journalists that I did not think Carter's insistence on civil rights would create difficulties between East and West in Europe. It was true that Brezhnev had complained to Giscard d'Estaing that Carter was 'breaking the rules of *détente*'; but it was also the case that the whole of Europe, plus the United States and Canada, had signed the Helsinki agreement, an essential part of which is the recognition of human rights. These off-the-cuff remarks of mine had been appreciated at the White House, and Carter said so in public, thereby causing me to restate my views, which I did by quoting Carter's own speech in London on the value of *détente* and on specific offers of negotiations made to the Soviet Union.

President Carter told me of a plan of his to help bring peace to the Middle East, which he felt confident about after discussions with King Hussein, President Assad, and Prime Minister Begin. Sadat was certainly willing to be involved, and he thought it not impossible to get the Israelis to accept the presence of Palestinians at talks in Geneva, as a people who have a right to their own country. Carter also invited Italy to help persuade the PLO to drop its rigid objection to the existence of the State of Israel; but I pointed out that if it really proved possible to get them both to sit at the same table, then mutual recognition would *ipso facto* have been achieved.

Carter surprised me by declaring himself firmly opposed to the neutron bomb, on the grounds that its limited destructive power might lead someone to use it, thereby setting off a process of nuclear escalation. His arguments were convincing, but how were we supposed to forget that the previous US administration had insisted that friendship with America had to mean acceptance of the neutron bomb? I felt I had to tell Carter this, and I also informed him that Brezhnev had written to all of us in Europe deploring the neutron bomb. In my view, the present-day responsibilities of the United States towards the rest of the world do not make a radical change of policy every four years permissible; especially since they are principally in dialogue with a country which is by no means given to habits of that kind. The fact that the House of Representatives has a life span of only two years may also prove an obstacle in an America which is no longer what it was in the early days of independence. But Carter had never been a member of the federal parliament, and seemed to have little interest in it.

I felt that Italian foreign policy was considerably assisted both by the frank relations established with Carter, and by certain public acknowledgements of Italy's reliability (including an important such statement by Burns, the Chairman of the Federal Reserve Board, who had perhaps had his doubts the previous year about the policies I had outlined). I was consequently dismayed when a State Department spokesman announced on the following 12 January that there was 'no change in the attitude of the US government towards communist parties, *including the Italian Communist Party*'. Why make such a pointless and interfering remark, when it was perfectly well known that relations between the parties in the Italian parliament were delicate? I had a telephone message to that effect sent to Ambassador Gardner, who was in Washington at the time, and he professed not only that he had nothing to do with the statement, but that he had actually tried to tone it down by stressing to journalists that the Carter administration fully supported the Italian government. The internal situations of the two countries, he added, sometimes follow different patterns. More or less the same idea (that internal politics sometimes oblige the USA to adopt certain attitudes) was put to the head of my press office that same evening by an important American lady journalist.

I was very upset by the whole affair, and let the fact be known, especially since I could see behind it some wretched little political manoeuvres of Italian origin, not unconnected with the government's increasingly difficult relations with the various parties. So much for the internal affairs of the United States!

On 30 May, while still deeply disturbed at the murder of Moro (after Moro was kidnapped, Carter wrote me a message of fervent support – including a prayer – for the defence of the democratic principles which the Italian government stood for; and he sent Secretary Califano to express American solidarity), I went to Washington for a meeting of the Atlantic Council, and in a

171

conversation with President Carter I heard nothing but praise for the Italian government, which at that juncture was enjoying the support rather than just the abstention of the Communists. When one can have a direct conversation, without the intervention of spokesmen, many mistakes can be avoided and many misunderstandings can be cleared up.

Carter told me he would like to visit Italy after the Bonn summit, but Leone's resignation and the subsequent presidential interregnum caused the visit to be cancelled. I don't believe the story published in *Newsweek* that he was advised not to go by the American security services because of Italian terrorism; though they must really have thought that our terrorists were capable of operating abroad, since the Italian Embassy in Washington was guarded by forty policemen backed up by tanks and helicopters during my visit there. There was also a great show of security forces at New York when I went there to speak at the United Nations disarmament debate; and indeed a graffito appeared on a wall (not the sort of literature one expects to find in New York!) which read 'Moro = Andreotti'.

Perhaps the presidential security men were still smarting from their humiliation during Kennedy's visit to Rome. Attracted by a cheering crowd as he and I came down the steps after paying homage to the Unknown Soldier, Kennedy had gone beyond the agreed programme by crossing the road, shaking people by the hand, and exchanging greetings with them. This caused a quite unnecessary panic amongst his vigilantes, one of whom had his pistol skilfully removed by an Italian policeman, without his noticing. It was returned to him at his hotel with the compliments of the Italian police.

The Bonn meeting took place on 16 and 17 July. Carter said he was sure that the Soviets, like the Americans, really intended to bring the SALT 2 negotiations to a conclusion; and he said he would not put obstacles in the way by insisting on this being tied to political developments within the USSR, though he would still lay maximum emphasis on human rights. I found myself sitting next to Carter at President Scheel's lunch, and so I asked him for a first-hand interpretation of the statement he had made in Berlin which appeared to accept the possibility of Eurocommunism. He asked me for my views on the subject, and I told him that a gradual Communist evolution would be good for the Warsaw Pact countries as well as for the Western Communist parties. He agreed, but made a point of saying that he certainly did not intend to encourage communism in Italy and France. We went on to talk about the European Monetary System, about which he had seemed rather cool at the meeting, perhaps because he had been advised that it was an anti-dollar and therefore anti-American manoeuvre. He paid great attention to my quite different interpretation of the EMS, and immediately gave instructions to Treasury Secretary Blumenthal to keep in close contact with Pandolfi, the Italian Minister of the Treasury. On his return to the United States, he wrote me a note of thanks for our co-operation at Bonn.

He also wrote that since he could not come to Rome himself for the time being, he would send his mother on a visit, in the hope that she might be received by the Pope and President Pertini.

Carter moved forward cautiously in his attempt to find a solution to the Arab–Israeli crisis. His idea now, he had told us, was not to follow the Geneva line, but rather to work towards a Sadat–Begin agreement which would be guaranteed by the United States. He sent me a letter in which he asked for Italy's support on the matter within the EEC; he forecast 'protests' by the other countries, but 'nothing more' (and indeed a 'resistance front' did come into being, but without violent demonstrations or threats of withdrawal).

I had a meeting with Brzezinski on 21 October, and he explained to me that this had proved to be the only possible solution, and that as soon as agreement had been reached with Tel Aviv, Sadat himself would oversee what it was hoped would be a practical solution to the Palestinian problem. With these assurances, Forlani and I went to Cairo, Tripoli, Amman, and Baghdad, both to support Carter's plan and to smooth the path of negotiations. Everywhere we went we were received with great courtesy and respect, even by those who did not share the view of the future for the Palestinian people which we were supporting. Italy more than any other country, therefore, was under an obligation to support the Camp David solution to the Palestinian problem, without any backsliding or temporizing. Otherwise the supporters of the resistance front would be right to see the peace agreement between Egypt and Israel as a general sign of weakness and as giving a free hand to the Israelis, even though this was paid for by the return of Sinai to Egypt.

Carter confirmed to me in writing that this was indeed the spirit of Camp David, and he guaranteed that the Palestinians would have direct control over their own political future. In another letter, he informed me that normal relations with China had been restored, and recalled my view as to the joint role of the Soviet Union, China, and the United States. He also mentioned that he was 'in contact with President Brezhnev in order to assure him that the restoration of normal relations with China was intended solely to promote the cause of peace in the world'. He then went on: 'I shall make clear to Brezhnev my continuing determination to strengthen relations between the United States and the Soviet Union.'

I replied that I appreciated his position, and I urged a direct Carter–Brezhnev summit as well as an early conclusion to the SALT 2 negotiations.

In January 1979, a certain amount of resentment was caused by a quadripartite meeting in Guadeloupe between Carter, Giscard d'Estaing, Schmidt, and Callaghan. Fear of a 'cabal' reared its ugly head, though what had really happened was simply that advantage had been taken of the fact that two of the heads of government had happened to be spending their New Year holidays in the Caribbean. Their meeting had not even been properly worked out beforehand, with the result that it produced a very rosy view of the future, more in keeping with seaside holidays than with the world of politics. (A few days later, in fact, the Shah left Iran, and there began a new year which was to be anything but tranquil.)

On 3 March, Carter wrote to me that he thought the SALT 2 talks would soon reach a conclusion, and this would serve, amongst other things, to calm the 'international turbulence' which was compromising world peace. His closing words were: 'I share your point of view about the importance of a meeting between President Brezhnev and me: the earlier this meeting takes place, the better it will be for US–Soviet relations.'

On 29 May, Cyrus Vance came to Rome and informed us that for the first time Begin had said that the Camp David agreement was a first step towards general peace in the area. He also told us that the SALT 2 agreement would soon be signed. (It was in fact signed on 18 June, and we all congratulated Carter at the summit meeting of the seven industrialized nations held in Tokyo nine days later. Once again the meeting was almost exclusively devoted to energy problems and the high cost of oil.)

When he got back to Washington, Carter wrote to the other six participants at the Tokyo summit – at least I assume so, since he had no reason to write solely to me – re-echoing and indeed developing the proposals he had made there: an absolute undertaking *never again* to import more oil than in 1977, and gradually to reduce oil imports so that they would be halved by 1990; public transport to be vigorously developed so as to decrease dependence on the motor car; vast sums to be spent on research to find a substitute for oil. 'If these policies meet with your approval,' he requested, 'I hope you will soon find an occasion to say so publicly.'

I had a press notice issued from my offices at the Palazzo Chigi in order to accede to Jimmy Carter's very reasonable request for support. And that, apart from an interview I gave on 19 July to his security adviser, David Aaron, was one of my last acts in my three years as Italian Prime Minister.

In 1979, I left government, and had no further occasion to meet Jimmy Carter, except at the official banquet which President Pertini gave in his honour during a brief trip to Rome. But the day he was defeated, I was one of the first to go to a meeting arranged earlier by the US Ambassador, Richard Gardner, who, I suspect, had hoped in his heart of hearts that he would be celebrating the re-election of a Democrat as President. Many of those invited offered their excuses at the last moment. You can't be too careful!

The endless legions of opportunists and turncoats were now beginning to revise their judgement of Carter.

# 28
# Mu'Ammar Ghaddafi

It may be that President Carter and President Sadat were acting in concert – though I don't think so – when, in the autumn of 1978, they each asked the Italian government to help them soften the Arab nations' opposition to the Camp David agreement. Sometimes the fact that Italy maintains a certain dialogue with all the Arab nations can come in handy . . . However, what we were being asked to do was by no means an easy task, because a resistance front had appeared on the scene and showed signs of out-and-out intransigence. It might be dangerous to get involved, especially since the US administration had radically altered its line in a matter of a few weeks, no longer thinking it necessary to involve the Soviet Union in seeking solutions to Middle East problems, as it had previously when influencing the Geneva Conference.

The argument was that the agreement between Egypt and Israel would produce movement in a dangerously stagnant situation; but its validity depended on whether the detailed prediction as to how subsequent events would develop turned out to be accurate. Otherwise there appeared to be a certain soundness in the view held by opponents of the agreement that the peace with Egypt would radically weaken the position of Israel's other neighbours. We sought and obtained first from Washington and then from Cairo a firm assurance that they saw the establishment of a Palestinian homeland as a matter of vital importance, and that Jimmy Carter was not so unwise as to offer such a homeland without first seeking assurances from the Israeli government.

On 15 November 1978, therefore, I set out with the Italian Foreign Minister, Arnaldo Forlani, on a trip to Tripoli, Cairo, Amman, and Baghdad.

Our first stop was Libya; and I have to admit that I had a certain interest in making the personal acquaintance of Colonel Ghaddafi, for his personality was (and still is) shrouded in a certain mystery, with largely contrasting tones of light and shade. Furthermore, there were a number of matters pending between Libya and Italy which only direct contact could resolve.

It would be inaccurate, not to say presumptuous, to suggest that we succeeded in persuading Ghaddafi to abandon the resistance front. However, our differences did not prevent us from holding polite and almost friendly conversations, and we parted without any ill feeling. Also useful, I think, were our preliminary conversations with Major Jallud, number two in the Libyan revolution, whom I had already met on several occasions in Rome.

At thirty-five, Jallud was two years younger than Ghaddafi. His substantial experience of international affairs comes partly from having studied in the United States, and partly from a number of official visits to Eastern (Moscow and Peking) as well as Western capitals. He was in command of the military base at Tripoli when the monarchy was overthrown, and succeeded in organizing the removal of British bases and the oil companies with courtesy. Many people were amazed, however, that the coup took them by surprise, for they were supposed to be renowned for their intelligence services, and the whole 'movement' had to face a mere few thousand men. Jallud was also responsible for negotiating the purchase of Mirage aircraft from France.

I do not wish to take anything away from Major Jallud's revolutionary orthodoxy if I say that Colonel Ghaddafi undoubtedly has a charisma all his own, and is steeped in social theory. From the very beginning of our meeting, it proved of value that I had read his green book, in which he sets out the theoretical basis of Islamic religious socialism. When I quoted a passage ('Man is not free unless he is the master of the house – or tent – in which he lives, and of the means of transport he uses'), it was greeted with a smile of satisfaction which I tried to use to advantage.

It proved of particular value in connection with an agreement which we outlined for the protection of Italians working in Libya, on the understanding that Under-Secretary Foschi would go and sign it within a few months.

We also talked about Malta, taking up an idea first put forward by Aldo Moro, that a collective guarantee and joint economic aid should be provided by six countries on the northern and southern sides of the Mediterranean, namely Italy, France, and Germany on the one hand, and Libya, Tunisia, and Algeria on the other. This would be a sort of ideal North–South bridge, but it was not all that likely that everybody concerned would agree. The Libyans were in favour in principle, especially as regards an understanding with Italy over Mintoff's island. This idea was later abruptly abandoned, however, and Italy embarked on its own scheme, which obtained the approval of parliament only with difficulty, and does not seem to have done much for peaceful relations among the Maltese. The agreement has now expired, and a renewal is being negotiated, but in the meantime Malta and Libya have drawn up a similar bilateral pact. Libya has been careful to indicate that, as far as it is concerned, the pact is not to be seen as having any anti-Italian significance.

At that 1978 meeting we also agreed to set up regular meetings of mixed economic commissions presided over by the Foreign Ministers of the two countries, and in the event this arrangement worked well. However, the nub of our conversations was, of course, the Middle East problem. Ghaddafi blamed Sadat for abandoning the united Arab nation, and also claimed he was naïve in supposing that the restitution of Sinai to Egypt would be a permanent arrangement. The Palestinians felt betrayed, he said, and American reassurances had to be taken with a pinch of salt, because of the massive influence of the Jewish lobbies in American politics, finance, and the press. He didn't deny that Carter had given certain assurances, but it was commonly held that Israel would never agree to any form of restitution and would use the period of transition to alter the make-up of the population. The US government's pro-Israel policy set them against the whole Arab world; and it was an illusion to suppose that Egypt's dissociation would counterbalance this.

When I pointed out that neither he nor the PLO's constitution recognized Israel's right to exist, he replied that in present circumstances this intransigent attitude was bound to become more entrenched, partly because Israel was showing not the least sign of sensitivity. Indeed, even UN resolutions (including No. 242, which he didn't like because it treated the Palestinians as mere refugees) were practically a dead letter.

Ghaddafi spoke slowly, pondering on every sentence, but displaying a certain lively sense of conviction when touching on what he considered essential points, such as devising a socio-political model which was different from capitalism (and neo-capitalism) as well as from schools of thought of Marxist- Leninist inspiration. According to him, the Libyan people understood this need for something new; and he was sorry that the shortness of our

178

visit prevented us from being present at one of the small-scale people's meetings at which that subject was debated.

Returning to the Israel–America–Egypt triangle, he said he understood the spirit in which our mission was undertaken, and had nothing against our visiting Sadat; but there was only one piece of advice we could give him, and that was to 'turn back'. Especially since he was bound to be sadly disappointed when the agreement was put into operation. He wished Italy well, and was convinced that Italian grounds for agreement with Libya far outweighed our different political allegiances (we were 'aligned', he was not). He also expressed the hope that we would defeat the terrorist threat; and at this point I listened as he set out his distinction between terrorism and a struggle for freedom. He condemned the former and claimed that the latter must be given every support. He failed to take up a remark I made about the terrible events at the 1972 Olympic Games at Munich, and repeated his criticism of 'excessive' American military aid to Israel, which made it necessary for equivalent aid to be given to 'the other side'.

Before we parted, I was surprised to hear him renew his condolences to the Moro family.

Such was my first meeting with Ghaddafi.

One unexpected result was that my daughter, who has a degree in archaeology, was included in an invitation from the Union of Women to visit Libya, though she was unable to go. I assume the invitation had something to do with a certain satisfaction I had noticed in Ghaddafi when I had praised his plans to resume a campaign of archaeological excavations.

Five years later, when I became Foreign Minister, I naturally found myself having to examine Italo–Libyan relations again. Up to that time I had taken only a marginal interest in them, from that special vantage-point, the Foreign Affairs Committee of the Chamber of Deputies. Apart from certain international questions, such as Italian interest at the Court of The Hague in the controversy between Libya and Malta over territorial waters, there were two dossiers on specifically Italo–Libyan matters. One concerned Libyan claims for compensation for damage to persons and property during the 'Italian period'; and the other concerned substantial sums owing for work done in Libya by Italian firms, many of whom were in danger of going bankrupt.

I willingly accepted an invitation from Tripoli to visit Libya, for I am convinced that when there are direct discussions and plain dealing, a way to solve problems can be found.

An exchange of notes is not always sufficient. On the question of reparations, for example, we were down a blind alley, for the Libyans were insisting on a case-by-case assessment from 1911(!) onwards. When we had objected that we had already settled the matter some time earlier by paying the Libyan government five billion lire, Ghaddafi had sent a reply to the effect that anything arranged with the monarchy was of no interest to him. Our only obvious answer was that there had been a change of regime in Italy, too, and so we could be responsible only for what had happened since 1946, when Italians had certainly not committed any acts of violence. In some cases, on the contrary, Italian property had been confiscated from people of modest means who certainly could not be described as usurpers. It was much better to take up the offer of talks rather than continue with a written dialogue.

This time Colonel Ghaddafi received me in a tent inside the barracks where he was living at the time. He no longer wore the elegant barracan and polo-neck sweater of the previous occasion, but a sort of blanket-cloak of rough wool. In the middle of the tent was a brazier to keep out the cold of the desert night.

He welcomed me and wanted to known why I had been . . . demoted to Foreign Minister. I explained in reply how the office of Prime Minister changed hands in a coalition government, and I told him about the simple majority whcih the Christian Democrats still enjoyed in parliament. He wanted to know how the Italian economy was faring (perhaps Libya was interested partly because of its stake in FIAT), and while I felt bound to admit that unemployment and inflation were at worrying levels, I also set out our plans for improvement. As far as our balance of payments was concerned, Libya was a good customer in the Italian market, but Italian firms working in Libya complained of long delays in receiving payment, even for work which had been completed.

Ghaddafi felt that Italian 'political instability' had unfortunately made it impossible to develop relations satisfactorily between our two countries. On the other hand, Libya had achieved stability after the revolution of 1969, and this allowed the Libyan people protection from the difficult international economic situation. He thought that the secret of Libyan stability lay in the present regime, which had brought the people to power through people's assemblies and committees. In Libya the struggle for power had ended because the masses had been involved in the government of the state. In other countries, too, instability would be overcome when the masses were involved in government. Libyan stability also derived from the practical application of the new socialism described in the green book. In the economic field, too, the principles established in the green book had made it possible to solve problems by involving workers in management and by creating people's management committees to take over the running of factories.

Libya, he went on, had solved its political and economic problems through people's assemblies and committees, which took the place of the traditional apparatus of government. The theory of freedom from need had also solved the problem of strikes, and had made it possible to bypass the stages described in Marxist theory as leading to progress. Peace movements and the Greens were moving towards applying the same theory, whether they had worked it out for themselves or not.

In Italy, too, he understood, there were peace movements whose value must be appreciated. I tried to explain that we were all working for peace, but he didn't seem convinced that such was the purpose of the missiles at Comiso. He saw them rather as a direct threat to Libya and other North African states. His concern was all the greater in that the base was American, and the United States seemed bent upon military intervention in the Middle East, partly to support Israel and help it to gain control of the other nations in the region. Libyans felt themselves to be a direct target of the United States, and had therefore adopted a policy of particular opposition to the base at Comiso. They hoped that their justified fears would induce the Italian government to avoid upsetting the equilibrium in the Mediterranean.

I said how pleased I was that Colonel Ghaddafi had brought up this subject, because it gave me an opportunity to clear up certain matters of a kind which he, as a military man, would understand particularly well. I explained that we had signed the Non-Proliferation Treaty, but that unfortunately the Soviet Union had for some years installed missiles which were a threat to Italy and Europe. Our position on the matter was, moreover, purely defensive, and we had not delegated powers to anyone, so no other power could use these weapons without our consent. All that we wanted was to re-establish equality with the missile power of the Eastern bloc countries. The fact that Comiso had been chosen as a missile base was not to be interpreted as indicating some special anti-Libyan intention, since the missiles have a range of about 1,500 miles and therefore would, on paper, be as potentially dangerous to Libya if they were installed in northern Italy as at Comiso. I also

181

pointed out that Libya ought, as a non-aligned country, to be equally worried by Soviet SS20 missiles. Indeed, Libya could take the initiative and persuade the non-aligned countries to make every effort in all quarters towards the removal of missiles from the whole of Europe. I reiterated that we were constantly trying to achieve *détente* with the Eastern bloc countries; and hence we viewed with optimism both the Stockholm Conference and the resumption of US–Soviet negotiations in Vienna. We must work actively for the banning of chemical weapons, and of the use of space for military purposes. We were therefore in agreement with the peace aims declared by Colonel Ghaddafi, and were of the opinion that the sums spent on missiles would be better used to help the development of poor countries. This was not a matter, however, on which we could make unilateral decisions.

Ghaddafi thanked me for my explanations, but insisted on reiterating that the missile installations were a source of fear for the Libyan people.

Since I noticed he had not brought up the subject of reparations, I myself took the initiative and referred to those who had suffered as a result of fascist oppression in the 1930s and the explosion of mines after the war. Legal obligations had been fulfilled when compensation was paid to King Idris (Ghaddafi interrupted me at this point to say that we had permanent obligations deriving from UN decisions – but it was precisely in that context, I replied, that Italy had paid the five billion lire), and perhaps it was technically impossible to find a formal way of settling differences over events which had happened so long ago. Why stop at 1911? I asked him in a half-serious tone of voice. Why not go further back and call the Turks to account for what had happened in Libya during the days of Ottoman rule?

Perhaps my unexpected way of presenting the problem slightly bewildered him, but he was clearly not displeased by it. He said that there was not a single family in Cyrenaica which had not had one of its members killed or injured during the fascist repression, and even before fascism there had been pillaging everywhere, so that even small peasants had been reduced to penury.

And what about the terrible injuries caused since the dreadful war years? At least fifty people were killed or seriously crippled every year as a result of this sinister hidden scourge of unexploded mines.

A solution to the problem must be found, because it was a serious obstacle to co-operation between the two countries. What was needed was a declaration of principle to prevent colonialism from ever recurring, whatever the source. It was therefore necessary to establish a new international law which would put a penalty on colonialism, and give universal application to Italian public condemnation of colonialism and fascism. But the Libyan people were in any case entitled to compensation. His aim was to warn the Italian government about what might happen in the future; the Libyans had been the victims of colonialism and might take action in the Libyan courts. They might expropriate Italian property, for example, by confiscating Italian ships or aircraft. He declared, however, that the Libyan government had no wish to go that far.

In historical and human terms, the basis of Ghaddafi's argument was understandable, but I could not accept his conclusions. I stressed the sense of responsibility shown by the Italian parliament and political parties in not reacting strongly to Ghaddafi's speech of 7 October, in which he had suddenly brought these matters up. I reminded him again of the payment that had already been made. At all costs we had to avoid a quarrel which would go on for a long time and poison relations between our two countries. On the other hand, I welcomed the idea of a specific gesture to show the Libyan people how friendly and supportive democratic Italy was towards them. On the spur of the moment I suggested that we might donate a hospital for the handicapped in Cyrenaica, if possible in an area where major damage had been done. Another possibility would be the setting up of seaside or mountain holiday camps in Italy for the descendants of those who had suffered under fascist repression, or for children who had been crippled by mines in the desert.

As regards the mines, it had not been possible to supply the Libyan government with a map of the minefields (I had looked into the matter myself when I was Minister of Defence), because no such maps existed in Italian or German archives. If they had ever existed, they had probably been lost during the war. However, I repeated our offer to send expert engineers to detect the mines and organize a programme of land reclamation.

This was the right approach to the problem – one which Italians would understand and Libyans were sure to appreciate for what it really meant. I recalled the occasion when the remains of twenty thousand Italian soldiers formerly buried in the cemetery at Tripoli had arrived in Bari. It was a delicate moment, and in the name of the Italian government I had opposed any emotional outburst – however understandable – declaring that we must not dwell on the past but turn our thoughts to building a new relationship with Libya. I reminded him, too, that the Italians who had been repatriated from Libya were not fascists but poor folk who had crossed the Mediterranean simply in search of work.

Ghaddafi listened very attentively, and recognized the constructive attitude adopted by the Italian government both on the occasion I had recalled and after the evacuation of Italians in 1970. He declared, too, that he was in favour of a practical and realistic solution to the problem.

He dwelt once again on the two factors underlying the policy of the Libyan government: (1) there had to be a new international law which would prevent colonialism and punish anyone who attempted to practise colonialism; (2) there was a risk that Italo–Libyan relations would deteriorate as a result of claims for compensation made by individual citizens who were seeking revenge for the heavy losses they had sustained.

There were thus moral and material reasons for Libyan behaviour. He did not want our relations to deteriorate in the future. We had enduring common interests which should spur us to improve our relations and find a way of burying the past. Our geographical position also constituted a permanent link. Consequently, every effort must be made to solve the problem and satisfy those Libyans who were seeking compensation. They still had a vivid recollection of the wrongs they had suffered, and of the serious loss of property and life (the man who killed Omar Al Mukhtar died a few years ago).

It was indeed true that the democratic government of Italy was not responsible for what the fascist government had done, but the years preceding 1922 were also involved, and amongst Italian politicians there were still some who had been active even then. And let it not be claimed that the Italian people had been opposed to fascism. At this point, Ghaddafi took me by surprise by producing photographs both of Piazza Venezia filled to overflowing with a crowd roaring its approval of the 'Founder of the Empire', and of other demonstrations of support for colonialism.

What could I say? Only that mass demonstrations are not always spontaneous, and that it was also a well-known fact that there had been many victims of the fascist dictatorship in Italy, too.

True – replied Ghaddafi – but Italian colonial activity began before the fascist period, and the ruling class of the time must bear some responsibility for it. At this point we spent a short time repeating our arguments (we had paid five billion lire and if it hadn't been distributed amongst the people that wasn't our responsibility; yes, but; but, yes . . .); then we agreed that we would examine further the possibility of finding some symbolic solution, reaffirmed our willingness to collaborate, and promised to provide visible evidence of that willingness through a greater number of visits and contacts.

In such an atmosphere, it would become increasingly likely that Ghaddafi could visit Italy, as he had been invited to do in 1971. This would be an important milestone in Italo-Libyan relations. If he came to Rome, he would also have the opportunity of meeting the Pope and resuming the Christian–Muslim dialogue which had been initiated at Tripoli at an important conference, attended by Cardinal Sergio Pignedoli amongst others. This conference had been much reported in the Catholic world and in Italian cultural circles generally, for Italy has a very ancient and distinguished tradition in Islamic studies. The frequent references to religious principles made by Colonel Ghaddafi in his writings ought to offer a suitable basis for discussion, and there was no doubt about Italians being open to such an approach.

We parted on cordial terms. For his part, Ghaddafi asked me to give Pertini and Craxi his cordial greetings, and declared himself reassured by my visit. (I hope that also applied to the missiles, but I am not sure.) I received a gift of a saddle and in return gave him a key-case with a reproduction of the Colosseum. The descendants of those martyred in the Colosseum have not yet claimed compensation from the Italian government.

There followed some months of comparative calm in our relations with Libya, and I received a pressing invitation to join Treki, the Libyan Foreign Minister, as co-chairman of a meeting of the mixed commission to be held in Tripoli at the end of July. I might perhaps have sent an under-secretary in my place, but the matter of debts to Italian firms had not been settled, and furthermore, the Libyan Ambassador (to use conventional terminology) had been assassinated in Rome, so it seemed to me that I would be performing a substantial act of courtesy by going myself.

It is true that there were disputes about these contacts, but I confess that I have difficulty in accepting the crude and oversimple classification of men as good or evil. God himself created a third state (Purgatory) and even a fourth (Limbo), the existence of which, as far as I know, has never been denied by the new theology. And yet Ghaddafi is universally cast in the role of devil. With the possible exception of earthquakes, there is no event anywhere in the world, and especially in Africa, which is not directly or indirectly attributed to the hand of Colonel Ghaddafi. In trying to damage his reputation, however, everyone ends up, in a sense, by giving him an appearance of unlimited power, thereby encouraging anyone who has tried all other remedies to turn to him. Apparently even the British coal-miners, when worn out by an interminable strike, did not disdain to contact him. Especially since one of the most publicized maxims in Libya reads: 'In the name of God, the Compassionate, the Merciful'.

The meetings in Tripoli with Treki and Jallud proved fruitful, in that a system was worked out for paying the Libyan debt to Italian firms by channelling it through ENI in the form of oil. A way out was also found for some of the pending 'criminal' cases, and I hope this may be put into practice. But from a political point of view what most concerned me was my meeting with Colonel Ghaddafi.

This took place at Benghazi on 31 July, and lasted for two hours. (He had sent his personal plane to fetch me from Tripoli.)

Colonel Ghaddafi lost no time in expressing the specific hope that he could count on Italy to help him establish better relations with other European countries, especially since it would shortly be Italy's turn to provide the President of the EEC.

Then he asked for news of the investigation into the murder in Rome of the Secretary of the Libyan People's Bureau (i.e. the Libyan Ambassador). The investigation was continuing, I replied, but those responsible had not yet been identified, in spite of all the efforts of the authorities. In Italy – and especially in Rome – there are a very large number of foreign residents or visitors, and it is very difficult to keep a check on them. That was probably one of the reasons why the investigation was proving difficult.

We then went on to discuss economic relations between our two countries. He expressed satisfaction at the agreement on payments to Italian firms, and thought this might lead to Italian companies being deeply involved in plans for the further development of Libya. This was in our common interest, I replied, and I dared express the view that he ought to convey an image of himself as more than just a trouble-maker. I was also very impressed by vast Libyan projects such as the plans for harnessing water which we had been told about.

In reply to a comment of mine, he repeated his condemnation of terrorism and his moral obligation to assist 'liberation' movements. He also told me that I was in an excellent position to bear witness to his opposition to terrorism, because in the years when the Red Brigades had been most active in Italy, they had in vain sought assistance from him in the form of money or . . . experts. There was nothing to liberate in Italy. And the rumour that he had sent people to America to assassinate President Reagan was false and stupid: 'the usual slanderous inventions of Israel'. (I observed with a smile that he was given a bad press not just by the Israelis but by many of his Islamic brethren as well.) He was both scandalized and amused when I told him that rumours had reached us to the effect that he was planning to assassinate Pertini, but that neither Pertini nor anyone else believed them.

I showed Colonel Ghaddafi a project for an Italian-built cardiology unit in Libya, in the hope that this would help overcome the long-standing dispute between the two countries, as outlined at our February meeting. He expressed his appreciation of Italy's current concern, and its condemnation of the colonial and fascist periods. Nevertheless, he must repeat his views. He hoped that the two countries would together find some uncomplicated way of settling the dispute. He was not in a position to comment on the project; but he felt, nevertheless, that some steps had been taken in the right direction. Perhaps the project should be expanded so as to achieve something more substantial. The Libyans had suffered a great deal, and there were still those living who remembered the suffering. For him there was one general imperative: if a repetition of colonialism was to be avoided, it must be punished. In other words, joint efforts must be made to establish a new international law against colonialism. Ghaddafi also mentioned that there was the problem of returning archaeological finds which had been stolen or confiscated and were apparently now in Italy. Then he went back to the question of clearing mines. This was a problem which concerned the United Kingdom and Germany as well, and ought to lead to a land reclamation project.

Ghaddafi was grateful for Italy's serious attempts to explain to others what Libyan policies really were. He also considered cultural co-operation between Italy and Libya to be a matter of importance, and was satisfied with what was being done in that area. He particularly hoped that the green book would circulate more widely amongst the young, in Italy as elsewhere, so that communist materialism could be countered. The 'third way' offered by the green book effectively superseded Marxism. It was necessary to support the setting up of cultural centres (libraries and radio stations) which could spread a knowledge of the green book.

My view is – and I told him so – that the best way to condemn and overcome the past is to intensify collaboration in the many areas where that is possible. That was what had been done, I said, and as far as Italy was concerned, there was a willingness to go further.

As regards clearing mines, I reminded him that Italy had presented a plan in 1981 and was still waiting to hear Libya's reaction to it. We would look into the question of archaeological finds. That was a problem which should be solved in the developing climate of collaboration between the two countries, which included the area of archaeology. This collaboration could also be used to increase tourism in Libya, which could give impetus to the development of the Libyan economy, and act as a means of improving Libya's image abroad.

It was a praiseworthy idea that the aims of the Libyan revolution should be better known, for the religious inspiration of its ideological and cultural content placed it on a very different plane from Marxism. Universities, research centres, and individual scholars could all help to achieve this.

On the question of the archaeological finds, Ghaddafi alluded to the fact that international aspects of the matter had emerged. I replied that I would prefer to ignore these aspects and solve the problem within the framework of stronger cultural relations between Italy and Libya.

I then moved on to the international situation, and asked Colonel Ghaddafi whether he was not a little more optimistic than the previous February, especially in view of developments in Lebanon. He replied that in his opinion the situation in Lebanon had indeed improved, especially following the withdrawal of American troops, even though this withdrawal had not been carried out in an amicable and honourable way; the United States had in fact been forced out of Lebanon. The presence of Israeli troops in Lebanon was, of course, a serious problem, and was the cause of spontaneous resistance on the part of the Arab population, as was also the case in the rest of the occupied territories and the Golan Heights.

He feared that a characteristic of President Reagan's personality was playing with fire. Only forty-eight hours earlier, the United States had violated Libyan air space over the Gulf of Sirte again. A conflict had almost broken out, even though the danger period had lasted for no more than five minutes. However, if the United States persisted in its activities, a catastrophe might occur. It was not acceptable to Libya that it should live permanently under threat from America.

Ghaddafi then touched on other matters. He said that the situation in Chad was still tense because of the continuing French occupation, but an agreement was in sight for a simultaneous withdrawal of troops. As for Sudan, he assured me that there were training camps there for terrorists from the United States and the United Kingdom, who had been sent into Libya but had been liquidated.

There were also radio stations operating in Sudan which spread terrorist propaganda. Perhaps Libya would be obliged to destroy them. At this point Ghaddafi spoke in unfriendly terms of Nimeiri, comparing him with Bokassa and Amin. (But hadn't Amin been Ghaddafi's guest after his expulsion from Uganda?)

The situation between Libya and Egypt, on the other hand, was calm; or at any rate the tension which had existed in Sadat's time was no longer there.

I repeated my old theory as to the importance of preserving the unity of the Arab world, and my view that such unity must include Egypt. Ghaddafi made a very cordial reference to the King of Morocco which I understood only later, when the pact of friendship between the two countries was announced.

He then went on to consider developments in the Gulf War, expressing the view that the situation had not yet been reached in which the two sides could negotiate or even meet. In his opinion, the only way to push the two sides towards coming to terms would be to place an embargo on arms supplies; but some countries did not agree.

In our survey of the international scene, there were various points where we disagreed. One was over El Salvador. He stressed the progress made by the Revolutionary Front, whereas I saw the importance of Napoleón Duarte as a true reformer who was opposed by the economic forces of the Right, and had spent long years in exile in order not to be subjected to the political dominion of the military Right. At the meeting in Costa Rica the following month, we Europeans were to support the efforts of the Contadora Group and defend Duarte, encouraging him to seek a negotiated peace with the rebels.

Coming back to relations with the United States, Ghaddafi said he liked the idea of a meeting of legal experts to sort out controversies over territorial waters in the Gulf of Sirte, and he explicitly stated that, as a non-aligned and non-alignable state, Libya really did desire a different relationship with the United States, based on mutual respect.

Since he knew I was to meet President Reagan at Los Angeles on 13 August, he asked me to tell him this, and a few other things as well.

In relation to this last matter, Italian and foreign newspapers wove a web of indiscretions, fantasies, and polemics. Is it really a waste of time to try to find points of contact in this madly turbulent world? Who gains from the isolation of Ghaddafi? Did we not receive recognition from Mrs Thatcher of the usefulness of our presence in Tripoli for protecting British interests after diplomatic relations with Libya were broken off?

In his usual October speech, however, Colonel Ghaddafi once more recited almost the whole litany of Italy's past wrongdoings. I had been given advance warning, in tones which suggested that I should not let it worry me too much. But words have their weight. However, a recent visit to Rome by Major Jallud (December 1984) has made it possible to embark on a cool examination of the various problems, and I hope that both parties will prove capable of really drawing a veil over the past.

# 29
# *Fidel Castro*

I was in Washington, on my way to the annual conference of the Inter-Parliamentary Union, when an American congressman – who did not normally miss Union meetings – told me that he could not go to Cuba because his electorate would never forgive him. And it is indeed the case (though the causes may have been different) that as powerful a politician as Edward Derwinski failed to stay away from the Union Conference and was eliminated in the Illinois primaries the following year.

The inaugural sessions of these conferences are usually very formal, but when Fidel Castro took the platform in 1981, his brief words of welcome were followed by a violent attack on all and sundry. The Americans were even accused of smuggling into the country swine fever, haemorrhagic conjunctivitis, and a virulent form of influenza. In their capacity as exporters of such unpleasant goods, Reagan and his administration were bluntly described as 'dangerous fascists'.

No one was safe from attack. The people of Northern Ireland, for example, were blasted for abusing the name Christian in one way or another, for preventing the necessary liberation of Ireland, and for indulging in bloody violence. Lengthy applause came from the visitors' gallery, while the stalls remained enveloped in an increasingly icy silence. As a member of the Executive Committee, Senator Stafford, the head of the US delegation, was sitting on the platform. He remained impassively in his seat, thereby relieving many others of the need to solve a tricky problem; for if he had got up and left the hall, he would not have been the only one to do so.

On my way out I met Raoul Roa, the President of the Assembly.

I had met him in Argentina on the occasion of the 150th anniversary of the Republic, and he had subsequently come to Rome as Foreign Minister. Moreover, his daughter had married an Italian, and they had kindly invited me to the wedding. I was therefore in a position to speak frankly to him, and I told him how worried I was. The conference was being wrecked by such a start, and irreparable damage might hence be done to a union which, for nearly a century, had been bringing together members of parliament of many different political hues, thereby introducing an element of *détente* and peace into a quarrelsome and warring world. Raoul thought one should not overreact. One had to appreciate that their state of mind was the result of American provocation; and then there was the need to maintain public morale (the speech was broadcast). He promised, however, that he would report my impressions to Fidel Castro.

Many delegations failed to turn up at the reception given by the government that evening, and I was one of those who absented themselves. Paolo Bufalini did go, but when he addressed the assembly the next morning, he said that he spoke in the name of Italy in deploring the application of the word 'fascist' to a people whose courageous behaviour had played a vital part in freeing Italy from fascism. It was significant that the man who spoke in the name of the Italian delegation was a Communist.

Meanwhile, an official came into the hall to tell me that Fidel Castro was waiting for me in the other wing of the parliament building. I do not deny that I was very interested in the possibility of talking to the Cuban leader, because it is only when they are seen in close-up that people's true character can really be understood. Here was a tall man in battledress, wearing boots which added to his height. There is something special about Fidel Castro, and when I saw him smile he seemed a quite different person from the one who had thundered and threatened the previous day.

I started the conversation by confirming what I had said to Raoul Roa, but I added that I had also noticed his *controlled moderation*. He looked at me in surprise, as though he suspected that I was pulling his leg. Not at all. What I had noticed, I explained, was that while he had accused the Americans of all sorts of incredible villainy, he had wisely said not a single word about the US base at Guantanamo, in spite of Cuba's historical claim to that territory.

There was one clarification I was anxious to have, however. In greeting the conference, he had described the Americans as liars because they accused him of supplying arms to the guerrillas in El

Salvador; was I to deduce, therefore, that the photographic evidence which the Americans had themselves circulated a few months earlier in support of their claim was just a propaganda invention?

Fidel Castro stared at me in curiosity – perhaps because he was not used to an approach of this kind – and surprised me by retorting that I had not listened carefully enough. He had not said that he *had not supplied* arms to the guerrillas in El Salvador, but that he *was not supplying* them, because he had come to the conclusion that neither side could achieve a military victory and that a *political* solution to the country's terrible problems had to be found. Naturally, the Cuban government was not to be held responsible for the current merciless anti-popular reaction there. I had the impertinence to tell him that his subtle use of verb tenses left me without any counter-argument, for I had been at a state school, whereas he had been educated by the Jesuits.

The ice was broken. For nearly two hours he talked to me about the state of siege in which the island of Cuba effectively found itself, having to cope with a very difficult economic and financial situation. However, his people had made extraordinary efforts and since the revolution they had rediscovered their taste for work. They had gradually improved agricultural production, and in particular had achieved moral standards which in the past had been undermined by a corrupt and parasitic ruling class. The tourists who had once flocked to Havana and the surrounding area saw the Cubans merely as playthings, whereas the Cuban youth of today were brought up to value formerly unknown ideals of dignity and pride. International Communist solidarity provided Cubans with the vital aid they needed to withstand the pressures brought to bear by the American economic bloc, but anyone who interpreted the revival of the Cuban people as simply a matter of accepting foreign models (as in the case of Grenada and Nicaragua) was wide of the mark. Havana had sent two hundred teachers to Managua to help them carry out their school development programme. So much for arms supplies! Certainly, Cuban support was not denied when requested by anyone fighting to free themselves from capitalist exploitation. But weren't the Italians proud of the fact that Garibaldi had also taken part in the resurgence of Latin America? In that connection, the Poder Popular representative would be talking to me about the desire to commemorate suitably the presence of Garibaldi in Havana during the period of Spanish domination. Garibaldi had encouraged the peasants by telling them that machetes could be used to fight for independence as well as to cut sugar cane.

I took up his frequent references to the 'American threat' and pointed out that on two separate occasions the United States had sacrificed vast numbers of lives in preventing Europe from succumbing to militaristic and dictatorial forces. We saw the Atlantic Alliance today as a protection against a third world war; and politically speaking it had been a success, for amongst other things it had made possible a gradual process of *détente* in East–West relations in Europe. My sincere wish was that relations between Washington and Havana might progress in a similar direction. I told him, too, that I had been very interested to learn of an attempt at mediation some time earlier by the Panamanian leader Omar Torrijos. How did I know about this? General Torrijos had himself talked to me about it when he came to Europe in October 1977 to explain the Canal agreement. Even though Torrijos was, alas, now dead (he had been killed when his plane had crashed a few weeks earlier), surely there were other men of peace who would try to work to achieve that kind of *détente*. Could the Organization of American States perhaps act in this way?

Fidel Castro rejected that suggestion, saying that the OAS was simply a North American tool; but he did not deny the truth of what Torrijos had told me, and indeed he added that there appeared to be some slight glimmer of hope now that the Carter administration was in power. But right now . . .

Apart from any other approaches, it was possible that Senator Stafford's visit might offer an occasion for an exchange of ideas. When it comes to relations between one nation and another, talking never does any harm. Fidel Castro made no comment, but I know that he and Stafford did meet. And perhaps some new Torrijos has appeared on the horizon.

Castro's personal knowledge of Italy was confined to the north-eastern border with Yugoslavia, which he had seen as a guest of Marshal Tito. For the rest, he had been able to look down on the country from an aircraft; and he said he admired our history and culture. It was in this area that I was able to appreciate something different from the dogmatism of his political convictions. He showed that he had quite a good knowledge of Latin literature, and could quote Suetonius and Cicero at the appropriate moment. Such were the things I heard and said during that first meeting with Fidel Castro; but there were to be others. Three days later, Castro came to a reception at the Italian Embassy, and stayed to talk to the whole of the Italian delegation for more than two hours. It was a frank and lively conversation, during which he took up again many of the subjects which he and I had discussed in our tête-à-tête. Now and again his chief of protocol would come and urge him to leave – he was supposed to put in at least an appearance at several other embassies – but Castro was disinclined to call a halt to a frank and indeed very interesting exchange of views. When he left, he said that since the Union conference would be held in Rome the next year, he might himself be among the Cuban delegates.

The work of the Havana conference went forward without a hitch, and in the Politics and Disarmament Committee (of which I was Chairman) we had a very lively debate which produced a good report. The effect of the first-day quarrels was overcome partly thanks to Carlos Rafael Rodriguez – an outstanding personality who had intelligent and frank discussions with many delegations. I had published an interview with him in my journal *Concretezza* in September 1947, and I too now had an opportunity to talk to him, about relations with the church amongst other things. He briefly explained the Cuban position, quoting from the theories and resolutions set out by the Central Committee of the Cuban Communist Party in 1976: it was a principle of the revolution that the right of the individual to profess or not to profess a religious faith should be recognized; but a natural, scientific view of the world excluded the possibility of any mystical or religious interpretation of natural, social, and human phenomena. Nevertheless, 'it will require long, patient, calm, and courageous work before religious ideology in all its different manifestations can be superseded'. For the time being all members of the community 'whether believers or not' are *indispensable* for the creation and development of a socialist society.

Before we left Cuba, Castro insisted on seeing me again, and he thanked the Italian delegation for its contribution to the success of the conference, hoping he had not tired us out during our long meeting at the embassy. He also thanked me for visiting the sacred places of the Cuban revolutionary movement – though there was in fact no political justification for his thanks, since my reason for spending Sunday at Santiago rather than on the trip to the beach arranged for members of the conference was that I feared the sunshine and the sea (which was very beautiful) would only make my usual migraine worse.

In any case, I had had a very interesting day, especially at Cuartel Moncada. If the guide's approach was the usual polemical one

('There was a widespread struggle – a struggle stirred up by exploiters, abusers, and unjust men who drove our people to rebellion and to the first great defeat of American imperialism'), he also quoted some rather different maxims of Fidel Castro, such as this one, which goes back to his days in Yugoslavia:

'Capitalism can cause a man to die of hunger, but Communism can also kill him by depriving him of freedom.'

When we left, I had the impression that there was in the air an acute feeling of apprehension that the international situation was deteriorating. 'If the Russians occupy Poland, the Americans will invade Cuba', was the sort of remark which was going the rounds. The fact that the Polish Foreign Minister was in Cuba at about that time tended to increase the sense of alarm, but I gave greater weight to what we had heard that week in our exchanges of ideas between delegations, including those of the Soviet Union and Poland. The crisis did not in fact get worse, and the *talentosos artistas* at the Tropicana continued to sing and dance as they had that evening.

In the spring of 1982, the Mayor of Rome went to Havana to unveil a plaque (in the former Town Hall, now the City Museum) commemorating the 130th anniversary of the visit to Cuba of the *libertador* Giuseppe Garibaldi. In September, the Cuban delegation to the Rome conference brought me a letter from Fidel Castro. It read as follows:

I always recall with particular appreciation the conversations we had in Havana last year. The conference was a very enjoyable experience for us, and it showed what an important international function the Inter-Parliamentary Union has in promoting frank and open discussion, personal contacts, and mutual understanding amongst the political leaders of the whole world.

Such work is now more useful and necessary than ever. During this last year, there has been a progressive increase in the speed at which the international situation has deteriorated. The economic situation, with its devastating consequences, especially for under-developed countries, has become more critical than ever. The prevailing climate of confrontation continues, thereby provoking confrontation politics, the arms race, and the threat of war.

These are the circumstances in which it is Italy's turn to host the sixty-ninth conference. Let us hope that, as the worrying times in which we live demand, this meeting will make an effective contribution towards persuading all right-minded political leaders in the world to take note of this reality and appreciate the urgency of the struggle to preserve peace, and to open the way to a genuine period of international co-operation.

Cuba, Sig. Andreotti, is taking part in this new Inter-Parliamentary conference with a sincere and constructive desire to achieve a common will, and to work alongside all those who believe that there must be no new war, and that the nations of the world must do their utmost to solve the worrying and pressing problems which beset mankind today.

Please accept once more my very sincere regards.

# 30
# *Enrico Berlinguer*

Communist collaboration with the other parties in support of my 1976–9 governments of national solidarity had in any case become very problematical; but it was Forattini's cartoon that finally killed it off. Enrico Berlinguer was shown bowed down under the weight of a giant edition of Karl Marx's *Das Kapital*, while I was comfortably riding on his back, ostentatiously holding in my hands that Machiavellian management manual known as *The Prince*. To make things worse, it was published by Mondadori, who chose the particular cartoon for the brightly coloured cover of a greetings booklet distributed to certain schools, where it aroused sarcastic comments, and provided an excuse for non-Communist teachers to poke fun at their Communist colleagues.

Berlinguer was very sensitive to public opinion, and especially to any waves of feeling which might reduce support for the Communist Party, to the advantage either of Socialists and Radicals or else of groups to the left of the Communists.

It was Luigi Longo who wanted Berlinguer to become Party Secretary, as a way of reconciling the rigorously traditional Marxism of Ingrao and Amendola's willingness to involve the whole of society. Berlinguer had been slow to settle on any particular attitude, and when obliged to take up a specific position, he had done so without allowing himself to adopt an inquisitorial attitude towards Ingrao and his friends. Hence he seemed to Longo the right person for a period of cautious transition to new policies which would, amongst other things, lead to a different relationship with the Soviet Union. Furthermore, Berlinguer had successfully led the Communist Youth Federation at international as well as national level; and after the disturbances of 1968 it was essential that very particular attention should be paid to the tangled web of youthful protest.

There is a well-known joke by Pajetta '– who specializes in the *castigat ridendo mores* approach – that Berlinguer's boyhood vocation had been to enrol in the party leadership. This points to something important in Berlinguer's earlier career, by emphasizing the fact that for a number of years he had had plenty of opportunity to follow Palmiro Togliatti's work as Party Secretary, and had had personal knowledge of some of the background to the evolution of policy which led Togliatti, though he had for many years enjoyed the trust of the Comintern, to write the courageous Yalta memorandum so shortly before his death.

Enrico Berlinguer was only three years younger than me, but when he was running the Youth Front I had already left the corresponding Christian Democrat job. After being a member of the Consultative Assembly (September 1945 to spring 1946), I was summoned by De Gasperi to work in politics alongside him, and was elected to parliament as early as 1946. I had consequently never had occasion to meet Berlinguer Junior, though I was often in contact with men of a much older generation, such as Mario Berlinguer. He was one of the survivors of the Chamber of Deputies of pre-fascist days, and made a name for himself after the Liberation as public prosecutor, along with Carlo Sforza, at the trial of those responsible for fascist crimes. It was in that capacity that I had approached him when I was a journalist for *Il Popolo*, and I was able to appreciate that beneath a mild exterior was a man who combined substantial toughness with a polite manner. I should like to take this opportunity of pointing out that, although a convinced republican, he had no hesitation in returning to Sardinia to pay homage to Queen Marie José, who had gone there on a brief propitiatory visit.

It was some years later, however, that I gained a closer acquaintance with Mario Berlinguer, in a strange and unilateral manner. We met in a corridor in parliament. He took me by the arm and, as we walked slowly up and down the lobby known as 'Il Transatlantico', he began talking to me about his family, and in particular about Enrico's marriage plans. I listened in surprise and embarrassment, but when he addressed me as Renzo, the penny dropped; he had mistaken me for a Sardinian Communist member of parliament whose facial features were apparently rather like mine, and who had a similar stooping gait. What was I to do? It was too late to tell him that he was speaking to the wrong person, because I would have run the risk of looking as though I had encouraged him to continue his confidential conversation. I crossed my fingers for fear that some colleague would interrupt us and the mistake would be revealed. But fortunately everything went without a hitch, and Mario took his leave, in the conviction that he had explained to his friend Renzo Laconi his views on certain matters that had nothing to do with politics.

Mario Berlinguer was automatically made a member of the Consultative Assembly because he had taken part in the Aventine Secession of 1924. He was then elected to the Chamber of Deputies in the second, third, and fourth post-war parliaments, and in the sixth became a member of the Senate. It was during his father's absence from parliament that his son Enrico was elected to the Chamber of Deputies, and it was during that same fifth post-war parliament that Luigi Longo set about designating his successor. Thus Berlinguer was elected Deputy Secretary at the Twelfth Communist Party Congress, and three years later (1972) the Thirteenth Congress acclaimed him Secretary – a post to which he was subsequently re-elected more or less without opposition candidates.

At exactly the same time as Enrico Berlinguer was ascending the Communist throne, I was Prime Minister of the pre-election government which, with the full acquiescence of all parties, was expected to be defeated in the Chamber of Deputies, so that a solution to the crisis of the centre-left formula could be sought in a general election. When the election was over, the Socialists refused even to sit at a preliminary negotiating table, if I invited the Liberals as well. Funny things happen in politics; two years earlier, I had been forced to abandon an attempt to form a government by the Social Democrats, who thought I was leaning too far towards the Socialists (perhaps because of my frank and fruitful collaboration with Luigi Bertoldi when I was parliamentary leader of the Christian Democrats). Yet it was now the Socialists who were my chief obstacle. However, I thought it my duty to push ahead all the same, and so there came into being what is known as the Andreotti-Malagodi government, which had to put up with the activities of 'rebels' for a year. As one could and can easily work out by simple arithmetic, the 'rebels' can harm you only when their votes are added to those of the Communists – but that frequently happened.

This is not the place for a retrospective survey of those twelve months when I led a government which was viewed with suspicion even by some Christian Democrats, though there were no alterna-

201

tives available at the time. When an alternative arose, I made no bones about handing over, and was pleased that in spite of all the difficulties, it had been possible to produce one or two more than run–of–the–mill achievements, such as the Political Consultation Protocol signed with the Soviet Union (our respective membership of opposed military alliances being left untouched, of course), and an official visit to Japan, a country to which Europeans pay all too little attention. The US government welcomed both initiatives whole–heartedly, and was prepared to say so, as I found when I went to the White House in April 1973.

My trip to Moscow was less warmly welcomed by the Italian Communist Party, for they insisted on seeing it as a sort of challenge, aimed at showing that it was possible to be on good terms with the Kremlin, even if Communist members of both houses of parliament were in fierce opposition to the Italian government. Soviet protests at permission being given for American submarines to use the naval base at La Maddalena were headlines in the Italian Communist press, though in fact the matter was hardly touched on, for the Russians knew perfectly well that we were not there to cast doubts on our own loyalty to the Atlantic Alliance. It was said that signals were received in the Soviet Union that we were to be received only by Kosygin and Podgorny and not by Brezhnev; but the rumour made no difference to me, and was not unattractive to the Soviets in that they certainly did not want to cut the umbilical cord with the Italian Communist Party, though they were increasingly keen on official relations between states. The story was published in Italy in *Il Globo* and denied by *l'Unità* – but not by the Soviets.

I mentioned fierce opposition from the Communists, but I have to acknowledge that there was no particular ferocity brought to bear by Berlinguer, formally at least. The Communist press, on the other hand, adopted a different tone, for it had to provide an image of a party that was fighting on *the ramparts of parliament* to overthrow a government which had 'swung to the right'. The Liberals had at an early (and later) stage been much courted by the extreme Left, but now they had become terrible reactionaries, while the work of the government was interpreted as ineffective or diabolical, or both.

Very much in the air was the problem of the referendum on Italy's divorce law. It was the large total of Communist votes which had effectively enabled the divorce law to be passed, but now they were not unwilling to seek a way of avoiding a referendum. Some of them, however, interpreted this willingness to negotiate as a specific sign of anxiety and weakness; and so their intransigence became more deeply entrenched. When I began suggesting the possibility of a double approach, by treating church and civil marriages differently, that is to say allowing divorce in the case of civil marriages only, I was shouted down first and foremost by the promoters of the referendum. In vain I politely pointed out that civil marriage was, perhaps unjustly, defined by the church as concubinage – to the extent that the Bishop of Prato had ended up in court for saying just that.

There was time to discuss the matter without haste, since the regulations for holding referendums were still lacking, though both the Episcopal Conference and the Socialist Party were pressing for them to be worked out. I saw Berlinguer briefly, and was given to understand that the Communists might agree to abstain if my suggested double approach were adopted, but that I had no authority to negotiate. He was irritated, but also amused, by the anti-divorce lobby's conviction that the wives of Communists would vote against divorce, in order to prevent their husbands from running off. He emphasized the fact that the Communist Party was not responsible for putting divorce on the parliamentary agenda in the first place, but that they were bound to support it. He hoped that, if it came to a referendum, public meetings would not be ill tempered. Also he was worried that some people's insistence that there was a clash between present Communist policy and Togliatti's wise decision to vote for the inclusion of the Lateran Pacts in the Italian constitution would have the effect of giving encouragement to those members of the party who were not insensitive to Radical and other lay calls for the Concordat to be denounced. In this sense, too, the divorce referendum was a nuisance.

In the preceding October, the Turin newspaper *La Stampa* had recalled that at a meeting held in 1947, in the presence of Togliatti, to explain why the Communists had voted for article 7 of the constitution, Enrico Berlinguer had appealed to working and student girls to fight immorality, including pornographic publications. Women's dignity had to be restored and defended, and it was to be found in their good taste, their sense of fashion, their dress, and their desire to achieve a modern way of life, as well as in their morality and in the spirit of sacrifice which abounds in the Italian tradition – the tradition of Irma Bandiera and Maria Goretti.

His mention of Maria Goretti, a child (now canonized) who was killed while defending her honour, caused the Turin journalist to say that Berlinguer's speech would not have come amiss 'not just from an ordinary, everyday Catholic, but from Pope Pius XII himself'.

Unfortunately, when it came to the debate on legalizing abortion, the position adopted by Enrico Berlinguer and his party did not coincide with that of the Pope. Yet he did make a point of saying: 'The Catholic Church is not an obstacle. Our position is reinforced by the support of many Catholics who are members of the Communist Party or stand with us in our struggle on behalf of the people.' The official incompatibility of Catholicism and communism had long since disappeared.

After my government fell, and Forlani (with whom we had worked in complete harmony) was replaced by Fanfani as Secretary of the Christian Democrat Party, a new centre-left government was brought into being, thanks to the Palazzo Giustiniani agreement engineered by Fanfani. Mariano Rumor was the new Prime Minister, but he soon had to hand over to Moro.

The shadow of divorce lay across parliament. De Martino had wisely suggested that before the divorce law was passed legislation on referendums should be finalized, so that Catholics could take advantage of it; and in the end this encouraged certain leading Catholics (Gabrio Lombardi and Franco Ligi) to take the plunge and appeal to the country. They felt sure the electorate would overturn the decision of parliament; while others, although convinced they would be defeated, observed that in any case a sense of history made it impossible to prevent a group of Catholics from trying to get rid of an unjust law by legal means. Attempts to find a compromise solution failed, as we have seen, because they were swamped by the two extreme camps, and the pre-referendum campaign brought about a real change in Italian political life. Photographs in newspapers and pictures on television showing the combined pro–divorce efforts of Communists, Socialists, Liberals, Social Democrats, and Republicans (not the Radicals, who criticized the divorce law as not strong enough) had the effect of making communication possible where it had seemed permanently impossible before. Giovanni Malagodi, the fearsome Minister of the Treasury in 1973, was not merely implicitly forgiven but hailed as the heir of Cavour and the fount of economic and financial wisdom.

Berlinguer kept on saying that it was not the Communists who had wanted the divorce law, or prevented a compromise, but he eagerly climbed on the bandwagon and turned it to good use in the regional elections the following year. We were now a long way from the days of De Gasperi when the danger was supposed to lie in the possibility that the combined strengths of Communists and Socialists might exceed that of the Christian Democrats. Now it was a matter of the Communist Party itself planning to overtake the Christian Democrats, albeit within an all-embracing design which still had to be worked out and was certainly full of contradictions.

It was no concidence that this change in the political scene happened at a time of economic disaster. Though it would be unjust to interpret it as deriving from political reversals (a glance at the international scene makes that clear), there is no doubt that the flight of capital, the downturn in investment, and a decreasing sense of responsibility were influenced by the loss of a firm anchorage in political stability.

Aldo Moro had been amongst those most upset at the way the reactivated opposition between Christian Democrats and 'lay' politicians had changed Italian political life, and for some time had been suggesting a platform for improving relations. It was not that he had mere party interests at heart. He realized, rather, that conditions were not right for rearranging the political set-up without the danger of arousing resentment and irresponsible behaviour. Certainly one had to face the fact that Italian society had changed, and that it was now visibly different from the cliché which was our customary term of reference. The judgement on divorce expressed by the Italian people was very different from what we Catholic members of the Chamber of Deputies had argued and voted for in parliament, but it also ran counter to the hopes and expectations of those who had organized the referendum. At any rate – Aldo Moro said at a meeting – there are so many unmarried couples living together at all social levels that perhaps the desire of certain supporters of divorce 'to regularize their position' shows that they still believe in the family.

During this period, Moro discreetly maintained a great number of contacts. Unfortunately his government went into crisis in late 1975 and early 1976 and this caused a break in relations between him and the Socialists, who were themselves going through a difficult period of internal stress, leading to the emergence of Craxi as Party Secretary.

Events preceding the general election of 1976 are fairly well known. The election itself brought the Communists a considerable increase in their representation in parliament, but they failed to overtake the Christian Democrats and so launch an attack to drive them from the centre of the political stage.

Berlinguer operated on two fronts. He maintained a dialogue with Moro, but wherever possible established alliances at local-authority and regional level to keep the Christian Democrats out. Rome city council was emblematic of this dual policy, which also received the support it needed from certain other parties, who accused the Christian Democrats of being lukewarm towards the Communists.

My political standing was fairly good at the time, because as Minister of the Budget and the South I had succeeded in getting through parliament a quite useful law for reactivating aid for the South, which met with even opposition approval. Furthermore, not only had I not raised matters of prestige or competence with Moro over the fact that La Malfa, who was Deputy Prime Minister, was more or less co-ordinating economic planning himself, I had actually been pleased about it; and my collaboration with La Malfa during those months allowed me to get to know him better and to build a friendly relationship with him.

As a result of discussions with the political parties, the President of the Republic decided to ask me to form a government. But how was I to do it? Everyone knew what they did not want, but scarcely anyone was able to produce an acceptable and workable political formula. As for an agreement with the Communists, the Christian Democrat Party was not alone in thinking this impossible.

A piece of news from Germany made things worse. Chancellor Schmidt declared, on behalf of the United States, France, and Britain as well as West Germany, that if the Communists were to enter government in Italy, that would have a serious unbalancing effect. This joint opinion of the four nations had apparently been worked out – and this made the whole situation more delicate – at an unofficial meeting held during the summit of the seven industrialized nations at Puerto Rico. But Moro and Rumor declared they knew nothing about it, in which case they had been seriously slighted. Trouble-shooters immediately set about repairing the damage – or so they thought – by saying that the meeting of the four had taken place within the sphere of normal consultations between the Powers responsible for the protection of Berlin.

What Berlin had got to do with it, I fail to understand, but a book written by Ducci, a former Italian Ambassador in London, reveals that Moro had also been invited to the working lunch concerned. Moro, however, had only just arrived at Puerto Rico, and had preferred to remain with the Italian delegation to study the papers for the summit, since his involvement with the election campaign and what followed had prevented him from doing so in Rome.

Furthermore, President Ford had made a speech in New Hampshire the previous February, in which he had taken up a subject dear to Henry Kissinger by declaring that the United States was opposed to a broadening of Italian government coalitions to include the Communists. The *Corriere della Sera* published a five-column headline which read: 'The American veto on Rome also applies to France and Spain'.

The only possible solution was a one-party government supported or tolerated by a large majority: what Luigi Cappugi ingeniously described as a government with 'no no-confidence'. The Italian language has infinite possibilities.

Because of the concatenation of circumstances I have described above, the Communists were the crux of the matter, but the Christian Democrat Party was not prepared to ask for their support. In fact I was asked always to refer to a *technical* rather than a *parliamentary* majority.

I worked out a plan of operations for the government, and even used the innovation of a fixed series of dates by which individual tasks had to be carried out. That is the kind of pragmatism I like – aimed not to avoid ideal aspirations, but to give them content.

I was glad to meet Berlinguer, partly to get an authentic version of two recent conversations he had had with Brezhnev, for there were several different versions in circulation. No doubt the attitude of Berlinguer at congresses cannot have aroused much enthusiasm amongst Moscow traditionalists; but it was also true that you could not easily give a spanking, as Suslov is supposed to have wished, to the leader of a party which had had such resounding election successes.

My own view is that the more effective relations are between Italy and the Soviet Union, the more stress must be laid on the autonomy (but not hostility) of the Italian Communist Party. And I had noted with satisfaction Berlinguer's praise of autonomy and pluralism. Moro had spoken of these ideas with approval, and had indicated their significance in the context of the apprehension expressed by Kissinger and Ford.

The idea of Eurocommunism seemed less substantial and clear, in spite of the joint Italo-French declaration of November 1975, and a public meeting in Paris in May at which both Enrico Berlinguer and Georges Marchais appeared. But what about the Atlantic Alliance?

At the very end of the election campaign, Berlinguer had said on television:

> We have already declared, and we now repeat, that we are opposed to Italy's leaving the Atlantic Pact, for reasons that we have explained on a number of occasions. Our view is that, since it has been possible, lately in particular, to improve *détente* by establishing a balance of power, to disturb this balance – and that is what would happen if a country were to leave one bloc or the other – would be to disturb the general process of *détente*. That is the basic reason why we think Italy should remain within the Atlantic Pact.

Since I had been involved in clashes in the Chamber of Deputies over this very matter in 1949, Berlinguer's acknowledgement of Italy's position seemed to me very significant, and I used it as a way of opening negotiations with him, and sounding out the possibility of 'technical' support from the Communists. The fact that the approach was being made by me and not by the Christian Democrat Party might, after all, prove convenient for the Communists, for they could go on attacking the Christian Democrat Party in public, while supporting the one-party Christian Democrat government, for reasons of higher policy. I was not personally persuaded by such a specious argument, but it might turn out to be useful, at least for the time being. We could go back to the subject in due course, to deal with any disharmony which might arise and cause difficulties; and that is exactly what we did. It was not all that logical either that, while an agreement on the presidency of the two houses of parliament had been reached (it allowed Pietro Ingrao to occupy a chair which had not accommodated a Communist since Terracini sat there in the days of the Constituent Assembly), we should refuse to negotiate with the Communists about support for the government. I am perfectly well aware that parliament and government are two quite separate entities, but support from outside government seemed to offer an acceptable arrangement, especially since there were no other solutions available, and, quite rightly, no one had fresh elections in mind.

In order to make the arrangement more palatable to the other parties, I suggested that trade unions should be consulted, as well as representatives of the Regions, Communes, and Provinces.

The Communists, naturally, were unwilling to accept any discrimination, and it proved difficult to overcome this preliminary problem, which I thought it best not to dwell on. All I wanted was advice and a sympathetic attitude to government plans, without any promises about future developments. The one thing I did make very clear, however, was that by supporting the government in such a difficult situation, and hence accepting a share of the inevitable unpopularity of the rescue programme, the right conditions would be created for *all* parties to get to know one another better and collaborate in working out Italy's future.

From the interest they showed in the government programme, and certain suggestions they made on specific points (young people, local finances, and foreign policy), I got the impression that Communist opposition was not totally entrenched. That was the conclusion I felt bound to draw, and I also felt that Berlinguer was aware that Italy might be staring financial disaster in the face, with all that would mean, especially for the working classes.

This feeling of mine was strengthened when I met the trade unions. Lama said he was opposed to stopgap measures, and showed some interest in my series of fixed dates, since it provided both a guarantee that things would get done and an opportunity for specific political checks to be carried out by parliament. He said that the government was bound to take due account of his trade union.

Berlinguer also made a small personal gesture which I interpreted as a good sign. (Don't forget that up to that time I had had little to do with him.) He sent me a cutting from the Belgian newspaper *Le Soir*, which said that the Left was making a lot of demands but that 'the Christian Democrat Party relies on these being watered down by Andreotti, the Italian Mazarin. He is a cunning old fox and a smooth operator, endowed with that cardinal's unctuousness which very few of the scheming politicians brought up in the confined atmosphere of Rome can claim to possess.'

At the other end of the scale there were those who threw up their hands in horror at my having discussions with the Communists. However, I was much assisted in parrying their objections by a comment which Indro Montanelli made on Radio Monte Carlo. He said that I should be judged on results rather than policies, and that anyway I was in a situation which demanded the greatest sympathy. 'If Andreotti wants to form a government, he needs either the Socialists or the Communists; that's not just my opinion, it's a matter of arithmetic.'

As I have already stated, there was no alternative. Without the Communists the Socialists wouldn't play; and there were sound and understandable reasons for that.

I formed a government and asked the two chambers for a vote of confidence. On 10 August, Enrico Berlinguer spoke in the Chamber of Deputies and confirmed that the Communists would abstain, as had already happened in the Senate. He said that for many reasons voting against the government would have been justified, but other factors led in the opposite direction. First of all (and he was certainly right about this), while the responsibility for providing Italy with a government lay primarily with the Christian Democrat Party ('in view of the fact that it still has, but only by a small margin, a simple majority in parliament'), it lay also with the Communist Party:

> Why have we reached this decision? Because on this occasion, as on every occasion, the Communist Party has based its conduct on the real needs of the working class and the country. And from these principles we have gone on to consider above all (I shall mention later some other considerations which have dictated our decision) that if we voted against the government, if, that is to say, we stifled at birth a government which sees the light of day after forty days of post-election negotiations and after far too many months of non-government, it would have meant that we too were helping to plunge Italy into an alarming state of political confusion.
>
> What political forces would have gained from such a situation? Certainly not, in our opinion, the working classes, employed or unemployed, nor their trade union organizations, nor those other categories of productive worker who, if they are to discuss and deal with problems that cannot be postponed, must have an effective government to turn to. And the essential point today is that this government must work alongside a fully functioning parliament which exercises all its constitutional prerogatives and all its rights both in the area of political and legislative action and in that of influencing and collaborating with the executive. A confused situation or one of prolonged crisis would certainly do no good to the Regions, Provinces, and Communes, which are in the alarming situation of being weighed down by appalling debts. The position of many local authorities is that they cannot guarantee to pay their employees during the coming months. We are of the firm opinion that if we had decided to prevent this government from taking office, we should have been playing into the hands of quite different interests and influences, including those of certain foreign countries which have tried and are still trying to prevent an improved prospect in Italy of unity amongst the masses, and of concord and collaboration between the democratic political parties.

210

That was the beginning of a period of three years during which the Italian political parties enjoyed a new relationship. It could and should have allowed them to move closer together, to compare ideas, and to work out valid plans for action over a specific period, as Vanoni did with his 1954 Plan. But while the new relationship did bring positive results – and substantial ones at that – in terms of disasters avoided and economic and financial recovery, what failed to occur was a political advance, precisely because each party insisted on preserving full and absolute freedom of manoeuvre, even though it voted for the government or prevented its fall by abstaining.

Berlinguer occasionally complained about statements made by some leading Christian Democrats that there was no prospect of any kind of joint government with the Communists. He assumed that these outbursts were responsible for grass-roots objections amongst the Communists to the 'blood donations' which the Communist Party was indeed giving to the one-party government. For my part, I pointed out to him that the attitude adopted on the fringes of his party towards the Christian Democrats had not changed in any way at all; and that the bewilderment displayed derived from asking a question that it was only too easy to ask: Why were they supporting a government which consisted entirely (with the sole exception of Rinaldo Ossola, a highly valued banking expert who had agreed to join us) of men belonging to a party which, so it was repeatedly said, was more or less the gateway to perdition?

This led to complaints about excessive pragmatism and the lack of a plan for the post-economic-crisis period, but when it came to discussing what that plan would be, there was talk once more of political pre-conditions and Christian Democrat attempts at a take-over.

Then, when Craxi came out with a sort of exaltation of Proudhon, and acknowledged that Marxist-Leninist theory was a thing of the past, Berlinguer hurried to Genoa to explain to the workers there that the government which they were propping up should not be used as an excuse for forgetting the theoretical basis of the Communist tradition.

Pinpricks or hammer blows like these made life difficult for Enrico Berlinguer.

It is always a matter of sound etiquette for a Prime Minister to maintain continuous and frank contacts with those parties in parliament which support his government in one way or another.

In the sort of government which I headed the frequency and frankness of contacts were absolutely vital; especially since there was a pretence that votes and abstentions were more or less random, because there could not be proper coalition meetings.

For ordinary business – but not much of our business was ordinary – Berlinguer suggested that Evangelisti, as Under-Secretary to the Prime Minister's Office, should maintain contact with Di Giulio, and for economic problems Giorgio Napolitano and Luciano Barca should be empowered to represent their respective parties. (Years later I heard echoes of a certain resentment on the part of some Communists who had been excluded from these diplomatic activities.) But there was always a direct line between the government and the Communists (as there was in the case of the other parties, too), or else Tonino Tatò would act as special intermediary.

I would divide this three-year period into three distinct phases: economic recovery; the crisis of 1978 and the Moro tragedy; and the decline of this very unusual 'coalition'.

The shadow of bankruptcy hung threateningly over us. The humiliation of having to provide gold as security before the West German banks would grant a hard-won loan to Rumor's government had left its imprint. The initial reaction of the political parties and trade unions that these things had to be accepted made it possible to adopt a series of measures to obtain release of the international loan arranged by the International Monetary Fund, which was rightly considered essential and extremely urgent. For my part, I tried to lessen the negative impression made on the parties by explaining, on television and elsewhere, that there was a direct connection between the measures we had taken and economic recovery. But I understood perfectly well that the Communists in particular were uncomfortable at agreeing to a freeze on cost-of-living bonuses for wages and salaries which were slightly above the average and the slowing down of wage-indexation (the price of newspapers, for example).

When inflation began to slow down and monetary reserves to build up, I repeatedly acknowledged that all parties had contributed. As soon as things improved, however, there occurred a phenomenon which was not too difficult to foresee: each political group resumed its freedom of action, and an attempt was made to abandon what I jokingly called 'blood-donation politics'.

In November 1977, I realized why Berlinguer could not make concessions on internal policies, once Italy had recovered from the crisis which had morally obliged him to do so. When he went to Moscow for the Soviet Communist Party Congress, he publicly took objection to the notion of Communist parties *which lead* and Communist parties *which are led*. Since he was deeply involved on the international front, he could already foresee the objections (or at least the resistance) of some of his followers, and he did not want this to be added to other reasons for grass-roots dissatisfaction.

When he came back from Moscow I could see that he was in a state of nervous tension. He was fascinated by the idea of abandoning old ideas and creating an advanced socialist society which would respect 'all individual and group freedoms as well as all civil and religious freedoms, and in which different political parties would coexist, and society, culture, and ideas would be pluralist'. At the same time, he nevertheless realized that it would be necessary to overcome obstacles and objections, and to refine the model before it could be applied to individual countries.

A Party Secretary cannot confine himself to working out long-term strategy, however. He must also offer party members short-term tactics and strategy which they can understand; and – so Berlinguer said – on his way towards total democracy, he was not assisted by the pre-planned obstacles which the Christian Democrats were continually putting in the path of the Communists. His party was in the ascendant, and he had no right to repress its energy for the benefit of the Christian Democrats and their one-party government. He acknowledged that I was always straight with him, but even I had never gone beyond the repeated invitation: 'Let's walk a stretch of road together, and then we'll see.' His conviction that the need to provide emergency support was now passed was partly confirmed (so he told me himself) by a conversation he had had with Ugo La Malfa. La Malfa had warmly praised Berlinguer's courageous speech in Moscow, and wanted to make it possible at once for the Communist Party to enjoy a greater *involvement*.

In late November and early December, Edward Gierek, the First Secretary of the Polish Communist Party, was in Rome on an official visit, and this gave me an opportunity of showing that, where state contacts at international level were concerned, we had no preconceived objections to anybody. I had made this clear by going to Moscow in 1972, and it was even easier to confirm this in Italy's current political and parliamentary situation. At any rate, Berlinguer was happy that the visit was taking place, and played an active part in it. Berlinguer, Aldo Moro, and Cardinal Wyszynski sat with me and our guest at the principal table, and we had a long conversation on how the Helsinki agreement might lead to developments in European security and co-operation.

The relaxed atmosphere of the meeting with Gierek was not allowed to deceive anyone, for at this same time Berlinguer was still publicly airing the idea of a general strike over unemployment and the need for a change in economic policy. Zaccagnini wisely expressed a certain sympathy, and tried to offer an olive branch to Berlinguer and Lama; but all he succeeded in doing was arousing objections from Carniti and Macario. Pierre Carniti approached Berlinguer, anyway, to tell him that the CISL trade union was not going to be pressured into doing anything, and that discussions had to be reopened with the government on the basis of the reply sent by the government to the Communists.

Attacks on the government became unremittingly and increasingly fierce. On 6 January 1978, *l'Unità* came out with a self-explanatory headline: 'Non-existent government'. As for the Socialists, Manca declared that the government could resign without a vote of no confidence.

To stir up even more trouble – if that was necessary – came a statement from the State Department in Washington to the effect that the United States had not changed its attitude to Communist parties, including the Italian Communist Party. Those members of the PCI who had been displeased at the way Berlinguer had distanced himself from Moscow were very sarcastic about this statement, and later on some attempt was made to deny its paternity. Nor could the increasing cry for a new government be stifled by a very complimentary statement about my government's achievements from that same Chancellor Schmidt who eighteen months earlier had drawn up what might be described as Italy's death certificate.

Symptoms of exhaustion in the government were produced by the vicious circle of public incomprehension caused by lack of public information. Indeed, these symptoms might well have appeared earlier, if one takes into account the existence of minefields such as the abortion dispute or the chaotic situation in the prisons, from which convicts frequently escaped. Other 'mines', such as arguments over the infamous Colonel Kappler's escape from hospital in Rome, were simply dummies. What on earth the Ministry of Defence had got to do with it is difficult to understand; and there is no doubt that if Lattanzio had stayed at the seaside no one would have thought of involving him. I tried to settle things by means of a compromise. I moved Ruffini to the Ministry of Defence and gave Lattanzio responsibility for transport and the merchant navy (the latter ministry having become vacant as a result of the death of Fabbri). But the atmosphere was embittered, and that was by no means the sole fault of the Communists.

On 14 January, I called a meeting of the leaders of the supposedly collaborating parties at the Chamber of Deputies. It was my birthday, and Natta gave me a tie – an object capable of a variety of different interpretations! It was clear, however, that the Communists were not alone in wanting there to be a close link between the government's political programme and the relative strengths of the political parties. There was nothing to be done but act accordingly, even without knowing where that might lead. Some kind of solution would surely be found, and it did not matter whether I or somebody else held the reins. Indeed, all the parties had let it be known that they did not preclude any individual as a possible new Prime Minister. In the event, it was I who was asked to form the next government.

Berlinguer examined closely the possibility of a *broad* government, but since he soon found that the Christian Democrat Party would not play ball, he settled for an agreement on what the government programme would be, and where support for it would come from in parliament. It was Moro's dedicated work which made it possible to overcome all obstacles. In this connection he had a decisive conversation with Berlinguer on 16 February (exactly one month before he was kidnapped) in which once again he explained his idea of creating a 'third phase'. It was not possible to establish when and how this would be done, but it would certainly depend on the extent to which collaboration and trust between the two parties produced positive results.

On the morning of 16 March, less than two hours before the (slightly) modified government presented its programme to parliament, Moro's escort was murdered and his incredible kidnapping was carried out. It was difficult not to connect the crime with the solving of the political crisis; but we had no idea whether it was a right-wing attempt to curb the Communists or an extreme-left attempt to punish them for what was judged to be overcompliance.

Berlinguer was one of the political leaders who rushed to the Prime Minister's office in dumbfounded disbelief. He immediately agreed to a shortened procedure which would allow the new government to be given a vote of confidence in both the Senate and the Chamber of Deputies that same day. If the hidden enemy was to be confronted, a government with full powers was required; and that itself would constitute a vigorous reply to this attempt at intimidation.

During the fifty-four days of Aldo Moro's Calvary, Berlinguer was always there to provide firm support for the government and the Christian Democrat Party in their opposition to the terrorists' absurd insistence that we should capitulate. I must make it clear, however, that no party was prepared to agree to the release of Red Brigades members currently in prison, or was ever in a position to suggest sound and acceptable alternative solutions. A large number of more or less subtle arguments were brought to bear on the subject, but almost all of them came later, and were used for polemical purposes. (The so-called 'humanitarian approach' was adopted only in order to find effective channels of communication; but there were really no differences of opinion about that.) There was a lot of talk about releasing Besuschio, a convicted Red Brigades member, as a symbolic gesture, but that really would not have achieved anything; for even if he had been pardoned by the President, he would still have had to face charges that required him to be held in custody, so he would have remained in prison anyway.

A gesture of goodwill was arranged towards a sick member of the Red Brigades, but on 9 May, Moro was murdered. The criminals, in their merciless ferocity, unfortunately continued until the end to reply on intimidating the Italian political system, but they underestimated its moral fibre. This was one of the toughest and most gruelling tests that members of the government and party leaders have ever had to face; and some of those responsible for the crime have, in their subsequent expressions of dissociation or repentance, fully confirmed that the attitude adopted by the state was necessary. What is most disconcerting, however, even in the writings of those who are prepared to be self-critical, is the total failure to give due consideration to the five lives sacrificed during the kidnapping of Aldo Moro. The government behaved responsibly, however, and never forgot their sacrifice.

On 14 October, Berlinguer and Natta came to see me. Because Moro's death had provoked considerable argument, the Communists wanted all parties to behave in a concerted and consistent way, so as not to encourage the terrorists by displaying so much as an apparent crack in the edifice. They were worried about certain criticisms of the special prisons or the activities of General Dalla Chiesa. They hoped that these were just personal opinions and did not represent the attitude of the Socialist Party as such. Berlinguer also took the opportunity to tell me of his disagreement with Marchais over Spanish and Portuguese membership of the EEC, and he told me about his conversations in Moscow. (Amongst other things, Brezhnev had asked why nobody ever talked about human rights in relation to China.)

Meanwhile, I was trying to establish the consensus between the parties on a sounder footing and test its solidarity, for it had been hard pressed when Leone was unjustly hounded out of the presidency of the Republic, and there had also been a repeated tendency for some groups to fly off at a tangent. I asked Pandolfi, as Minister of the Treasury, to draw up a three-year economic plan which would involve all the parties in support of the government, plus the trade unions and representatives of the Regions. But did the parties really want to continue with the status quo?

On 24 November, Berlinguer still seemed willing to go along with the government programme, but demanded that efforts be made to put it into full operation 'without anybody using delaying tactics or backsliding'. (He had in mind the police reform and the so-called Reale Law No. 2.) Craxi felt, however, that it was impossible to go on with the present one-party government *ad infinitum*, and suggested a new one-party government, half of whose members, less one, would be 'experts' trusted by the various parties. Longo quite liked the idea of a government crisis, or at least a round of talks to test party positions, for he did not like the government's bill on pensions, and for political reasons he did not want it to be the Communists who broke ranks after their congress.

For some weeks there was a trial of strength, so to speak, between these occasional sudden dissensions and my attempt to pin the parties down to supporting the government in a more specific political programme and a more pronounced European commitment.

The birth of the European Monetary System was an event of importance, but its *immediate* effects were bad. At the Common Market meeting in Brussels we had had to delay joining the EMS, primarily because of justified anxieties on technical grounds at the Banca d'Italia. When I got back to Rome, I consulted the political parties, and suggested that we needed time to think about it; but within a few hours I was forced to take a decision on my own responsibility. On the one hand, direct pressure was brought to bear, and promises were made, by Helmut Schmidt and Valéry Giscard d'Estaing; and on the other, I was made aware that the delay was interpreted by the Chancelleries as a weakening of Italian commitment to Europe. Therefore once I had got Ciampi, as Governor of the Banca d'Italia, to agree (he spent the whole night at my offices), I was obliged to ask parliament point-blank for Italy to join the EMS at once.

In theory, those who protested were right, but in practice it was impossible for us to do anything else. The Communists voted against joining (they demanded a delay, such as two days earlier I had thought possible), and the Socialists abstained. This was another hammer-blow to the already ailing government support.

I was aware that preparatory meetings for the Communist congress had been critical of the party's support of the government. Berlinguer was certainly not insensitive to these scattered alarm signals, even though they were to a considerable degree the result of a mood which had its origin in provincial party cadres, some of which were the offspring of the 1968 troubles, and all of which were always very worried about being overtaken on the Left.

As the year 1979 began, the outlook for the government was not good. I met Berlinguer on 24 January, and we spoke about the correspondence with Brezhnev over a policy which might be more effective in improving *détente*. There was no disagreement between the government and Berlinguer on this, but he told me quite frankly that a government crisis was inevitable. (Berlinguer spoke with the same calm and apparently detached tone of voice whether he was promising to vote for you or telling you that some particular experiment was now over.) He considered the following to be unacceptable: the decision to join the EMS; the principles applied in making recent appointments to top positions in state economic enterprises (quite independently of the individuals chosen); the 'obvious' fact that the government was to be identified with the Christian Democrat Party; and too little success in the fight against terrorism.

Berlinguer also told me (a little later) that they didn't like the composition of the government, and that but for the Moro tragedy they would have decided to vote against the government right from the beginning. And so the list of complaints went on: indecisiveness and parliamentary boycotts over the agriculture agreements and reform of the police; the fact that a hundred Christian Democrat members of the Chamber of Deputies had declared that they would never agree to working with the Communists, something they stubbornly avoided doing even at regional level, where it would have served a useful general purpose; and Zaccagnini's statements in Washington to the effect that the Communists were fed up with supporting the government (Galloni had said the same thing in 1976), and that the Socialists would revive the Centre-Left as soon as they felt like it.

What about the Socialists? Were they really waiting for the elections to the European Parliament, so that they could register success there and so approach the Italian general election in triumph ('always assuming . . .'). Berlinguer thought that the Socialists were particularly annoyed at the Italian Communists' direct contacts with the British Labour Party and the West German Social Democrats.

He kept on saying that the grass-roots Communists were becoming increasingly worried. And certain irresponsible statements, such as the insinuation that Lama was sacrificing the workers to the Communist Party's freedom of manoeuvre, were bound to cause confusion and objections. And what about *Il Popolo*'s attacks on the Communists over events in Cambodia – a country whose problems were very difficult to analyse?

The last item on Berlinguer's list of complaints was his almost total disapproval of the personnel and management of the state radio and television organization.

It was clear to me that the government had little hope of survival, though it was difficult to see an alternative.

Meanwhile, the country's problems of government were complemented by crimes serious enough to make the headlines. A working man who had assisted the forces of justice in the fight against terrorism was murdered in Genoa. Judge Alessandrini was murdered in Milan.

It was in this atmosphere that I outlined a three-year plan to the Chamber of Deputies and asked the parties to express an opinion on it, though I realized how slight my chances of success were. But I was inviting them to behave responsibly. While pointing out that since the government had taken office in 1976 the dollar had fallen from 860 lire to 830, and the rate of inflation had been almost halved, I stressed that what the country needed was not a formula but a practical policy. It was vital to preserve solidarity on the major problems of the day: protecting employment, defending the lira, preserving peace at home, and maintaining Italy's international position.

I took due note that the parties were not agreed as to whether my government should carry on, but that none contested the facts I had set before them. I went to the President's Palace. The President was just back from Alessandrini's funeral, where he had been deeply

219

moved by the dignified behaviour of magistrates and public. He told me that he already knew the views of the parties and would ask me to form another government in two days' time. That is indeed what happened, and so I began the round of consultations again.

Having seen all the other party secretaries, I had a private meeting with Berlinguer on 12 February. He asked the Christian Democrat Party to clarify its position, and did not exclude the possibility that the Communists might adopt an attitude of constructive opposition. But it seemed like an empty gesture to me, because the emphasis *l'Unità* had given to a very tough speech which Berlinguer had delivered a few days earlier in Sardinia was effectively a rejection of the note which I gave him. He said the Communist Party's official reply would reach me within forty-eight hours.

At an early stage, the Socialists thought they would remain outside a two- or three-party government, and would abstain in parliament, but then they asked for members of the independent Left to be included, claiming to have the Communist Party's agreement to this; but the Communist delegation flatly refused to accept the idea, much to the annoyance of Craxi.

Matters became complicated in the days that followed. When I abandoned my attempt to form a government, La Malfa spent an unsuccessful week trying to do the same thing, and there then took place a mysterious little game of musical chairs. First of all it was suggested that Saragat should be Prime Minister with La Malfa and me as Deputy Prime Ministers, then that was altered to me as Prime Minister with Saragat and La Malfa as Deputies, and finally it was settled that I should be Prime Minister, with La Malfa as the sole Deputy. I had been invited to try to form a government on the unusual condition that whatever happened I should present my programme to parliament. La Malfa was convinced that an early election was unavoidable, though everybody else continued to disagree. Immediately after the cabinet had been chosen, La Malfa died. It was a sadly disturbing epilogue to two and a half years of exceptional government activity.

The Communists and Socialists voted against me, and I really did not think the government could rely for its existence on Democrazia Nazionale, a group which had broken away from the MSI-National Right as a result of internal dissensions.

By a curious paradox, the demise of my government was brought about by two senators from my own party. They agreed with me that the parties which had supported one-party governments for the last three years must not be allowed to gain the impression that I was using diversionary tactics or attempting a temporary salvage operation. These two rebels caused the government to be defeated by 150 votes to 149. It seemed appropriate to me that the government should fall by one vote.

I had clearly stated to those who were prepared to listen – and to those who were not – that if some different alliance of parties had been feasible, I would not have stood out against it. Craxi, however, had brushed aside the possibility of other groupings, though Cipellini's speech in the Senate had seemed less clear cut. The reliable statistical data on results achieved which I had supplied in parliament could provide any party with plenty of scope for justifying its own activities to the electorate; and the electorate was now going to have its say.

Enrico Berlinguer seemed to be the most worried of all, and since I knew he was frequently to be seen at football matches, I jokingly suggested he should play an attacking game by proudly stressing the crucial role his party had played in 'rescuing Italy from danger'. He looked at me and smiled. It was clear that the last thing he intended was to adopt passive, defensive tactics.

Parliament was dissolved on 2 April, and a general election was called for 3 and 4 June, one week before the elections to the European Parliament. Unfortunately the law does not permit these two elections to be combined.

This time the election programmes on state radio and television were accompanied by a certain amount of activity amongst the independent television stations. On 2 June, I myself joined Guido Carli and Luciano Lama in a relaxed independent television broadcast which was enlivened by pictures of Lama adjusting the microphone-cord around my neck. Natta had given me a tie; and now Lama was adjusting a collar strap. What a lot of interest in my neck!

At least the election result gave me as a Christian Democrat the satisfaction of seeing all the gloomy forecasts about a collapse in the party's fortunes proved false. (Voters listen more carefully than political pundits and those with an axe to grind.) It also provided something quite novel: a substantial fall in the Communist vote, with seven fewer senators and twenty-six fewer members of the Chamber of Deputies.

National solidarity went out of the window, and when I was asked to form another government, I found that the Communists were personally polite, but that was all; while the Socialists wanted a 'lay' (or rather a non-Christian Democrat) Prime Minister, which was naturally bound to attract the other parties.

A few of my aides were worried at the way I was being kept out, and complained that my scrupulous observance of my obligations as Prime Minister (which included causing the government to scuttle itself) had not inspired a spirit of helpfulness in others. How naïve can one be! Fancy thinking that in political life people get ahead thanks to other people's gratitude!

So I returned to private life – or rather to extra-governmental life (for I was elected Chairman of the Foreign Affairs Committee) – and had few occasions to talk to Enrico Berlinguer. He, like the other party secretaries, was also a member of the Foreign Affairs Committee, but he didn't attend regularly. I appreciated his appearance, however, at the opening meeting, at which I was elected Chairman.

It so happened that in February 1984 we travelled to and from Moscow together as guests in President Pertini's plane, along with a Vatican delegation, for the funeral of Yuri Andropov. For technical reasons we had to land at Budapest and Vienna, so the journey was a long one and gave me a chance to discover two new sides to Berlinguer. D'Alema Junior and I took on Berlinguer and Pertini at cards; and our opponents were by no means always the winners. On the journey home, however, Berlinguer and I let others get on with their harmless card-games while we had a long conversation. We recalled moments of crisis, analysed situations and developments, and commented on foreign affairs. Berlinguer had had advance notice of an audience with the new Soviet leader, Chernenko, who had devoted all his time to state rather than party delegations during the period of our visit. Pertini and I had had a conversation with him the previous evening, and I had then had a meeting with Gromyko.

Berlinguer was not touchy about these meetings, and shared my views as to the value of making a clear distinction between governments and parties in international relations. I am not convinced that all his fellow Italian Communists would agree, and I could foresee a certain disgruntlement over what might be construed as competition with what some people think *ought* to be a natural link in Italo-Soviet relations.

Berlinguer was certainly no extrovert, but he talked to me at length about his family as well as about young people in Italy, educational freedom, and the need to avoid the reactionary attitude of those groups who objected to mass parties as such.

222

On the basis of what had happened in the years 1976–9, he acknowledged that I had always taken care to adopt the principle 'to each his own'. But he would insist – with almost mechanical precision – on listing all his complaints, past and present, about the Christian Democrats and the Socialists.

Berlinguer was afraid that there might be a resurgence of terrorism in Italy, and he agreed that it was essential to get a clear message to the neo-Red Brigades that both the political parties and the trade unions were utterly opposed to them. But he wanted to be quite sure (and he wasn't) that everyone was of the same opinion. He asked me to make strenuous efforts to ensure that the fight against terrorism was a European matter, and he declared himself totally in favour of fighting the drug problem with equal vigour, especially since the two problems were connected. He was passionately dedicated to the European Parliament, for he recognized its constructive potential and its ability to help give Italy an unusual reputation for unity.

I am grateful to the memory of Andropov, in the sense that without his death I should perhaps never have encountered the *private* Berlinguer, as I did on this occasion, when he was unusually willing to talk about things other than political and economic crises, as had always happened between us in the past.

Berlinguer died in June 1984, sadly struck down at the end of a public political meeting in Padua by a form of circulatory disease. That and cancer are the two diseases which account for the deaths of nearly all politicians.

In September, I was invited to the Festa dell'Unità for a foreign affairs debate with Paolo Bufalini, and I felt the presence of Berlinguer. Although a tough opponent, he always behaved correctly and showed a sense of responsibility. In certain unpleasant episodes that have occurred since then, I could no longer feel that presence. I have been comforted, however, by a cordial letter from the Berlinguer family, who wished to remind me that their beloved Enrico had 'respected and admired' me.

# 31
# Ronald Reagan

I first met Ronald Reagan in 1972. He was Governor of California at the time, and President Nixon had sent him on a 'friendship' tour of European capitals. After a few hours of conversation, I found I was gaining an extremely favourable impression of him, partly because of something which very rarely occurs in talks of this kind. If a subject came up of which he had no direct knowledge, or about which the State Department had not prepared a note for him, he would confess quite frankly that he was unable to express an opinion, without taking refuge – as nearly everyone does – in those generic, all-embracing clichés which often make such conversations either pointless or confusing. He was very proud of his state's progress (not only in the industrial field but also in population, for California was about to overtake New York), and showed a great deal of interest in our plans for Southern Italy and in statistics about the North–South divide.

He spoke with feeling about the Californians of Italian origin, mentioning not only Giannini, who founded the Bank of America, but many other men who had made their mark in a great variety of fields. There was Enrico Fermi and his research team, whose work was now being continued in universities and research centres; there was Luis Martini, a Piedmontese who was responsible for giving a vital impetus to the American wine-growing industry; there was Joseph L. Alioto, who became Mayor of San Francisco, and Professor Vittorio Nino Novarese, a Hollywood celebrity.

I was in a position to impress Reagan, because I had been to California more than once, and could therefore speak on many topics from personal experience.

I was somewhat surprised to learn that the Republican Convention had preferred Reagan to Bush or any of the other big names from Washington or the international scene, but I certainly did not join the ranks of those stupid and presumptious commentators who decried him by almost scornfully referring to his origins as an actor, and forgetting that he had been in charge of a state which was more important than two-thirds of the nations belonging to the UN. Perhaps there are some political pundits who consider it a matter of merit and distinction if a politician has never had a trade or profession in his life.

In his election campaign, Reagan laid great emphasis on the need to restore strength, prestige, and authority to the United States, and he bitterly attacked the economic policy of the Carter administration, with its supposed waste. The amusing thing is that he was applauded and cheered even by the recipients of social security benefits, who should have realized that if Reagan won the election and kept his promises, they were going to fall on hard times. He was skilful, however, in avoiding any argument with Carter about the Tehran hostages, because in that way he avoided not only possible accusations that he was taking advantage of a national tragedy, but also the need to commit himself to any particular future action, should he inherit the 'hot potato'.

I would describe Reagan's success as an emotional one, and indeed the landslide victory of the last few days was a just reward for his highly skilful campaign management. At the same time, his chances of victory were considerably enhanced by two millstones round Carter's neck: the hostages in Iran, and his failure to get the SALT 2 agreement ratified.

There are many obscure aspects to the way the hostage crisis was handled, especially in relation to the helicopter attack, whose failure was as disastrous as it was easily foreseeable. The only possible explanation is that an incorrect calculation was made (based perhaps on the pathetically irresponsible views of some influential Iranian exile) as to the ease with which it would be possible to stir up popular local support for the American action. It was announced that a military commander would publish his memoirs of the enterprise, but perhaps the security services managed to put a stop to it. There is one aspect of the Tehran hostages affair, however, of which I have some personal knowledge. Pierre Salinger mentioned it, though somewhat inaccurately, in his book *America Held Hostage*, but it remains difficult to explain.

A few days after the hostages from the US Embassy in Tehran had been taken, although I was unwell, I contacted a Paris lawyer who belonged to a practice which had looked after Khomeini's interests during his exile in France, and still maintained contact with him. This lawyer had in fact been sent to see me by Khomeini after the (still unexplained) disappearance of the Imam Mussa Sadr, spiritual leader of the Lebanese Shi'ite Muslims. I now told him my view of the situation: if a way out were not found at once, and if more days went by with this crisis as headline news in newspapers and on televison screens throughout the world, it would be difficult to find a solution which did not involve one of the parties losing face. Could something be done? The lawyer consulted the Iranian government; he then flew to Italy to talk to me about it, and immediately afterwards (on 25 November) I received a proposal to be forwarded to Washington – which I did at once. It was central to this proposal that an American jury should be empanelled to look into the serious charges levelled at the Shah by the new regime in Iran. The jury would be supplied with a dossier of evidence, which was to be given wide publicity, using, amongst other means of dissemination, the public information channels available in the United States.

I had good reason to believe that, since there was no extradition treaty available, this procedure might be sufficient to get things moving. The fact that there could be no extradition would not make any difference, because it was a question of no bilateral extradition agreement existing, not of whether extradition was applicable.

Forty-eight hours later, I received the following reply via Ambassador Gardner: 'The US government appreciates and is very grateful for the proposal received. It considers, however, that the steps being taken at the United Nations, and other initiatives, make it inadvisable to follow up the proposal. The US Ambassador in France will contact the lawyer.'

There was nothing left for me to do but report to Paris that I had received this dispatch, and I was now free to go into a clinic for a gall-bladder operation, content to have done what I felt I had to, even if it came to nothing.

More than a year went by without the hostages being freed. The American presidential election was to take place on 4 November – the anniversary of the taking of the hostages. Carter either hoped or let others hope that he would just manage to have the hostages freed by that date, for he had sent special aircraft to Frankfurt, together with the voting certificates of the sixty-two unfortunate American citizens. According to a reliable source, Khomeini had already decided to release the hostages on the agreed fairly tough conditions (I do not know what subsequently happened about them), but he was not going to give an indirect helping hand to a President who had mounted an attack on his country, and who had publicly praised the Shah when he spent the New Year with him in 1978.

What Carter had actually done on that occasion was to talk about respect for human rights, and the Shah's enemies had interpreted that as a criticism and a warning to the Iranian state police.

As for SALT 2, which Carter and Brezhnev had signed in Vienna, what caused amazement everywhere was the great wave of feeling against ratification which swept through Congress immediately afterwards. Now, it is true that parliamentary ratification procedures take place after governments have signed, but you would have thought that, on such an important and well-publicized matter, advance soundings would have been made amongst senators and representatives as a precaution. It was subsequently claimed that obstacles had arisen over the question of the hostages, but a lot of time had gone by between June and November.

In my opinion, Carter was doubly damaged by what happened. The hawks criticized him for signing SALT 2, while the doves deplored the sorry figure cut by the United States on the international scene, and the deterioration of relations with the Soviet Union.

Certainly, the failure to ratify SALT 2, and the defeat of Carter by the Iranian students (so-called) are not in themselves a satisfactory explanation for Reagan's overwhelming victory. There was a feeling that the time was ripe for a change, and there was something for everybody in the Republican programme, even if in a sometimes paradoxical way. Taxes were to go down, for example, and at the same time there was to be a big increase in military spending. And although it was said in Catholic circles that many parts of the Republican programme were unacceptable, they felt bound to acknowledge that Reagan was the only candidate who openly declared himself in favour of an anti-abortion amendment to the constitution.

In 1982 Reagan came to Italy, but he spent only a few hours there, between a Paris summit and a visit to Queen Elizabeth in England; and those few hours were largely devoted to the Pope. Lunch at the President's Palace began at least an hour late, with some lightning handshakes before sitting down at table, and without even the usual little 'parade' when coffee was served, because those responsible for his programme whisked him off to the Palazzo Chigi, where the

227

secretaries of the political parties involved in the government were waiting for him. Each of them was allowed four minutes' conversation, including interpreting.

However, the visit had been preceded by his *friend* Pertini's highly successful trip to the United States, as well as by two hours of talks with Spadolini, who had been given a lift in Reagan's plane from Paris to Rome.

Less would have been said about the brevity of his trip to Rome, however, if the next day's newspapers had not appeared with pictures of Ronald on horseback beside Queen Elizabeth II in the Home Park at Windsor, near London. Naturally, the usual scandal-mongers raised the spectre of Italy's supposedly poor security. As though things were better in the United States, where Reagan had miraculously escaped assassination a few months earlier.

When *Time* magazine invited me to write something about this forthcoming trip of Ronald Reagan's, I suggested a few likely items for an agenda (Madrid conference, North–South dialogue, a coherent overall strategy for the Middle East, USA–Europe triangular operations, African problems). I also prefaced them with a piece of advice for him: remember that America's real friends are the ones who don't worry about whether the President is a Republican or a Democrat; and beware of flatterers who will try to ingratiate themselves by speaking ill of some of your predecessors. And you will have to put up, I added, with a paradox which is very widespread in Europe. There are many people who would like the US government in Washington to look after everything and everybody, taking on board every international crisis and problem; but every time the US takes up an international stance, these same people will complain about what they claim is American interference in other people's business.

I don't know whether Reagan reads *Time* magazine. But at least he has a press office.

# 32
# Sandro Pertini

I never met Pertini during the occupation of Rome, because, soon after being freed from Regina Coeli prison in a masterly operation, he went to Northern Italy, where he was to play an important part in the decisive stages of the uprising.

Once Italy was reunited, his lively personality was much in evidence, for he made no concessions to the Roman bent for diplomacy and compromise. He once caused a furore at a public political meeting, for example, by threatening to have Umberto of Savoy strung up in the Piazzale Loreto if he came to Milan for monarchist propaganda purposes. Nevertheless, he was anxious to make it clear that he had nothing to do with the macabre hanging of the corpses of Mussolini and the fascists shot at Dongo, and indeed he had made a vigorous personal protest about it to the Committee of Liberation.

I recall a meeting in De Gasperi's office at the Palazzo Chigi (which then housed the Foreign Ministry) during the cabinet crisis of December 1945. The Liberals were being difficult by threatening not to take part in a new government if an agreement was not reached. The argument had been going on for some hours, when Pertini's patience gave out (though the Liberal representative, Leone Cattani, was a true gentleman whom Pertini respected and with whom he was on friendly terms), and he proposed a five-party coalition without the Liberals. I saw De Gasperi grow pale at this suggestion, and realized the need to gain time. Since it was already late evening, I took the liberty of suggesting that we should adjourn until the following day, but I succeeded in getting approval only for a break for dinner. We had dinner brought up from Il Falchetto – a favourite restaurant of that very Roman poet, Trilussa, whose

Sandro Pertini

regular dining companion was the industrialist Giovanni Armenise. At the time, the latter was setting up his first penicillin factory, and he scandalized De Gasperi by singing the praises of contraceptives (which he insisted on calling by the much less scientific name 'preservatives'). Pertini and everyone else particularly enjoyed the fettuccine, which were served in a corner room of the Palazzo Chigi. It was on the balcony of this room that, twenty years earlier, Mussolini should have been given his come-uppance by a rifle shot from Tito Zaniboni. But at the last moment the attempt failed.

The only one of us not to enjoy the meal was De Gasperi. In fact he left the table more than once to telephone the Royal Palace; and he received a very specific reply to his query: ditching the Liberals would mean going back on the armistice agreement between the Crown and the Committee of National Liberation. He therefore asked for a personal interview with Umberto of Savoy as Lieutenant-General of the Realm, and an audience was arranged for 11 p.m. De Gasperi was hoping to persuade the Royal Palace to give him a free hand, but he felt that this was not the moment to leave the Crown exposed, and while the party delegations were preparing to resume discussions he . . . fainted! It would be unfair to suggest that he was pretending, because there is no doubt that he was in a state of nervous tension, but the fact remains that when he came to, he persuaded those present to adjourn the meeting until the following morning, and on his way home he went to his appointment with Umberto of Savoy. A journalist saw his car turn left instead of right at the Piazza Venezia and gave the alarm, but nobody managed to make anything out of it during the night. The next day the Liberals decided to remain in the coalition. Pertini was dismayed. Nenni, whose moderate approach was shared by De Gasperi, suggested that no obstacles should be placed in the way of arrangements for the referendum on the monarchy, but Pertini seemed unconvinced.

From that time onwards, there were numerous occasions when Pertini's open dissent from his party's policies was quite evident. His views gained vehement expression in 1948 when, in spite of his desperate attempts to prevent it, the Socialists decided to form a Popular Front with the Communists, after the Social Democrats, led by Saragat, had broken away. The primacy of the Socialist Party was at stake, and although Pertini took great care not to come into collision with the Communists, he was not willing to allow them to overtake the Socialists. As far as one could tell, he was the only leading Socialist to oppose the Popular Front, but he had to put up with it. Perhaps when he went to Caprera for the celebrations connected with the centenary of Garibaldi's death, Pertini will have felt deep down a certain pride that he was not amongst those responsible for 'Garibaldi's' election defeat on 18 April 1948.

Pertini played a very active role in parliament, and in 1955 was particularly influential in the election of Giovanni Gronchi as President of the Republic. Owing to a miscalculation, the Christian Democrat leadership had rejected the idea of a second term of office for Luigi Einaudi, though he openly aspired to it. Moreover, Merzagora had appeared on the scene as an independent candidate in spite of having twice been elected to the Senate as a Christian Democrat in the very safe Vimercate constituency. Some friends and I tried unsuccessfully to have Einaudi adopted as a candidate at a mass meeting of Christian Democrat voters (senators, members of the Chamber of Deputies, and representatives of the regions); so we then joined forces with the other Christian Democrat minority groups in raising the party flag over the candidature of Gronchi, whose support sprang from a reaction to what had happened at the Christian Democrat congress in Naples, when the new broad majority had gone too far in pushing him into the wings.

Both Socialists and Communists had offered us their votes (perhaps principally because Gronchi's position as President of the Chamber of Deputies made him unwelcome to the government majority). And it was Pertini who to a considerable extent saw to the success of the operation. He invited me to his house one evening to discuss detailed tactics. The meeting was to remain secret; even his wife Carla had been persuaded to go out for the evening so that no one should know of our discussion. I went to Pertini's house by the Tiber on foot and arrived very punctually, only to find to my astonishment that the entrance courtyard was full of people in prayer around a statue of the Madonna Pellegrina, who was at that time being taken around the streets of the parish after dark each night. What was I to do? As I stood in momentary hesitation, the lift door opened and Pertini appeared in his dressing-gown to let me in at the front door. He gazed at me in wide-eyed amazement, quite unable to understand why I had come to his house in a religious procession. But the faithful were so immersed in their prayers that, in a cold sweat, I managed to slip into the lift without anyone noticing.

Years later, Pertini became Giovanni Leone's Vice-President in the Chamber of Deputies, and often found it easier to obtain support for his activities amongst other political groups than amongst his own. And when Leone was elected President of the Republic, it was natural that his place as President of the Chamber of Deputies should be taken by Sandro Pertini, after Bucciarelli Ducci.

During this period, 1969 to 1972, I was leader of the Christian Democrat parliamentary group and was in daily contact with the President of the Chamber of Deputies. The secret of maintaining a good rapport with Pertini was twofold. The first thing was always to be quite straight with him, avoiding any action which might take him by surprise; and the other was to support him in seeking to establish agreed procedures with other political groups, so that the Chamber and its committees could function correctly and smoothly. So great was his concern not to witness 'incidents' in the Chamber, or be present at tiresomely fruitless sittings, that it must sometimes even have prevented him from sleeping, for he would telephone me in the early morning to talk about his impressions or intentions, or to invite me to go and discuss some point with him at once. Puffing at his pipe, and with his peaked cap on, he would go round and round the outside of the Chamber of Deputies building, to the greetings of the street-cleaners and lorrymen, who at that early hour were unloading the huge rolls of newsprint for *Il Tempo*.

The general election of 1976 brought an appreciable increase in the Communist vote, and immediately afterwards the political parties agreed that a Communist and a Christian Democrat should be put at the head of the two chambers in parliament. Moro would have been very glad to be the Christian Democrat, but withdrew his candidature in order not to upset Fanfani; while the Communist candidate was Pietro Ingrao. No one had kept Pertini informed of the negotiations, with the result that he learned of their outcome almost entirely from the press. He was deeply hurt at the way things had been done, and on the day when the election took place he remained ostentatiously at his station on the podium, looking down on the formal procedure by which his chosen successor was elected.

Throughout his life, however, Sandro Pertini has often made a comeback in ways which have compensated for periods spent out in the cold. His time came in the summer of 1978.

Giovanni Leone had been forced to resign as President of the Republic, as a result of a malicious press campaign led by Camilla Cederna. Once the Communists went and told him they were supporting her campaign, it could no longer be withstood. She was his foremost accuser, and though later found guilty of

233

defaming him, she had by that time obtained what she wanted. Whatever constitutional law has to say on such matters, it would have been very rash to allow a vote to be taken in the two chambers against the President of the Republic. Every effort to postpone matters until the last six months of his term of office proved fruitless, though in such circumstances his resignation would have been quite a different matter. 'Crucify him, crucify him.' As it was, many self-righteous people stood to one side, and a few servile hacks, who had excelled themselves at the beginning of Leone's term of office with splendid words of praise and adulation, now set about insulting him and his family in a thoroughly shameful way. All it needed was for someone to describe his beautiful wife Vittoria as old and ugly! *Sic transit gloria mundi.* Giovanni Leone deserved better; especially since he had always avoided ministerial or higher office in order not to lose contact with the university world and the legal profession. Perhaps he had in mind the unscrupulousness of certain politicians when he looked back with nostalgia on the prostitutes and small-time thieves in the law courts of Naples.

The situation created by this sudden vacating of the presidency was quite different from what had occurred before previous presidential elections, when a programme of sophisticated and laborious negotiations had been put into operation – and had almost always proved a failure. The parliamentary support which kept the government in office was of a very unusual kind, and had now exhausted its possibilities. Consequently there was no prospect at all of arranging things on that basis. Nor was there a sound basis for using this vital selection procedure as a possible springboard for restoring good relations at least between the Christian Democrats and the Socialists.

In order somehow to acknowledge that the highest positions of state should be shared amongst the political parties, the Christian Democrats did not put forward a candidate for the presidency. The only Christian Democrat who might have received substantial support was Guido Gonella, but his role was reduced to that of flying the party flag in the tentative early ballots.

Pertini had no hesitation in indicating his willingness to stand, but he was not the official Socialist candidate. (Giuliano Vassalli and Antonio Giolitti had more support than him within the Socialist Party.) Every day during the disconcerting ritual of ineffectual ballots, fresh little groups of official and unofficial candidates appeared on the scene, until finally an agreement to vote for Pertini was reached. The Christian Democrat Party proposed him, and on the morning of 8 July 1978 he was elected with as many as 832 votes. The next day he returned to his old seat in the Chamber to take the oath as President of the Republic, and the speech he made was full of human warmth as well as moments of direct popular appeal.

For the first time, Sandro Pertini *mattered*, and he certainly was not going to give up the opportunity of getting his revenge occasionally (and justifiably). Meanwhile, he made an intelligent choice of head of his press office in Antonio Ghirelli who, as a prestigious Neapolitan sports correspondent, was a skilful purveyor of images to the public. Later on his collaboration with Pertini was broken off, and the result of the parting was that Ghirelli published an account of his experiences as press officer, which revealed a love–hate relationship between the two, and provided a disconcerting series of indiscretions.

Although he claimed not to have the gift of faith (but woe betide anyone who criticized Don Bosco, for Pertini had been at a Salesian school), the new President took great care to establish good relations with the Vatican. Although he was close to death at the time, Pope Paul VI insisted that Pertini's audience should take place, and shortly before he died he was thoughtful enough to send a message to Pertini saying how much he had enjoyed seeing him. Pertini himself was so moved by all this that it was his sole subject of conversation when he had lunch with Fanfani, Ingrao, and me soon afterwards. His relationship with John Paul II was even warmer, and he took delight in having been the Pope's guest at table, and in having spoken to him on the telephone several times, including an occasion when the Pope congratulated him on Italy's victory in the World Cup football final, at which Pertini was present in no uncertain fashion. In a public speech made in 1979, the Pope congratulated Pertini on the exemplary affection which he obviously still felt for his mother.

As President, Pertini was also very keen on the armed forces. On the very day of his installation, he was on his way to pay homage to the Unknown Soldier, immediately before going to the President's Palace, when he reminded the Chief of the General Staff of his own military service during the First World War; and the same subject came up again a few weeks later, when he called a significantly early meeting of the Supreme Defence Council. Furthermore, he insisted on having General Arnaldo Ferrara of the Carabinieri on his regular staff in addition to the other military personnel already attached to the President's Palace, so that he could keep a closer watch on problems of security.

There was always the possibility that Pertini's personality might cause the government problems. (I shall never forget the furore he caused in 1973 when he said to Costantino Belluscio, 'I wouldn't be surprised if there's a microphone in my room. The telephones in my flat and my study are under surveillance.') But since he and I had learned to get on together years earlier in the Chamber of Deputies, it was easy for me to establish at once an atmosphere of mutual respect for our separate duties as public servants. In recognizing the President's right to a certain personal freedom of action, moreover, I was being consistent with my ideas on the moral rights of those in positions of public authority, which I had upheld during Giovanni Gronchi's presidency in a polite argument with Luigi Sturzo. The first occasion on which Pertini took advantage of his presidential freedom of action was when he sent a message to Brezhnev, interceding on behalf of a Soviet citizen who had been sent to prison for a political offence. I was personally responsible for giving this humane and civilized gesture the go-ahead, allowing it to bypass any consultation with the Foreign Minister. Since, however, it is always the government's task to 'cover up' for the Head of State, there were occasions when we had to mend a few fences. For example, Pertini caused a considerable stir by giving an interview to Camilla Cederna, who had so relentlessly attacked his predecessor. He was criticized for this even by journalists who profoundly admired him, and he wrote a note to one of them (Enrico Mattei) confessing that he had made a mistake. In order to sort the matter out, I too granted Camilla Cederna an interview, thereby diverting attention from President to Prime Minister. And so the fuss died down.

A more dramatic episode in my relationship with Pertini occurred during the political crisis of early 1979, by which time any semblance of national solidarity had been completely shattered. Pertini had told a Socialist delegation that he was very sorry to hear of the declining health of his old friend (and foe!) Pietro Nenni, because this would have been his great moment. (But he did not respond to an invitation to turn to the generation of the forty-year-olds.) His idea, on the contrary, was that the next government should be headed by Saragat, with two Deputy Prime Ministers in the form of La Malfa and a *Christian Democrat*. I received an unexpected telephone call offering me the vice-premiership, but I pointed out that since I was a member of a team, I must consult my party on a matter of such political importance. Pertini, however, assured me that Zaccagnini, the Party Secretary, had already agreed to the appointment. So an official announcement was issued by the President's Palace to the effect that the three of us had been summoned to a meeting at nine o'clock the next morning. What happened still retains an element of mystery.

Shortly before this historic non-event was due to take place, I received a request to go and see the President half an hour earlier, and Pertini then told me that there had been a misunderstanding with Zaccagnini. The Christian Democrat Party was anxious to retain the premiership, and Pertini felt that that was only right. So the Saragat–La Malfa–Andreotti triumvirate remained, but it was the first two who were to be the vice-premiers. When the other two came in, my embarrassment was certainly very visible, but Pertini explained with great simplicity that there had been a misunderstanding. He confirmed that he was designating me to lead the government, and asked the others to collaborate with me. La Malfa accepted without demur, whereas Saragat wanted to impose as a condition that the government should be broadened to include the independent Left; but there was no way this could be effected. I tried to win Saragat over by offering him the Foreign Ministry, but his objection proved to be one of principle. That is how the Andreotti–La Malfa government came into being, but alas it came to a rapid end when La Malfa unexpectedly died – an event which deeply affected Pertini as well as me.

It was at this point that a plot was set in motion which deeply upset me. The idea was that immediately after the inevitable general election, I should at all costs be obliged to abandon the premiership, and to facilitate this plan an absurd rumour about the oil industry was circulated, in which a central figure was no less than Mazzanti, the Socialist Chairman of ENI, the state oil and gas agency. The rumour suggested that behind the contract negotiated by Mazzanti with Saudi Arabia were 'mysterious interests' involving the presidency of the Council of Ministers and certain Socialists. The practical result was that Italy failed to receive a quantity of oil at an attractive price and without involving the multinationals; but a subtler consequence was the reaction in Pertini, who began to behave towards me, I noticed, with unusual coolness. The affair caused me some bitterness, and I shall not feel happy until it is revealed whether some Italian individual or party stood to gain from a contract which ENI considered to be one of the most prestigious it had ever managed to sign.

The attempt to estrange Pertini and me continued for some time even after I had ceased to be Prime Minister.

On 7 January 1980, for example, he sent me a copy of an astonishing letter written to a member of the Chamber of Deputies, whose surname he had removed. The letter was accompanied by a note which read: 'In all conscience I had to send you this copy for your information. Sincerely, Pertini'. Pertini expressed regret that this fellow had informed an aide rather than himself of my apparent wicked intention of stirring up a hornets' nest against him, in the hope that he would resign and I would take his place.

'However,' he went on, 'I assume this to be one of those many items of gossip which circulate in the lobbies of parliament [this was not in fact the case], but if by any chance it were shown to have some foundation in fact, I would certainly know how to deal with it: I would repay the ill-deed with interest.'

This stupid and malicious invention was even made public by someone or other, and so I published my reply to Pertini – having first obtained his permission, as protocol required. In it I expressed regret that there were those willing to spread falsehoods about me and to stir up trouble between the two of us. 'For several decades,' I wrote, 'you have been aware of my attitude towards you. Perhaps there is someone who finds irksome my total loyalty to you and our mutual friendship, which has been a source of strength in tackling many difficult problems during my three years in government.'

It is true that when Pertini sent me a letter of Christmas greetings in 1968, he also wrote: 'our political world gives us more bitterness than satisfaction'; but I have feelings of friendship towards him as a person rather than because of his position, and I would rather not have received such an expression of bitterness from him, even though it was oblique and hedged about. The fact is that I am still as Pertini described me in another letter, dated 5 February 1962: 'My dear Andreotti, you are no sectarian. You have a deep respect for other people's opinions and for your friends, even – or perhaps I should say especially – when they are your political opponents, as I am.'

In 1979, however, the Socialists decreed that I was to be ostracized by them – not so much, I suspect, out of dislike for me as to permit open competition for the premiership. Unlike 1976, there were now plenty of candidates, and Bruno Visentini was the punters' favourite, as a change from a Christian Democrat. It was Craxi who got the job, however, in spite of his not being known as a great friend of Pertini. But there is an unwritten law going back to the days of the monarchy, which says that the Head of State must be on friendly terms with the Prime Minister of the day. There was certainly no way in which Pertini could insist on my remaining in office, though a few days earlier he had passed on to me some warm tributes to the effect that my reputation on the international scene was increasing; and furthermore he had threatened to report me for dereliction of duty if I resigned without there being a vote of no confidence.

The Socialists promised to allow parliament to run its full term, in view of their pledge to the electorate that they would make Italy governable. A single government did not succeed in lasting out to the next general election, however, and in three years there were as many as three different Prime Ministers: Francesco Cossiga (twice), Arnaldo Forlani, and Giovanni Spadolini (twice). Pertini unsuccessfully told each of them to remain at the helm unless they received a substantial vote of no confidence. And I don't doubt that he did so in good faith.

When Spadolini found himself in a difficult situation (the Minister of the Treasury, Andreatta, had actually accused the Socialists of being infected with national socialism, that is, Nazism), Pertini gave him a helping hand – and also tried to prevent a political crisis – by describing Andreatta's behaviour as 'disgusting'. At the same time he chose to ignore a comment made by the Minister of Finance, Formica, to the effect that the Christian Democrats were murderers because they had failed to save Aldo Moro's life. This remark was also offensive to Pertini, for he had been very supportive of the government during those tragic weeks, and had personally come across to embrace me when I declared in the Chamber of Deputies that we were not afraid of terrorists, since they could deprive us of our lives but not our souls. However, a new order of chivalry (Knights of the Disgusting Order) had now been created, and it would do no harm if a few such knighthoods were handed out each year, as happens with the Knights of Labour.

Pertini's vitality amazes everyone, for he even undertakes the exhausting travel and heavy engagement schedules of journeys abroad. The list of his admirers is now international, and includes the King of Spain, who smiles upon him and gives him pipes as presents, as well as other Heads of State who are delighted to see him kiss the flag of the host country during military parades.

Pertini is now in his eighties, and amazes everyone with his little unrehearsed gestures. On a number of occasions he has asked for 'extras' to be tacked on to the end of exhausting days filled with official engagements. In Spain he wanted to go and see flamenco dancing, and in New York he wanted to experience a luxury discothèque called the Regine. The security services tremble at these additions to the programme, but in Madrid the King and Queen themselves accompanied him, with the result that Pertini has on a number of occasions passionately defended monarchy – but only when it operates outside Italy, of course. He was fascinated, too, by his first visit to America, and has spoken about the country with enthusiasm. What impressed him was not only the enormous expanse of the big cities, but also the politeness and will to work of the people. There was the New York girl, for example, who kissed him twice of her own accord when they met in the street; and the first lady of San Francisco much impressed him by her attractiveness. (Whether in Spain, capitalist America, or anywhere else, socialist Pertini is as ready to pay homage to female beauty as the republican poet Carducci was to Queen Margherita of Italy.) Pertini's story of this visit to America, which he is always willing to tell, is a piece of genuine, spontaneous publicity for the American continent.

Pertini particularly enjoyed the very special reception he was given at the New York Stock Exchange. Everybody stopped their noisy activity for a moment and began to clap him, joyfully hurling bundles of contract notes in the direction of the gallery where Pertini stood.

I feel sure, however, that in all his visits abroad, there was no moment which moved him more than his visit to the concentration camp in Bavaria where his brother died. Alas, the Nazis prevented his brother from ever saying, as Sandro often does, with a wink towards someone who aspires, or is thought to aspire, to the presidency: 'Me old? All my family have been over ninety when they died.'

Franz Josef Strauss had written to Pertini, requesting the honour of accompanying him on that melancholy pilgrimage. Pertini embraced him warmly, and mentally inscribed his name amongst those whom he holds most dear.

# 33
# Margaret Thatcher

The first time I met the Right Honourable Mrs Margaret Hilda Thatcher (*née* Roberts) was in 1975, at a session of the European Parliament in Strasbourg. She had come to visit fellow Conservatives amongst the Euro-MPs, and their leader, Scott Hopkins, wanted other members of the Parliament to meet her. She gave the impression of being an appealingly frail woman, but there was a suggestion of tough obstinacy in her glance which was fully confirmed in our five minutes of general conversation.

Four years later, on 4 May 1979, the Conservatives won an impressive election victory, in spite of forecasts that the country would view a female leader with suspicion. (An unlikely prejudice, surely, in the land of Queen Victoria!) So James Callaghan – a gentleman if ever there was one, and a convinced European in a party which is cool about Europe – gave up 10 Downing Street to Mrs Thatcher, who settled in there with the avowed intention of making it a lengthy tenancy.

The only consolation left to the previous Conservative leader, Edward Heath, was conducting the European Youth Orchestra.

As soon as she had settled in, Mrs Thatcher invited me to meet her in London on 15 June, to discuss together those problems which were to be on the agenda a week later at a meeting of the European Council, summoned in Strasbourg by Giscard d'Estaing. The British turn-out in the elections for the European Parliament had been very low indeed at 23 per cent, but Mrs Thatcher was anxious to underline the fact that her party, unlike Labour, was genuinely pro-Common Market. Nevertheless, that very support for the EEC meant that nobody should be surprised if she took a stand on certain issues, such as the Community budget, fishing rights, and the agricultural policy. There was nothing unreasonable about such statements, and indeed they largely coincided with the Italian point of view. What mattered, however, was to make clear the spirit in which they were expressed, so as to avoid their being interpreted as weakening the bonds uniting the Ten.

The Strasbourg meeting revealed a fair consensus of opinion on the need to establish a clear-cut strategy in moving towards the harmonization of Community policies, though it was perhaps rather naïve to make forecasts up to 1990. Mrs Thatcher and I agreed that our two governments would keep in close contact in deciding what suggestions to make to the European Commission, which had in the meantime been asked to draw up a report for a later Dublin meeting. She also supported a proposal which President Pertini was particularly keen on, namely that the communiqué should mention aid for refugees from Vietnam.

In late June, there was a Tokyo summit of the seven most industrialized nations. This was the first international appointment in Mrs Thatcher's diary and the last in mine (at least for the time being). One amusing detail remains in my mind. The Japanese had organized everything down to the last detail with clockwork precision, partly through fear of terrorist action. The forces of law and order were there in such great strength that even the barber who came to shave me was escorted by two policemen and a policewoman. Each of us had his exact time-table, and I was due to come down in the lift and get into my car exactly ninety seconds after my colleague Mrs Thatcher. She, however, took this one advantage of her sex, that she would be a few minutes late, thereby putting those responsible for protocol in a terrible tizzy; since I was already at the hotel entrance, was I to set off, or should the pre-established order of precedence be respected? This same little comedy was enacted on each of four days.

The summit was principally devoted to the energy crisis, with its economic and financial repercussions. For the twin problems of inflation and the impossibility of maintaining an adequate oil supply were on pretty well everybody's mind – though Forlani, Pandolfi, and I thought that Schmidt, Genscher, and Lambsdorff were unduly concerned about West Germany's rate of inflation, when Italy had 13 per cent, France 10 per cent, and the United States and Canada 8 per cent.

The point was repeatedly made that anyone who has suffered

burns in his youth (as in the Weimar Republic) is likely to be terrified of the least flame for the rest of his life. But we Italians were rather proud of having practically halved our inflation rate over the previous three years. Mrs Thatcher's inflation rate was 10¼ per cent (2 per cent up on the previous year), but she didn't have much to say about that; indeed, she didn't have much to say throughout the summit. She wanted it to be seen that she thought of herself as a new girl who would stick to the golden rule that there is often more to be gained by listening than by talking. (There is a splendid Romanian proverb which praises God for having given us two ears but only one tongue.)

Now that the extent of North Sea oil reserves was known, Mrs Thatcher was not over-concerned about oil, though she vigorously supported every plan for cutting down consumption. (Later on I found this to be a constant characteristic of her approach.) Nevertheless, she shared my slight scepticism when Jimmy Carter announced that before long solar energy would supply one-fifth of the United States' needs. (What extravagant claims our rulers succeed in making on the basis of notes supplied by *experts!*) On the other hand, we all congratulated Carter on the SALT 2 agreement; but he didn't say anything about problems of ratification, and they later wrecked the whole operation.

It was not difficult to reach agreement on the development of nuclear energy, though Mrs Thatcher complained about delays in the programme, while stressing the need for ever higher safety standards and the avoidance of nuclear proliferation. The atom must be used primarily for peaceful purposes, and so on.

Under Callaghan's premiership, Britain had thought fit not to join the newly created European Monetary System, but, if I remember correctly, Mrs Thatcher didn't bat an eyelid when it came in for praise. It was too early for her to reach a decision on the subject, but in conversation with me she said that, in September, Britain would take a 'small step forward'.

When I had met her in 1975, Mrs Thatcher seemed to me more strong-willed than she did at Strasbourg in 1979, and much more than in Tokyo. Was it a question of her moving from opposition to government, or was it the inevitable personal process of accustoming herself to the exercise of power?

When Mrs Thatcher came to visit Cossiga in October 1979, I received a courteous note of apology from London, regretting that the brevity of her visit prevented her from meeting me. There was a courteously added assurance that the conversations which we had begun in Strasbourg would continue.

In August 1983, I joined the Italian government again as Foreign Minister, and so had many more opportunities to talk to Mrs Thatcher: at two Anglo-Italian meetings in London (September 1983 and October 1984); when I accompanied President Pertini to Britain in February 1984; at meetings of the European Council in Athens, Brussels, Fontainebleau, and Dublin; at a meeting of the seven most industrialized nations in London; and at two funerals. One was that of Andropov in Moscow, and the other was in New Delhi, after the assassination of Indira Gandhi.

It was now perfectly clear, I must admit, that Mrs Thatcher was no longer learning the ropes or feeling her way, and the flash of steel was no longer confined to her eyes. For the tragic Argentine attack on the Falkland Islands had caused her to clad herself entirely in armour, as the coal-miners and other British trade union groups were to discover to their cost.

I noticed this transformation at our first ministerial meeting, when I referred to a suggestion, worked out with Claude Cheysson, that when it came to a UN vote, it might be possible for Britain to relax its intransigent attitude towards the resumption of negotiations with Argentina. Now that there had been a change of regime in Argentina, it seemed sensible to resume what the generals' folly had caused to be broken off – especially since the Argentinian people (at least half of whom have Italian blood) find it hard to accept what Italy regards as European solidarity, but what they regard as at least indifference, if not incomprehensible hostility. But Mrs Thatcher brought any discussion of that subject to an abrupt halt. The mere mention of it was almost a provocation. Nor did the repeated UN Assembly vote have the slightest effect, even though the motion was supported by the USA, with abstentions by the other EEC members. Equally unsuccessful was an attempt at reconciliation sponsored by the Swiss government.

On the other hand, our respective positions were very close on the responsibilities accepted by NATO in 1979 as regards restoring the balance in European missile defences. On every occasion we both agreed that scrupulous adherence to this principle – plus increasing contacts by both our countries with the Soviet Union and the other East European states – was the only way to induce Moscow to re-establish contact with Washington, and persuade the two superpowers to commit themselves fully to a search for agreement.

Another link between our two countries was our respective contributions to the multinational force in the Lebanon, whose job was to prevent further disasters (after the Sabra and Chatila massacres), and to push the various political factions in the Lebanon in the direction of mutual understanding and collaboration.

Mrs Thatcher had to overcome some serious practical difficulties before she could arrange landing rights for Italian military aircraft at the British base in Cyprus whenever the necessity should arise. Later on, both governments were invited by Egypt to send ships and experts in search of those famous mines in the Red Sea which still remain a total mystery.

Where negotiations with Mrs Thatcher become more complicated is in relation to Common Market matters. I am sure she is a convinced European, and I also see the need for sympathetic understanding of the difficulty she has in dealing with widespread antagonism towards the EEC at home. But I am not sure whether she will be able to support the plan for a progressive, if gradual and partial, integration of the Ten or Twelve, together with a drawing together of their social and economic systems. Her idea of a free exchange area to be associated with consultation on matters of foreign policy deserves consideration; but it is something quite different from the Europe contemplated in the Treaty of Rome.

Furthermore, Mrs Thatcher is right when she protests at the burdensome waste caused by agricultural surpluses. Some steps have already been taken to put this right, and speedier action is necessary, but without abrupt changes of direction which would be politically and psychologically unacceptable. She was wrong, however, to start asking for a reduction in the British contribution to the EEC, because the right way to obtain fair financial shares is by redistributing costs, not by means of 'fiscal' privileges. However, the Council accepted Mrs Thatcher's request at the Stuttgart summit, and the benefit she gained was confirmed at Fontainebleau, though not without some expression of discontent and displeasure in the European Parliament.

In any case, the argument about *waste* is a two-edged weapon. If the overproduction of tomatoes and other fruits and vegetables in Southern Europe is wasteful, what about the costly support of that pretty useless vegetable called rape in the North? When I once put this question to Mrs Thatcher, she told me that these were 'details'.

There is an Italian biography of Mrs Thatcher, whose title, *The*

*Iron Lady*, is inspired by Ronald Reagan's definition of her as 'the strongest man to be found in the United Kingdom'. And it is interesting to learn that this certificate of masculinity awarded by the President of the United States has met with her approval.

I feel sure, however, that she must have obtained much more satisfaction from the praise of her femininity contained in a speech by Sandro Pertini, which ended with an elegant kiss of the hand such as Joan of Arc never dreamed of receiving.

# *Index*

249

# Index